THE NETWORK PRESS™
DICTIONARY OF
NETWORKING

INTRODUCING NETWORK PRESS™

Welcome to Network Press, the new and expanded successor to Sybex's acclaimed Novell Press® book series. These books represents a significant change in how you will access the best networking knowledge in the future. Readers who value Sybex's Novell Press books now have an independent source in Network Press for unbiased information on Novell, Microsoft, and other network environments.

Network Press, building upon Sybex's twenty-year history of technical and publishing excellence, is dedicated to expanding the range and depth of publications available to you. You'll find the same dedication to quality, contents, and timeliness that you have come to expect from Sybex. Look to Network Press for a truly comprehensive body of knowledge on the complete spectrum of networks and networking issues.

With striking new covers, emblematic of networks that form the natural world, and completely updated contents, you'll soon find that the book you need looks a lot like this . To be assured of unparalleled quality in your computer book selections, look for the Sybex logo.

All previously released Novell Press titles remain available from Sybex. New editions will be released as part of the expanding Network Press family of titles.

For more information, please contact:
Sybex Inc.
2021 Challenger Drive
Alameda, CA 94501
Tel: (510) 523-8233/(800) 227-2346
Fax: (510) 523-2373

THE NETWORK PRESS™
DICTIONARY OF
NETWORKING

Second Edition

PETER DYSON

NETWORK ™
PRESS
SYBEX

*The first edition of this book was published
under the title* Novell's Dictionary of Networking

San Francisco • Paris • Düsseldorf • Soest

ACQUISITIONS MANAGER: Kristine Plachy
DEVELOPMENTAL EDITOR: Guy Hart-Davis
EDITOR: Abby Azrael
TECHNICAL EDITOR: Jim Huggans
BOOK DESIGNER: Lisa Jaffe
TECHNICAL ARTISTS: Cuong Le and Rick Van Genderen
DESKTOP PUBLISHER: Lynell Decker
PRODUCTION COORDINATOR: Sarah Lemas
COVER DESIGNER: Archer Design
COVER PHOTOGRAPHER: Charles Krebs

Library of Congress Card Number: 95-70853
ISBN: 0-7821-1818-6

Manufactured in the United States of America

10 9 8 7 6 5 4 3 2 1

FOR MARIANNE, JIM, AND BARKIS.
NOW WHERE'S THAT PHONE?

ACKNOWLEDGMENTS

People usually think of writing a book as being a solitary process, but nothing could be further from the truth. I had lots of help in writing this book, and this is my chance to say thanks to all the people who provided advice and technical assistance along the way.

At Sybex, thanks to Kristine Plachy, Acquisitions Manager; Guy Hart-Davis, Developmental Editor; Abby Azrael, my ever patient Editor; Jim Huggans, Technical Editor; and Cuong Le and Rick Van Genderen, Technical Illustrators. I also appreciate the hard work of the Desktop Publisher, Lynell Decker, and Production Coordinator, Sarah Lemas. And thanks to Gary Masters who helped me to hatch this project in the first place.

Also, thanks to the people who reviewed the lists of words that formed the basis of this book, particularly Tom Charlesworth, who has been heard to describe the TCP/IP specifications as "a thumping good read."

And finally, thanks to Nancy; as always, in a class by herself.

INTRODUCTION

Networks are currently one of the fastest growing and most important developments in the computer industry. Not only are more and more PCs becoming parts of networks, but networked PCs are being incorporated into larger enterprise-wide applications, so that everyone in a company can access and share data.

With the expanding technology of networking comes the terminology to describe it. This *Network Press Dictionary of Networking* provides definitions for all the terms you might encounter when dealing with networks of any type.

Who Should Use This Book?

This book is designed to meet the needs of people who work with networks, communications, and mobile computing systems. Whether you are networking previously unconnected computers or downsizing from a mainframe, this book is for you. Network users of all levels are faced with an almost bewildering barrage of terms, abbreviations, and acronyms in books, magazine and newspaper articles, advertisements, and their day-to-day conversations. Jargon is a useful shorthand, but it can easily become incomprehensible and unmanageable, even to the most seasoned network administrator.

What You'll Find in This Book

Along with clear explanations of the jargon and slang associated with networking, you'll find definitions of networking technical terms, abbreviations, and acronyms. The list that follows gives you a brief overview of topics that this book covers:

- Chips, memory, and adapters
- Communications
- Disks and storage media
- Industry standards
- Internet terms and abbreviations
- Leading hardware and software companies
- Microprocessors
- Mobile computing
- Networking theory and concepts
- Novell NetWare 3.*x* and 4.*x* commands
- Operating systems and environments
- Protocols
- Security and network administration
- Workstations

How This Book Is Organized   This book is organized for easy reference. Entries are arranged in alphabetical order, ignoring punctuation and spaces, with terms that begin with an uppercase letter (or all in uppercase) before those in all lowercase letters. So *Internet* comes before *internet*, and *link layer* comes before *link-state routing algorithm*.

Symbols, such as * and ?, are listed at the beginning of the book in ASCII order. Numerical entries appear at the beginning of the letter that the number starts with when spelled out, so you'll find *802.x* at the beginning of the E section.

The information within each entry is presented in the following order:

- Entry name, presented in alphabetical order, letter by letter
- Abbreviation or acronym, or the spelled-out term if the abbreviation or acronym is the main entry, where applicable
- Pronunciation, if it isn't obvious (the term is said just as it's spelled)
- Definition
- Cross references to other dictionary entries that provide additional or related information on the topic, where applicable

If an entry has multiple definitions, each one is numbered to separate it from the next.

Within a definition, terms that are also separate entries in the diction-ary, and which are directly relevant to the term being defined, appear in *italic*. This system allows you to follow a topic through a chain of en-tries that you select. However, common terms, such as network, server, and modem, and terms that do not add additional value to the entry in which they occur, are not italicized.

Some definitions are with the abbreviations or acronyms for terms, and some are with the spelled-out term, depending on which you are most likely to encounter in the networking world. But you will find both versions listed, with a *See* reference to indicate where you will find the information.

And Finally... Through more than 15 years' involvement in practical computer applications, including the management of minicomputer sys-tems, PC-based networks, large-scale data communications systems, software development, and technical support, I have become intimately familiar with computer and networking terminology. This dictionary is a direct result of that experience, and it represents a practical and down-to-earth approach to computers and computing.

Everyone who has worked on this dictionary has tried to make sure that it is as complete and accurate as possible. But if you think that we have missed a word or two that should be included in a future edition, please write to the following address:

Network Press Dictionary of Networking
c/o SYBEX Computer Books
2021 Challenger Drive
Alameda, CA 94501
USA

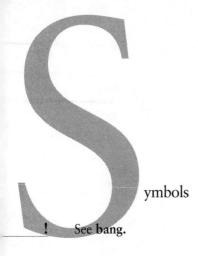ymbols

!	See **bang**.	?	See **question mark**.
*	See **asterisk**.	@	See **at-symbol**.
.	See **star-dot-star**.	.	See **period and double-period directories**.
/	See **slash**.		
\	See **backslash**.	..	See **period and double-period directories**.

a-b box A switching box that allows a peripheral device such as a printer to be shared between two or more computers. It can be switched manually or through software.

abend Contraction of ABnormal END. A message issued by an operating system when it detects a serious problem, such as hardware or software damage. An abend can halt the file server.

ABORT REMIRROR A Novell NetWare server utility that unmirrors a mirrored disk so you can make changes to the disk, such as resizing the *partition*. When the changes are complete, you can reset the mirroring and synchronize the data on the changed partition. You can also use this command to stop the remirroring process.

See also **disk duplexing, disk mirroring, MIRROR STATUS, REMIRROR PARTITION.**

accelerator board An add-in, printed circuit board that replaces the main processor with a higher-performance processor. Using an accelerator board can reduce upgrading costs substantially, because you won't need to replace the monitor, case, keyboard, and so on. However, the main processor is not the only component that affects the overall performance of your system. Other factors, such as disk-access time and video speed, contribute to a system's performance.

See also **graphics accelerator board, Intel OverDrive.**

access

1. To retrieve data from a storage device, such as a hard disk.

2. To log in to a computer system or network.

AccessBuilder Remote access software from 3Com Corporation that lets you access network resources over a dial-up connection from a remote location.

See also **mobile computing.**

access control list Abbreviated ACL. In Novell NetWare, a list containing information about which other objects can access it;

3

trustee and the *Inherited Rights Filter* are contained in the ACL.

access method   The set of rules that determines which node in a network has access to the transmission media at any moment.

Attempts at simultaneous access are either managed by a collision detection mechanism such as *CSMA/CD,* or prevented by use of a *token passing* method.

access protocol   The set of rules that workstations use to avoid collisions when sending information over shared network media. Also known as the media-access control protocol.

access rights   See **rights.**

access server   A computer that provides access for *remote users* who dial in to the system and access network resources as though their computers were directly attached to the network. An access server can be a computer designed for this purpose and sold as part of the network, or it can be a computer on the network that has multiport *central processing unit* (CPU) cards installed.

See also **communications/modem server, mobile computing.**

access time   The period of time that elapses between a request for information from disk or memory and the arrival of that information at the requesting device.

Memory-access time refers to the time it takes to transfer a character between memory and the processor. Disk-access time refers to the time it takes to place the read/write heads over the requested data. *RAM* (random-access memory) may have an access time of 80 nanoseconds or less, while hard-disk-access time could be 10 milliseconds or less.

account   On *local area networks* (LANs) or *multiuser* operating systems, an account is set up for each user. Accounts are usually kept for administrative or security reasons. For communications and online services, accounts are used as a method of identifying a subscriber for billing purposes.

See also **user account.**

accounting   The process of tracking the resources used on a network. The *network administrator* can charge for files accessed, connect time, disk space used for file storage, and service requests, by assigning account balances to users. The users can then draw from their account balances as they use network services.

Most of the popular network operating systems include an accounting utility; NetWare 3.*x*, for example, has *SYSCON*, which includes an accounting option.

account policy   On networks and *multiuser* operating systems, the set of rules that defines whether a new user is permitted access to the system and whether an existing user is granted additional rights or expanded access to other system resources.

In *Windows NT 3.5 Server*, account policy also defines the way in which passwords are used in a *domain* or in an individual computer.

ACF   See **Advanced Communications Function.**

ACK   Abbreviation for acknowledgment. In communications, ACK is a *control code*, ASCII 06, sent by the receiving computer to indicate that the data has been received without error and the next part of the transmission may be sent.

See also **NAK**.

ACONSOLE   A Novell NetWare 3.*x* workstation utility that controls a modem attached to the workstation. ACONSOLE is used to establish an asynchronous remote console connection to a server. The *RS232 NetWare Loadable Module* (NLM) must be loaded on the server to which you want to connect. In NetWare 4.*x*, use *RCONSOLE* to perform this function.

acoustic coupler   A *modem* that includes a pair of rubber cups that fit over the mouthpiece and earpiece of a standard telephone handset (to prevent external noise from being picked up); see the accompanying illustration. An acoustic coupler allows you to connect your computer to a telephone system that does not have the standard RJ-11 connections used with conventional modems.

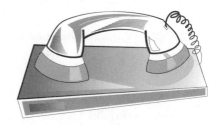

ACOUSTIC COUPLER

across-the-wire migration   A method of migrating file-server data, trustee rights, and other information to a Novell NetWare 4.1 server. You can also use

5

across-the-wire migration to upgrade from *LAN Manager, LAN Server*, and from earlier versions of NetWare; a similar process known as *BMIGRATE* allows users to migrate from *Banyan VINES*.

ACS   See **Advanced Communications Service.**

active hub   A device that amplifies transmission signals in a network, allowing signals to be sent over a much greater distance than is possible with a *passive hub*.

An active hub may have ports for *coaxial*, *twisted-pair*, or *fiber-optic* cable connections, as well as LEDs to show that each port is operating correctly.

See also **repeater.**

adapter   A printed circuit board that plugs into a computer's *expansion bus* to provide added capabilities.

Common adapters include video adapters, hard-disk controllers, and input/output (I/O) adapters, as well as other devices, such as internal modems, CD-ROMs, and network interface cards (NICs). One adapter

can often support several different devices. Some modern PC designs incorporate many of the functions previously performed by these individual adapters on the *motherboard*.

adaptive routing   A mechanism that allows a network to reroute messages dynamically, using the best available path, if a portion of the network fails.

See also **alternative route.**

ADCCP   Abbreviation for Advanced Data Communications Control Procedures. A *bit-oriented, link-layer, ANSI-standard communications protocol*.

See also **HDLC.**

ADD NAME SPACE   A Novell NetWare server utility that creates space for long, non-DOS file names, such as those used in the OS/2, Windows 95, or Macintosh System 7 operating systems. To user, first load the *name space NetWare Loadable Module* (NLM) on the server, and then add support for that name space to the *volume* in which the files will be stored.

address

1. The precise location in *memory* or on disk where a piece of information is stored. Each *byte* in memory and each sector on a disk has its own unique address.

2. The unique identifier for a specific *node* on a network. An address may be a physical address specified by switches or jumpers on the *network interface card* hardware, or a logical address established by the network operating system.

3. To reference or manage a storage location.

See also **address bus, DNS, e-mail address, memory address**.

address bus
The electronic channel, usually from 20 to 64 lines wide, used to transmit the signals that specify locations in *memory*. The number of lines in the address bus determines the number of memory locations that the processor can access, because each line carries one bit of the address. A 20-line address bus (used in early Intel 8086/8088 processors) can access 1 megabyte (MB) of memory, a 24-line address bus (used in the Intel *80286*) can access 16 MB, and a 32-line address bus (used in the Intel *80386DX*, Intel *80486*, and Motorola *68020*) can access more than 4 gigabytes (GB). A 64-line address bus (used in the DEC Alpha APX) can access 16 exabytes (EB).

addressing space
The amount of *RAM* (random-access memory) available to the operating system on a server running Novell NetWare. Under NetWare 4.*x*, the maximum is 4 gigabytes (GB).

Address Resolution Protocol
Abbreviated ARP. A *protocol* within *TCP/IP* and *AppleTalk* networks that allows a *host* to find the physical address of a *node* on the same network when it only knows the target's logical *address*.

Under ARP, a *network interface card* contains a table (known as the address resolution cache) that maps logical addresses to the hardware addresses of nodes on the network. The next time a node needs to send a packet, it first checks the address resolution cache to see if the physical address information is already present. If so, that address is used and network traffic is reduced; otherwise a normal ARP request is made to determine the address.

ADMIN object   A user *object*, created during installation of NetWare 4.*x*, that has the *rights* to create and manage other objects.

ADMIN has Supervisor rights, and can therefore populate the *NDS* tree.

Advanced Communications Function   Abbreviated ACF. A set of program packages from IBM that allows computer resources to be shared over communications links using the concepts of *SAA* (Systems Application Architecture).

For example, ACF/TCAM (Advanced Communications Functions/Telecommunications Access Method) and ACF/VTAM (Advanced Communications Functions/Virtual Telecommunications Access Method) allow the interconnection of two or more *domains* into one multiple-domain network.

Advanced Communications Service   Abbreviated ACS. A large data-communications network established by AT&T.

Advanced Interactive Executive   See **AIX**.

Advanced Peer-to-Peer Networking   See **APPN**.

Advanced Program-to-Program Communications   See **APPC**.

advanced run-length limited encoding   Abbreviated ARLL. A technique used to store information on a hard disk that increases the capacity of run-length limited (RLL) storage by more than 25 percent and increases the data-transfer rate to 9 megabits per second.

See also **run-length limited encoding**.

advertising   The process by which services on a network inform other devices on the network of their availability. Novell NetWare uses the *Service Advertising Protocol* (SAP) for this purpose.

AFP   A Novell NetWare *NLM* that provides support for the *AppleTalk Filing Protocol* (AFP) so that Mac users can access applications or files from a NetWare server just as though they were stored on a local drive.

See also **AFPCON, ATCON, ATCONFIG, ATPS, ATPSCON, ATXRP**.

AFP   See **AppleTalk Filing Protocol**.

AFPCON   A Novell NetWare *NLM* that lets you configure the *AFP* system on your file server.
See also **AFP, ATCON, ATCONFIG, ATPS, ATPSCON, ATXRP.**

aftermarket   The market for related hardware, software, and peripheral devices created by the sale of a large number of computers of a specific type.

AIX   Abbreviation for Advanced Interactive eXecutive. A version of the *Unix* operating system from IBM that runs on IBM RS/6000 workstations, PS/2 desktop computers, minicomputers, and System 370/390 mainframe computers.

alias object   In Novell NetWare 4.*x*, a *leaf object* that references the original location of an object in the directory.

ALLOW   A Novell NetWare 3.*x* workstation utility used to view, set, or modify the *Inherited Rights Mask* for a file or directory. You can also view the current *rights* settings for a file or directory.
In NetWare 4.*x*, use the *RIGHTS* utility for this purpose.

alphanumeric   Consisting of letters, numbers, and sometimes special control characters, spaces, and other punctuation characters.
See also **ASCII, EBCDIC, Unicode.**

alpha testing   The first stage in testing a new hardware or software product, usually performed by the in-house developers or programmers.
See also **beta testing.**

alternative route   A secondary communications path to a specific destination. An alternative route is used when the primary path is not available.
See also **adaptive routing.**

AMD   Abbreviation for American Micro Devices. Manufacturer of microprocessors, specializing in clones of *Intel's* popular *80386* and *80486* chips:
• **AMD386DX.** An 80386DX clone
• **AMD386SX.** An 80386SX clone
• **AMD486DX.** A clone of the popular 80486DX microprocessor from Intel
• **AMD486DX2.** A clock-doubled clone of the 80486DX2 chip
• **AMD K5.** A *pin-compatible* clone of Intel's *Pentium* processor,

available in late 1995, containing 24K of on-board cache (8K data, 16K code), a built-in floating-point processor, a 32-bit address bus, and a 64-bit data bus

See also **Cyrix, NexGen, P6.**

American National Standards Institute   See ANSI.

American Standard Code for Information Interchange   See ASCII.

AMPS   Acronym for Advanced Mobile Phone Service. Currently the cellular telephone standard in the United States, an *analog*, cellular communications system developed by AT&T. AMPS uses *frequency-division multiplexing* (FDM) and operates in the 825 to 890 megahertz (MHz) range.

analog   Describes any device that represents changing values by a continuously variable physical property, such as a voltage in a circuit. Analog often refers to transmission methods developed to transmit voice signals rather than high-speed digital signals.

ANI   See **automatic number identification.**

anonymous ftp   A method of accessing an *Internet* computer with the *ftp* file-transfer program. Anonymous ftp does not require you to have an account on the target computer system. Just log in with the user name anonymous and use your *e-mail address* as your password.

You can use anonymous ftp with only those systems set up to offer the service.

In the Unix world, the term is lowercased, but in the world of Windows and OS/2, you'll sometimes see it in all capital letters.

See also **Archie, archive.**

ANSI   Abbreviation for American National Standards Institute. A nonprofit organization of more than one thousand business and industry groups, founded in 1918, devoted to the development of voluntary standards.

ANSI represents the United States in the *International Standards Organization* (ISO) and is affiliated with *CCITT*. ANSI committees have developed recommendations for the programming languages COBOL, FORTRAN, and C, as well as the *SCSI* interface and the *fiber-distributed data interface* (FDDI) fiber-optic standard.

answer mode   A function that allows a modem to answer an incoming call, detect the protocol being used by the calling modem, and synchronize with that protocol. On a Hayes-compatible modem, answer mode is controlled by the command ATS0=*n*, where *n* specifies the number of rings that the modem waits before answering.

anti-virus program   A program that detects or eliminates a computer *virus*. Some anti-virus programs are *terminate-and-stay-resident* (TSR) programs that can detect suspicious activity on your computer as it happens; others must be run periodically as part of your normal housekeeping activities.

An anti-virus program locates and identifies a virus by looking for characteristic patterns or suspicious activity in the system, such as unexpected disk access or .EXE files changing in some unusual way. It recognizes the virus by comparing information from the system against a database of known viruses, which is kept on disk.

Be sure you test an anti-virus program carefully on your network before you employ it everywhere; some programs impose an enormous overhead on normal network operations.

See also **virus**.

API   See **application program interface**.

APPC   Abbreviation for Advanced Program-to-Program Communication. A set of protocols developed by IBM as a part of its *SNA* (Systems Network Architecture), designed to allow applications running on PCs and mid-range *hosts* to exchange data easily and directly with mainframes. APPC can be used over an SNA, *Ethernet*, *X.25*, or *Token Ring* network.

APPC/PC is a PC-based version of APPC used over a Token-Ring network.

Apple Computer, Inc.   Manufacturer of the successful Macintosh and Quadra series of computers based on Motorola chips. The company was founded by Steve Wozniak and Steve Jobs in a garage on April 1, 1976. However, as is often the case with innovative startup companies, most of the original founders have moved on to other ventures.

In 1993, Apple entered the consumer electronics marketplace with a personal digital assistant known as Newton, combining *fax, electronic mail*, and other functions into a unit small enough to fit into a pocket.

In 1994, Apple launched a new series of computers called the Power Macintosh (or Power Mac), based on the PowerPC, capable of running either the Macintosh operating system or DOS/Windows programs under software emulation. In a further attempt to narrow the gap between Macintosh and DOS/Windows systems, the Power Mac 6100/66 DOS Compatible system has both a PowerPC chip and an Intel 486DX2 chip inside, and you can switch from one operating system to the other with a single keystroke.

Early in 1995, Apple announced plans to license the Macintosh operating system and other technology to allow independent manufacturers to create Macintosh clones.

Apple Desktop Bus   A *serial communications* link that connects low-speed input devices, such as a mouse or keyboard, to the computer on the Macintosh SE, II, IIx, IIcx, and SE/30. Light pens, trackballs, and drawing tablets may also be connected via the Apple Desktop Bus. Most Apple Desktop Bus devices allow one

device to be daisy-chained to the next, up to a maximum of sixteen devices.

Apple Macintosh   See **Macintosh**.

AppleShare   Network software from *Apple Computer* that requires a dedicated *Macintosh* computer acting as a centralized server and includes both server and workstation software. AppleShare uses the *AppleTalk Filing Protocol* (AFP).

AppleTalk   An Apple Macintosh network *protocol*, based on the *ISO/OSI model*, which gives every Macintosh networking capabilities. AppleTalk can run under several network operating systems, including Apple Computer's AppleShare, Novell NetWare for the Macintosh, and TOPS from Sun Microsystems.

AppleTalk (see the illustration on the next page) includes specifications for the *data-link layer* as LocalTalk, EtherTalk, or TokenTalk, and the *network layer* as Datagram Delivery Protocol. The *transport layer* contains four protocols: Routing Table Maintenance Protocol (RTMP), AppleTalk Echo Protocol (AEP), AppleTalk Transaction Protocol

(ATP), and Name Binding Protocol (NBP). The *session layer* includes AppleTalk Data Stream Protocol (ADSP), AppleTalk Session Protocol (ASP), Printer Access Protocol (PAP), and Zone Information Protocol (ZIP). The *presentation layer* adds the *AppleTalk Filing Protocol* (AFP) for access to remote files on shared disks.

A revision of AppleTalk was released in 1989 to increase support to sixteen million nodes, and add enhancements needed for large networks.

AppleTalk Filing Protocol   Abbreviated AFP. AFP is located in the *presentation* and *application layers* of the *AppleTalk protocol stack*. AFP lets users access remote files as though they were local, as well as providing security features that can restrict user access to certain files.

application   Abbreviated app. A computer program designed to perform a specific task, such as accounting, scientific analysis, word processing, or desktop publishing.

Layer 7: application layer	AppleShare			
Layer 6: presentation layer	AppleTalk Filing Protocol (AFP)			
Layer 5: session layer	ASP	ADSP	ZIP	PAP
Layer 4: transport layer	ATP	NBP	AEP	RTMP
Layer 3: network layer	Datagram Delivery Protocol (DDP)			
Layer 2: data-link layer	Local-Talk	Ether-Talk	FDDI-Talk	Token-Talk
Layer 1: physical layer	network interface card and cabling			

APPLETALK

13

In general, applications can be distinguished from system software, system utilities, and computer language compilers, and they can be categorized as either stand-alone or network applications. Stand-alone applications run from the hard disk in an independent computer, so only one user at a time can access the application. Network applications run on networked computers and can be shared by many different users. Advanced applications such as *groupware* and *e-mail* allow communications between network users.

See also **application metering, client/server architecture, LAN-aware.**

application layer   The seventh, or highest, layer in the ISO/OSI model for computer-to-computer communications. This layer uses services provided by the lower layers but is completely insulated from the details of the network hardware. It describes how *applications* interact with the *network operating system*, including database management, *electronic mail*, and *terminal emulation* programs.

See also **ISO/OSI model.**

application metering   The process of counting the number of executions of the copies of an application in use on the network at any given time, and ensuring that the number does not exceed certain limits.

Application metering is usually performed by a network management application running on the file server. Most application metering software will allow only a certain number of copies (usually that number specified in the application software license) of an application to run at any one time, and will send a message to any users who try to exceed this limit.

See also **concurrent license.**

application program interface   Abbreviated API. The complete definition of all the operating system functions available to an *application* (the functions the application can use to perform tasks such as managing files and displaying information on the computer screen) and how the application should use those functions. In operating systems that support a *graphical user interface*, the API also defines functions to support windows, icons, pull-down menus, and other components of the interface. In *network operating systems*, an API defines a standard method that applications can use to take advantage of all the network features.

application server A special type of *file server* optimized for a specific task, such as communications or a database application, that uses higher-end hardware than a typical file server.

See also **superserver**.

application-specific integrated circuit Abbreviated ASIC. A computer chip developed for a specific purpose, designed by incorporating standard *cells* from a library rather than created from scratch. Also known as a gate array, an ASIC can be designed and manufactured very quickly. The only drawback is that much of the chip remains unused.

APPN Abbreviation for Advanced Peer-to-Peer Networking. IBM's SNA (Systems Network Architecture) *protocol*, based on *APPC*. APPN allows nodes on the network to interact without a mainframe *host* computer and implements dynamic *network directories* and dynamic *routing* in an SNA network.

APPN can run over a variety of network media, including *Ethernet, token ring, FDDI, ISDN, X.25, SDLC*, and higher-speed links such as *B-ISDN* or *ATM*.

arbitration The set of rules used to manage competing demands for a computer resource, such as memory or peripheral devices, made by multiple processes or users.

See also **contention**.

Archie A system used on the Internet to locate files available by *anonymous ftp*. Once a week, special programs connect to all the known anonymous ftp sites on the Internet and collect a complete listing of all the publicly available files. This listing of files is kept in an Internet Archive Database, and when you ask Archie to look for a file, it searches this database rather than the whole Internet; you then use anonymous ftp to retrieve the file.

architecture

1. The overall design and construction of all or part of a computer, particularly the processor hardware and the size and ordering sequence of its bytes.

2. The overall design of software.

See also **client/server architecture, closed architecture, complex instruction set computing, open architecture, reduced instruction set computing**.

15

archive

1. To transfer files to some form of long-term storage, such as magnetic tape or optical disk, when the files are no longer needed on a regular basis but must be maintained for periodic reference.

2. On the Internet, a site containing a collection of files available via *anonymous ftp*.

See also **erasable CD**.

ARCnet

Acronym for Attached Resources Computing network. A network available from the Datapoint Corporation and other vendors that can connect a wide variety of PCs and workstations (up to a maximum of 255) on *coaxial, twisted-pair,* or *fiber-optic cable*. ARCnet uses a proprietary *token-passing* access method at speeds of up to 2.5 megabits per second (Mbps). ARCnet Plus is Datapoint's proprietary product that runs at 20 Mbps.

ARCnet is very popular for smaller networks, because it is relatively easy to set up and to operate, and also because the components are inexpensive and widely available.

See also **token-ring network**.

ARLL

See **advanced run-length limited encoding**.

ARP

See **Address Resolution Protocol**.

ARPANET

Acronym for Advanced Research Projects Agency Network. A research network funded by the Defense Advanced Research Projects Agency (DARPA) to link universities and government research agencies, originally built by BBN, Inc. in 1969. It was the backbone for the now huge *Internet. TCP/IP* protocols were pioneered on ARPANET. In 1983, the military communications portion was split off into the MILNET.

AS/400

A series of minicomputers from IBM, first introduced in 1988, that replaces the System/36 and System/38 series of computers. The AS/400 can serve in a wide variety of network configurations: as a host or an intermediate node to other AS/400 and System/3x computers, as a remote system to System/370-controlled networks, or as a network server to a group of PCs.

ASCII

Acronym for American Standard Code for Information Interchange, pronounced "askee." A standard coding scheme that assigns numeric values to letters, numbers, punctuation characters, and control characters to achieve compatibility among different computers and peripheral devices. In ASCII, each character is represented by a unique integer value, from 0 to 255; see Table A.2 in the appendix.

See also **ASCII extended character set, ASCII file, ASCII standard character set, EBCDIC, Unicode.**

ASCII extended character set

The second group of characters, from 128 to 255, in the ASCII character set. The extended ASCII character set is assigned variable sets of characters by computer hardware manufacturers and software developers, and it is not necessarily compatible between different computers. The IBM extended character set used in the PC (see Table A.3 in the appendix) includes mathematical symbols and characters from the PC line-drawing set.

See also **ASCII, ASCII file, ASCII standard character set, EBCDIC, Unicode.**

ASCII file
A file that contains only text characters from the ASCII character set. An ASCII file can include letters, numbers, and punctuation symbols, but does not contain any hidden text-formatting codes. Also known as a text file or an ASCII text file.

See also **ASCII, ASCII extended character set, ASCII standard character set, binary file.**

ASCII standard character set
A character set that consists of the first 128 (from 0 to 127) ASCII characters. The values 0 to 31 are used for nonprinting control codes (see Table A.1 in the appendix), and the range from 32 to 127 is used to represent the letters of the alphabet and common punctuation symbols. The entire set from 0 to 127 is referred to as the standard ASCII character set (see Table A.2 in the appendix). All computers that use ASCII can understand the standard ASCII character set.

See also **ASCII, ASCII file, ASCII extended character set, EBCDIC, Unicode.**

ASCII text file
See **ASCII file.**

ASIC
See **application-specific integrated circuit.**

Association of Banyan Users International
Abbreviated ABUI. The Banyan user group, with 1700 members worldwide,

concerned with all hardware and software related to the Banyan system, including *Banyan VINES*.

asterisk   In several operating systems, you can use the asterisk (*) as a *wildcard character* to represent one or more unknown characters in a file-name or file-name extension.

See also **question mark**.

asymmetrical multiprocessing

A multiprocessing design in which the programmer matches a specific task to a certain processor while writing the program.

This design makes for a much less flexible system than *symmetrical multiprocessing* (SMP). SMP allocates tasks to processors as the program starts up, on the basis of current system load and available resources.

asynchronous communications

See **asynchronous transmission**.

asynchronous communications server   A *local-area network* (LAN) server that allows a network user to dial out of the network into the public switched telephone system, or to access *leased lines* for asynchronous communications. Asynchronous

communications servers may also be called *dial-in/dial-out servers* or *modem servers*.

Asynchronous Transfer Mode

Abbreviated ATM. A method used for transmitting voice, video, and data over high-speed *local-area networks* (LANs). ATM uses continuous bursts of fixed-length packets called cells to transmit data. The basic packet consists of 53 bytes, 5 of which are used for control functions and 48 for data.

ATM is a connection-oriented protocol, and two kinds of connection are possible: permanent virtual circuits (*PVCs*), in which connections are created manually, and switched virtual circuits (*SVCs*), in which connections are made automatically. Speeds of up to 2.488 gigabits per second have been achieved in testing. ATM will find wide acceptance in the LAN and *wide-area network* (WAN) arenas as a solution to integrating disparate networks over large geographical distances. Also known as *cell relay*.

asynchronous transmission   A method of data transmission that uses *start bits* and *stop bits* to coordinate the flow of data so the time intervals between individual characters do not need to be

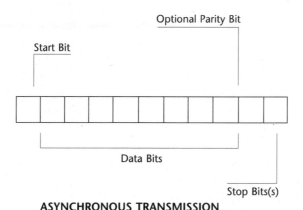

equal. *Parity* also may be used to check the accuracy of the data received. The accompanying illustration shows a single data word sent by asynchronous transmission.

See also **communications parameters, data bits, synchronous transmission.**

AT command set   A set of standard instructions used to activate features on a *modem*. Originally developed by Hayes Microcomputer Products, the AT command set is now used by almost all modem manufacturers.

The code AT is short for ATtention, and it precedes most of the modem commands. On a Hayes or Hayes-compatible modem, the ATDP (ATtention Dial Pulse) command initiates pulse dialing, while the ATDT (ATtention Dial Tone) command initiates touch-tone dialing.

See also **modem.**

ATCON   A Novell NetWare NLM that lets you monitor activity on *AppleTalk* network segments.

See also **AFP, AFPCON, ATCONFIG.**

ATCONFIG   A Novell NetWare *NLM* used to configure NetWare for the Macintosh.

See also **AFP, AFPCON, ATCON.**

ATM   See **Asynchronous Transfer Mode.**

Optional Parity Bit

Start Bit

Data Bits

Stop Bits(s)

ASYNCHRONOUS TRANSMISSION

19

ATOTAL   A Novell NetWare 2.*x* and 3.*x* workstation utility that displays all the *accounting* charges for a particular server. Use the *SYSCON* utility to determine chargeable services and to set the associated charge rates.

ATPS   A Novell NetWare *NLM* that supports the *AppleTalk* Print Services (APS) protocols. ATPS gives all users access to all available printers.
   See also **AFP, AFPCON, ATCON, ATCONFIG, ATPS, ATPSCON, ATXRP.**

ATPSCON   A Novell NetWare *NLM* used to configure *AppleTalk* Print Services.
   See also **AFP, AFPCON, ATCON, ATCONFIG, ATPS, ATXRP.**

at-symbol   In an *e-mail* address the @ symbol is often used to separate the UserID from the domain name of the computer used for mail.
   See also **bang path.**

ATTACH   A Novell NetWare 3.*x* workstation utility used to *attach* to servers other than the one you are currently logged in to. Attaching to a server makes its file system and other resources available without requiring you to log out of your current server.
   In NetWare 4.*x*, use the *LOGIN/ utility instead.* You can use ATTACH in *login scripts* in NetWare versions 2.*x*, 3.*x*, and 4.*x*.
   See also **MAP.**

attach   To establish a connection between a workstation and a network file server; particularly, to access additional servers after logging in to one server.

Attachment Unit Interface
   See **AUI.**

attenuation   The decrease in power of a signal with increasing distance. Attenuation is measured in *decibels*, and it increases as the power of the signal decreases. The best cables (those exhibiting the least attenuation) are *fiber-optic* lines, and the worst cables are unshielded, untwisted-pair lines, such as the silver, flat-satin cables used in short-run telephone and modem lines.
   In a *local-area network* (LAN), attenuation can become a problem when cable lengths exceed the stated network specification; however, the useful length of a cable

may be extended by the use of a *repeater*.

attribute

1. A file attribute is a technique for describing access to and properties of files and directories within a file system. In Novell NetWare, file attributes include Archive, Read, Write, Create, Execute, and Shareable. File and directory attributes include Delete inhibit, Hidden, Purge, Rename inhibit, and System. A user cannot override attributes, but they can be changed by a user who has at least the Modify right. You may see the term attribute used interchangeably with the term property.

2. A screen attribute controls a character's background and foreground colors, as well as other characteristics, such as underlining, reverse video, and blinking.

3. In DOS and other operating systems, a characteristic that indicates whether a file is a read-only file, a hidden file, a system file, or has changed in some way since it was last backed up.

See also **FLAG, NDIR.**

ATXRP A Novell NetWare *NLM* that sends a print job from a NetWare print queue to an *AppleTalk* network printer.

See also **AFP, AFPCON, ATCON, ATCONFIG, ATPS, ATPSCON.**

AUDITCON A Novell NetWare workstation utility that creates a log file to allow an independent auditor to verify that network transactions are accurate and that confidential information is secure. When *auditing* is enabled, an auditor can track when files or directories are created, deleted, modified, salvaged, moved, or renamed. Changes to security *rights* can also be tracked.

auditing The process of scrutinizing network security-related events and transactions to ensure that they are accurate, particularly reviewing attempts to create, access, and delete files and directories. Records of these events are usually stored in a security log file, which can only be examined by users with special *permissions*.

audit trail An automatic feature of certain programs or operating systems that creates a running record of all transactions. An audit trail allows you to track a piece of data from the moment it enters the system to the moment it leaves and to determine the origin of any changes to that data.

AUI Abbreviation for Attachment Unit Interface. A 15-pin socket used by some *Ethernet* devices. AUI connections adapt between two different cabling types and work with a wide range of wiring schemes. Also known as a DIX (for Digital, Intel, Xerox) connector.

authentication In a *network operating system* or *multiuser* system, the process that validates a user's login information. Authentication usually involves comparing the user name and *passwords* to a list of authorized users. If a match is found, the user can log in and access the system in accordance with the *rights* or *permissions* assigned to his or her *user account.*

auto-answer A feature of a modem that allows it to answer incoming calls automatically.

See also **answer mode, dial-back modem.**

auto-dial A feature of a modem that allows it to open a telephone line and start a call. To auto-dial, the modem sends a series of pulses or tones that represent a stored telephone number.

See also **callback modem.**

AUTOEXEC.BAT A contraction of AUTOmatically EXE-Cuted BATch. A special DOS *batch file,* located in the *root directory* of your startup disk, that runs automatically every time you start or restart your computer. The commands contained in AUTOEXEC.BAT are executed one by one, just as if you had typed them at the system prompt. An AUTOEXEC.BAT file can be used to load hardware device drivers, set the system prompt, change the default drive to the first *network drive,* and log the user in to the file server.

In *OS/2,* you can select any batch file to be used as AUTO-EXEC.BAT for a specific DOS session, so you can tailor specific environments for separate DOS sessions, each using a different AUTOEXEC.BAT file.

See also **AUTOEXEC.NCF, boot, bootstrap, CONFIG.SYS, SERVER.**

AUTOEXEC.NCF A Novell NetWare batch file usually located on the NetWare *partition* of the server's hard disk, used to set the NetWare operating system configuration. AUTOEXEC.NCF loads the *local-area network*

(LAN) drivers, the *NetWare Loadable Modules* (NLMs), and the settings for the *network interface boards*, and then binds the *protocols* to the installed drivers.

See also **NetWare command files.**

automatic number identification
Abbreviated ANI. A method of passing a caller's telephone number over the network to the recipient so the caller can be identified. ANI is often associated with *ISDN* (Integrated Services Digital Network), and is sometimes known as caller ID.

automatic rollback
In a Novell NetWare network, a feature of the *Transaction Tracking System* (TTS) that abandons the current transaction and returns a database to its original condition if the network fails in the middle of a transaction. Automatic rollback prevents the database from being corrupted by information from incomplete transactions.

See also **backing out.**

A/UX
A version of the *Unix* operating system that runs on the Macintosh.

A/UX is based on the *System V* release 2 of Unix and includes a number of Apple features, such as support for the Macintosh Toolbox. This support allows applications running under A/UX to use the familiar Macintosh user interface. You need a Macintosh II with a Motorola *68020* or higher microprocessor and at least 4 megabytes of memory to use A/UX.

AUX
The *DOS* name for the auxiliary device, usually the default *serial communications* port, also known as COM1.

AWG
Abbreviation for American Wire Gauge. A measurement system that specifies copper wire by thickness; as thickness increases, the AWG number decreases. Some common conductor gauges are:
- **RS-232-C:** 22 or 24 AWG
- **Thick Ethernet:** 12 AWG
- **Thin Ethernet:** 20 AWG

See also **cabling standards, EIA/TIA 586, Type 1–9 cable.**

B

backbone   That portion of the network that manages the bulk of the traffic. The backbone may connect several different locations or buildings, and other, smaller networks may be attached to it; see the accompanying illustration. The backbone often uses a higher-speed *protocol* than the individual *local-area network* (LAN) segments.

back-end processor   A secondary processor that performs one specialized task very effectively, freeing the main processor for other, more important work.

back-end system   The server part of a client/server system that runs on one or more file servers, and provides services to the *front-end applications* running on networked workstations. The back-end system accepts query requests sent from a front-end application, processes those requests, and returns the results to the workstation.

See also **client/server architecture**.

corporate backbone

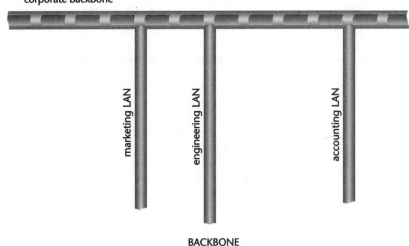

marketing LAN

engineering LAN

accounting LAN

BACKBONE

background

1. On a computer screen, the color on which characters are displayed; for example, white characters may appear on a blue background.

2. In an operating system, a process that runs in the background generally runs at a lower level of priority than a foreground task and does not accept input from the user. Only multitasking operating systems support true background and foreground processing, but some applications can mimic it; for example, many word processors can print a document while still accepting input from the keyboard.

See also **foreground, multitasking.**

background authentication

The process used to give a workstation access to a particular server. In Novell NetWare, *password* authentication uses a public key encryption scheme to protect password information before it is transmitted over the network. All this activity takes place in the *background*, and all the user has to do is enter his or her password.

background noise

Any unwanted signal that enters a line, channel, or circuit; for example, electrical interference on a telephone circuit.

See also **noise.**

backing out

The process of abandoning the current transaction and returning a database to its original condition if the network fails during the transaction. This process prevents the database from being corrupted by information from the incomplete transaction.

See also **automatic rollback, Transaction Tracking System.**

backslash

1. In *DOS, OS/2,* and other operating systems, you must use the backslash character (\) to separate directory or subdirectory names in a *path* statement or when changing to another directory.

2. A shorthand name for the *root directory*.

3. In *Microsoft Windows,* you can use the backslash key with the Ctrl key (press Ctrl-\) in the *File Manager* to deselect all the currently selected files.

See also **slash.**

backup   An up-to-date copy of all your files. There are several reasons to make a backup:

- Insurance against possible hard-disk or file-server failure. Hard disks often fail completely, taking all your work with them. If this failure occurs, you can reload your files and directories from the backup copy. A backup is your insurance against disk failure affecting the thousands or possibly tens of thousands of files you might have on your file server.

- Protection against accidental deletion of files or directories. Again, if you mistakenly delete a file or directory, you can retrieve a copy from your last backup.

- As an *archive* at the end of a project, when a person leaves your company, or at the end of a financial period such as year-end close.

Your decision when or how often to make a backup depends on how frequently important data on your system changes. If you rely on certain files always being available on your system, it is crucial that you make regular, consistent backups. Here are some backup tips:

- Keep multiple copies— redundancy should be a part of your backup plan.

- Test your backups to make sure they are what you think they are, and you can reload the information you need.

- Store your backups in a secure off-site location; do not leave them right next to the computer (if the computer is damaged by an accident, the backup may be damaged as well).

- Replace your backup media on a regular basis.

- Consider making incremental backups of critical data at more frequent intervals.

See also **archive, differential backup, disk duplexing, disk mirroring, full backup, incremental backup.**

backup program   An application that you use to make *archive* or *backup* copies of important data files.

Most operating systems offer commands for making backups, but many are limited in capability. The most cost-effective backup programs are from third-party vendors.

See also **disk duplexing, disk mirroring, full backup, incremental backup, tape cartridge, tape drive.**

27

backward compatibility
Full compatibility with earlier versions of the same application or computer system.

bad sector
An area on a hard disk or floppy disk that cannot be used to store data, because of a manufacturing defect or accidental damage.

An operating system will find, mark, and isolate bad sectors. Almost all hard disks have some bad sectors, often listed in the *bad track table*. Usually, bad sectors are a result of the manufacturing process and not a concern; the operating system will mark them as bad, and you will never even know they are there.

bad track table
A list of the defective areas on a hard disk, usually determined during final testing of the disk at the factory. Some disk-preparation programs ask you to enter information from this list to reduce the time that a *low-level format* takes to prepare the disk for use by the operating system.

balun
A contraction of BALanced UNbalanced. A small device used to connect a balanced line (such as a *twisted-pair cable*) to an unbalanced line (such as a *coaxial cable*). The balun matches impedances between the two media.

bandwidth

1. In communications, the difference between the highest and lowest frequencies available for transmission in any given range.

2. In networking, the transmission capacity of a computer or a communications channel, stated in *megabits per second* (Mbps). For example, *Ethernet* has a bandwidth of 10 Mbps, and *fiber-distributed data interface* (FDDI) has a bandwidth of 100 Mbps.

bandwidth on demand
A feature of *wide-area networks* (WANs) that allows the user to dial up additional bandwidth as the application demands. Most network traffic does not flow in steady and easily predictable streams, but in short bursts, separated by longer periods of inactivity. This pattern makes it very difficult to predict peak loads. Bandwidth on demand allows the user to pay for only the amount of bandwidth used.

See also **virtual data network**.

bang   A name given in the *Unix* and *Internet* worlds to the exclamation point (!) character.

bang path   An old-style *UUCP e-mail address* that uses excla mation points to separate the sequence of computer names needed to get to the addressee. Bang paths list addresses—general to specific—from left to right, which is the reverse of the sequence used by other addressing schemes.

See also **at-symbol, domain name, e-mail address**.

Banyan VINES   A network operating system from Banyan Systems. VINES (a contraction of VIrtual NEtworking Software) is based on a special version of the Unix System V operating system. The accompanying illustration shows the VINES architecture. This Unix layer is hidden from view by VINES and is not available for other applications. VINES provides all server functions, including those of a *communications/modem server*, and offers many options for connecting to minicomputers, mainframes, and other network file servers. VINES supports up to

Layer 7: application layer	VINES File Service		VINES Applications Services	
Layer 6: presentation layer	VINES Remote Procedure Calls (RPC)		Servers Message Block (SMB)	
Layer 5: session layer	Socket Interface			
Layer 4: transport layer	VINES Interprocess Communications Protocol (VICP)	VINES Sequenced Packet Protocol (VSPP)	Transmission Control Protocol (TCP)	User Datagram Protocol (UDP)
Layer 3: network layer	VINES Internet Protocol (VIP)	Internet Protocol (IP)	X.25	
Layer 2: data-link layer	Network Driver Interface Specification (NDIS)	X.25 HDLC		
Layer 1: physical layer	network interface card and cabling			

BANYAN VINES

four *network interface cards* per server for any topology and automatically manages protocol binding and translations required between the network interface cards for routing to different local-area network (LAN) segments. A complete set of network management tools is built into the console.

Workstations can run DOS, Microsoft Windows, Unix, or OS/2, and they can store native-form files on the server. Macintosh computers can also attach to the network. VINES offers special support for very large LANs and *wide-area networks* (WANs) with multiple file servers. VINES also allows PCs that support multiple processors, such as the Compaq

System Pro, to use multiprocessing to divide the file server processing load.

See also **Enterprise Network Services, StreetTalk.**

baseband network   A technique for transmitting signals as direct-current pulses rather than as modulated signals. The entire bandwidth of the transmission medium is used by a single digital signal, so computers in a baseband network can transmit only when the channel is not busy; see the accompanying illustration. However, the network can use techniques such as *time-division*

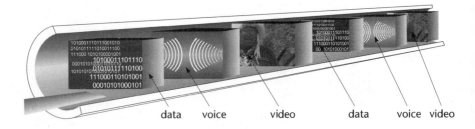

data   voice   video   data   voice video

BASEBAND NETWORK

multiplexing to allow channel sharing.

A baseband network can operate over relatively short distances (up to 2 miles if network *traffic* is light) at speeds from 50 kilobits per second up to 100 megabits per second. *Ethernet*, AppleTalk, and most PC *local-area networks* (LANs) use baseband techniques.

See also **bandwidth, broadband network, frequency-division multiplexing.**

baseline The process of determining and documenting network throughput and other performance information when the network is operating under what is considered to be a normal load. Measured performance characteristics might include error-rate and data-transfer information, along with information about the most active users and their applications.

basic input/output system
See **BIOS.**

Basic Rate ISDN Abbreviated BRI. An *ISDN* (Integrated Services Digital Network) service that offers two bearer channels: a 64-kilobits per second (Kbps) *bandwidth*

used for data transfer and a data-link, 16-Kbps channel used for signaling and control information.

See also **Primary Rate ISDN.**

batch file An *ASCII file* that contains operating system commands and other commands supported by the batch processor. Batch files are used to automate repetitive tasks. The commands in the file are executed one line at a time, just as if you had typed them at the system prompt. A DOS batch file must have the file-name extension .BAT. An OS/2 batch file has the extension .CMD.

See also **AUTOEXEC.BAT.**

baud A measurement of data-transmission speed. Originally used in measuring the speed of telegraph equipment, it now usually refers to the data-transmission speed of a modem or other serial device.

See also **baud rate.**

baud rate In communications equipment, a measurement of the number of state changes (from 0 to 1 or vice versa) per second on an *asynchronous communications* channel.

Baud rate is often assumed to correspond to the number of bits transmitted per second, but baud rate and bits per second (bps) are not always the same. In modern high-speed digital communications systems, one state change can be made to represent more than one data bit. A rate of 300 baud is likely to correspond to 300 bps; however, at higher baud rates, the number of bits per second transmitted can be higher than the baud rate. Bits per second is a more accurate statement of modem capability. For example, 2400 bps can be sent at 1200 baud if each state change represents two bits of information.

In the past, mismatched baud rates were one of the most common reasons for communications failures. However, modern modems can detect and lock onto one of a range of rates. Some modems can even change rates in response to changing line conditions during the course of a transmission.

See also **baud, bits per second.**

BBS   See **bulletin board system.**

bcc   Abbreviation for blind carbon copy. A list of recipients of an *e-mail* message whose names do not appear in the normal message header, so the original recipient of the message does not know that

copies have been forwarded to other locations.

beaconing   In a *Token Ring* network, the process of informing other *nodes* that *token passing* has been suspended because of a severe error condition, such as a broken cable. Communication cannot resume until the condition is resolved.

Bell communications standards

A set of data-transmission standards developed by AT&T in the 1980s that rapidly became the de facto standard for modem manufacturers. Although several of these standards are still widely used in the United States, the *CCITT V series* definitions are now generally accepted as the defining standards for modem use, data compression, and associated hardware.

benchmark program   A program that attempts to provide a consistent measurement of system performance. Some examples are Dhrystone, which measures microprocessor and memory performance; Whetstone, which measures speed of arithmetic operations; and Khornerstone, which measures overall system performance, including disk drive access speed, memory access speed, and processor performance.

The Systems Performance Evaluation Cooperative (SPEC) developed a set of ten tests to measure performance in actual application environments. The results of these tests are known as SPECmarks.

Some popular PC benchmark programs have been shown to provide wildly overoptimistic results, particularly when run on processors other than the one for which they were originally written.

BER   Abbreviation for bit error rate. The number of erroneous bits in a data transmission or in a data transfer, such as from CD-ROM to memory.

Berkeley Software Distribution Unix   See BSD Unix.

Berkeley Unix   See BSD Unix.

beta site   A location where beta testing is performed before a hardware or software product is formally released for commercial distribution.

See also **beta software, beta testing**.

beta software   Software that has been released to a cross-section of typical users for testing before the commercial release of the package. See also **beta testing**.

beta testing   The process of field testing new hardware or software products before the product's commercial or formal release. Beta testing is usually done by a cross-section of users, not just programmers. The purpose of beta testing is to expose the new product to as many real-life operating conditions as possible.

If the beta tests indicate a higher-than-expected rate of *bugs*, the developer usually fixes the problems and sends the product out again for another round of beta testing. Preliminary versions of the product documentation are also circulated for review during the beta testing.

See also **alpha testing**.

BGP   Abbreviation for Border Gateway Protocol. A *routing protocol* designed to replace *EGP* (External Gateway Protocol) and interconnect organizational networks. BGP, unlike EGP, evaluates each of the possible routes for the best one.

BGRCON   A Novell NetWare *NLM* that lets you look at configuration information for a NetWare Server for OS/2 bridge.

Big Blue   A nickname for *International Business Machine Corporation* (IBM), which uses blue as its corporate color.

binary   Any scheme that uses two different states, components, conditions, or conclusions. In mathematics, the binary or base-2 numbering system uses combinations of the digits 0 and 1 to represent all values. The more familiar decimal system has a base of 10 (0–9).

Unlike computers, people find binary numbers that consist of long strings of zeros and ones difficult to read, so most programmers use *hexadecimal* (base-16) or octal (base-8) numbers instead.

binary file   A file consisting of *binary* information. Usually, a binary file is a program or data file in machine-readable form rather than in human-readable ASCII text.

BIND   A Novell NetWare server utility used to bind a *protocol* to a *network interface card* or *device*

driver. The default when you install NetWare or add boards or drivers using *INSTALL* is to bind the *IPX* protocol.

bindery   A database maintained by the Novell NetWare 2.*x* and 3.*x network operating systems*. The bindery contains information about users, servers, and other important network configuration details. The bindery is crucial to NetWare's operation, and is constantly consulted by the operating system. The bindery files (NET$BIND.SYS and NET$BVAL.SYS in NetWare 2.*x*, and NET$PROP.SYS, NET$VAL.SYS, and NET$OBJ.SYS in NetWare 3.*x*) are hidden, and should be located on the fastest drive available, and are located in the SYS: volume.

In NetWare 4.*x*, the bindery is replaced by *NetWare Directory Services* (NDS).

See also **BINDFIX, BINDREST**.

bindery services   A feature of Novell NetWare 4.*x* that provides *backward compatibility* with NetWare systems still using the *bindery*. Also known as bindery emulation.

BINDFIX A Novell NetWare 2.*x* and 3.*x* workstation utility used to repair a damaged server *bindery*. The utility locks the bindery files and then copies them to files named with an .OLD extension. After the bindery is rebuilt, BINDFIX reopens the bindery so that the server can be accessed once again. In Novell NetWare 4.*x*, a similar function is performed by the *DSREPAIR* command.

See also **BINDREST**.

BINDREST A Novell NetWare 2.0 and 3.*x* workstation utility used to delete the current copy of the *bindery* and restore the old copy that existed before *BIND-FIX* was run.

BIOS Acronym for basic input/output system, pronounced "bye-os." In a PC, the BIOS is a setof instructions that lets the computer's hardware and operating system communicate with applications and peripheral devices, such as hard disks, printers, and video adapters. These instructions are stored in *ROM* (read-only memory) as a permanent part of the computer. They are always available at specific *addresses* in memory, so all programs can access them to perform their basic *input/output* functions.

IBM computers contain a copyrighted BIOS that only IBM machines can use. Other companies, such as Phoenix, Award, and American Megatrends, have developed BIOS types for other manufacturer's computers. If you use a non-IBM computer, the BIOS company's copyright message and BIOS version number are displayed every time you turn on your computer.

As new hardware is developed, new BIOS routines must be created to service those devices. For example, BIOS support has been added for higher-capacity floppy disk drives and for larger hard disks. If you are experiencing problems accessing these devices after adding them to an existing system, your computer's BIOS may be out of date. Contact your computer supplier for information about BIOS updates.

See also **BIOS extensions, shadow memory**.

BIOS extensions In the PC, extensions to the main *BIOS* (basic input/output system) that enable the computer to work with add-on devices, such as hard-disk controllers and VGA adapters. The *ROM* (read-only memory) chips

35

containing BIOS extensions can be located on the *motherboard* or on *expansion boards* plugged into an *expansion bus*. The BIOS extensions are loaded automatically when you *boot* the computer.

bis   A term describing a secondary *CCITT* recommendation that is an alternative or extension to the primary recommendation. For example, the CCITT *V.42* standard refers to error correction, and the *V.42 bis* standard refers to data compression.

See also **ter**.

BISDN   Abbreviation for Broadband Integrated Service Digital Network. A high-speed communications standard for *wide-area networks* (WANs) that handles high-*bandwidth* applications,

such as video, voice, data, and graphics.

SMDS (Switched Multimegabit Data Services) and *ATM* (Asynchronous Transfer Mode) are two BISDN services that can provide a huge bandwidth for WANs.

bisynchronous communications   A *protocol* used extensively in mainframe computer networks. With bisynchronous communications, both the sending and receiving devices must be synchronized before data transmission begins.

Data is collected into a package known as a *frame*. Each frame contains leading and trailing characters that allow the computers to synchronize their clocks. The structure of a bisynchronous communications frame is shown in the accompanying illustration.

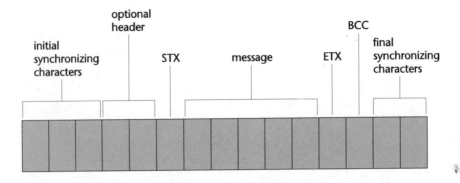

optional header

BCC

initial synchronizing characters

STX   message   ETX

final synchronizing characters

BISYNCHRONOUS COMMUNICATIONS

The STX and ETX control characters mark the beginning and end of the message. BCC is a set of characters used to verify the accuracy of the transmission.

A more modern form of this kind of protocol is *SDLC* (Synchronous Data Link Control), which is used in IBM's proprietary networking scheme, *SNA* (Systems Network Architecture).

See also **asynchronous transmission.**

bit   Contraction of BInary digiT. A bit is the basic unit of information in the *binary* numbering system, representing either 0 (for off) or 1 (for on). Bits can be grouped to form larger storage units; the most common grouping is the 7- or 8-bit *byte*.

See also **octet.**

bit-oriented protocol   A *communications protocol* in which data is transmitted as a stream of *bits* rather than a stream of *bytes*.

A bit-oriented protocol uses specific sequences of bits as control codes, unlike a byte-oriented protocol, which uses reserved characters. *HDLC* (High-level Data Link Control) and IBM's *SDLC* (Synchronous Data Link Control) are both bit-oriented protocols.

See also **byte-oriented protocol.**

bits per second   Abbreviated bps. The number of binary digits, or *bits*, transmitted every second during a data-transfer procedure. Bits per second is a measurement of the speed of operation of equipment, such as a computer's data bus or a modem that connects a computer to a transmission line. Speed in bits per second is not the same as *baud rate*.

blackout   A total loss of commercial electric power. To avoid loss of computer data due to a blackout, use a battery-backed *UPS* (uninterruptible power supply).

See also **brownout, power conditioning.**

block   In communications, a unit of transmitted information that includes header codes (such as addresses), data, and error-checking codes.

See also **checksum, error, detection and correction.**

block suballocation   A mechanism used in Novell NetWare 4.*x* that allows files to share the same block space by dividing each 8K hard-disk block up into smaller 512-byte segments. Files needing extra space can use these smaller segments rather than wasting a whole new disk block, making for more efficient disk-space use.

BMIGRATE   A Novell NetWare utility program used to migrate from the *Banyan VINES* network operating system to Novell NetWare 4.1. BMIGRATE operates in a manner similar to that of the standard *MIGRATE* utility and uses the *across-the-wire migration* method.

BNC connector   A small connector with a half-turn locking shell for coaxial cable, used with *thin Ethernet* and *RG-62* cabling. The accompanying illustration shows both male and female connectors.

boot   To load an *operating system* into *memory*, usually from a hard disk, although occasionally from a floppy disk. Booting is generally an automatic procedure that begins when you turn on or reset your computer. A set of instructions contained in *ROM* (read-only memory) begins executing. The instructions run a series of *power-on self tests* (POSTs) to check that devices such as hard disks are in working order, then locate and load the operating system, and finally

pass control over to that operating system.

Boot may be derived from the expression "pulling yourself up by your own bootstraps," and is sometimes called bootstrap.

See also **cold boot, warm boot.**

bootable disk   Any disk capable of loading and starting the operating system. Bootable floppy disks are becoming less common, because operating systems are growing larger. In some cases, all the files needed to start the operating system will not fit on even the largest-capacity floppy disk, which makes it impossible to boot from a floppy disk.

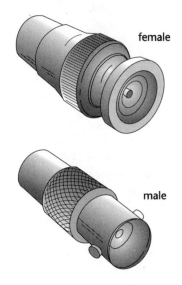

female

male

BNC CONNECTOR

BOOTCONF.SYS   A Novell NetWare configuration file that specifies how a diskless workstation boots the operating system from the file server. If the file server contains several different *remote boot* image files, BOOT-CONF.SYS determines which one will be loaded onto the workstation.

See also **diskless workstation**.

boot ROM   A type of *ROM* (read-only memory) that allows a workstation to communicate with the network file server and to read an image file containing a DOS *boot* program. In this way, a workstation without a local disk can boot DOS from the file server.

See also **diskless workstation**.

bootstrap   See **boot**.

Border Gateway Protocol
See **BGP**.

bounce   The return of an *e-mail* message to its original sender due to an error in delivery. There may be a simple spelling mistake in the *e-mail address*, the recipient's computer system may be down, or the recipient may no longer subscribe to or have an account on the system. A returned e-mail message will usually contain a description of why the message bounced.

bps   See **bits per second**.

breakout box   A small device that can be connected into a multi-core cable for testing the signals in a transmission. Small LEDs in the breakout box indicate when a signal is transmitted over one of the lines. Switches or short jumper cables can be used to re-route these signals to other pins as required for troubleshooting.

bridge   A hardware device used to connect *local-area networks* (LANs) so that they can exchange data. Bridges can work with networks that use different wiring or network *protocols*; see the illustration at the top of the following page.

A bridge operates at the *data-link layer* of the ISO/OSI model for computer-to-computer communications. It manages the flow of *traffic* between the two LANs by reading the *address* of every *packet* of data that it receives.

See also **brouter, gateway, ISO/OSI model, router**.

BrightWorks   A package of network management utilities from

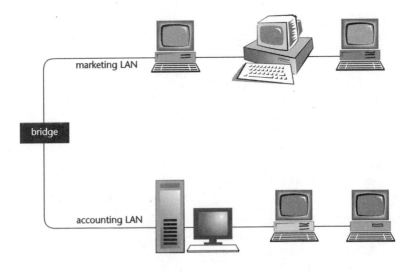

BRIDGE

McAfee Associates that includes hardware and software inventory, *application metering*, remote control of clients, virus detection, and a help-desk utility.

broadband network   A technique for transmitting a large amount of information, including voice, data, and video, over long distances using the same cable; see the illustration to the right. Sometimes called wideband transmission, it is based on the same technology used by cable television.

The transmission capacity is divided into several distinct channels that can be used concurrently by different networks, normally

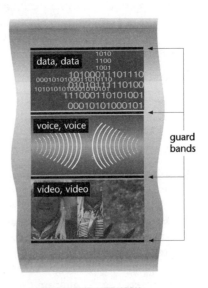

BROADBAND NETWORK

by *frequency-division multiplexing* (FDM). The individual channels are protected from each other by guard channels of unused frequencies. A broadband network can operate at speeds of up to 20 megabits per second.

See also **baseband network, multiplexer.**

BROADCAST A Novell NetWare server utility used to send a message from the server console to users logged in to the network. It can send a message to all users or to a specific user, group, or workstation connection number.

broadcast To send a message to all users currently logged in to the network.

See also **multicast.**

broadcast storm Congestion on a network that occurs when a large number of *frames* are transmitted by many workstations in response to a transmission from one workstation.

brouter A networking device that combines the attributes of a *bridge* and a *router*. A brouter can route one or more specific

protocols, such as *TCP/IP*, and bridge all others.

See also **gateway.**

brownout A short period of low voltage, often the result of an unusually heavy demand for power. A brownout may cause your computer to *crash*. If your area experiences frequent brownouts, consider using a *UPS* (uninterruptible power supply) as a battery backup system.

browser

1. An application program used to explore *Internet* resources. A browser lets you wander from node to node without concern for the technical details of the links between the nodes or the specific methods used to access them, and presents the information—text, graphics, sound, or video—as a document on the screen.

2. A small application used to scan a database or a list of files.

See also **HotJava, Mosaic, Web browser, World Wide Web.**

BSD Unix Abbreviation for Berkeley Software Distribution Unix, also known as Berkeley Unix. Derivatives of the *Unix* operating system, developed at the

University of California, Berkeley. BSD additions to Unix include virtual memory support, networking support, interprocess communication, support for additional peripherals, and *file system* and *security* enhancements.

buffer   An area of *memory* set aside for temporary storage of data. Often, the data remains in the buffer until some external event finishes. A buffer can compensate for the differences in transmission or processing speed between two devices or between a computer and a peripheral device, such as a printer.

buffered repeater   Any device that amplifies and retransmits a signal so that it can travel greater distances. A buffered repeater can also control the flow of information to prevent *collisions*.

See also **repeater**.

bug   A logical or programming error in hardware or software that causes a malfunction of some sort. If the problem is in software, it can be fixed by changes to the program. If the fault is in hardware, new circuits must be designed and constructed. Some bugs are fatal and may cause a

program to *crash* or cause data loss, others are just annoying, and many are not even noticeable. The term apparently originates from the days of the first electromechanical computers, when a problem was traced to a moth caught between two contacts inside the machinery.

See also **bug fix**.

bug fix   A release of hardware or software that corrects known *bugs* but does not contain new features. Such releases are usually designated by an increase in the decimal portion of the revision number; for example, the revision level may advance from 2.0 to 2.01 or 2.1, rather than from 2.0 to 3.0.

built-in groups   The default groups provided with *Windows NT* and *Windows NT 3.5 Server* that define a collection of *rights* and *permissions* for members. Using built-in groups is an easy way of providing access to commonly used network resources.

bulletin board system   Abbreviated BBS. A computer system equipped with one or more modems, serving as a message-passing system or centralized information source, usually for a particular special interest group. Bulletin board systems are often established by software vendors and by different PC user groups.

bundled software   Programs in a combined hardware and software package sold for a single price. *DOS* and the Macintosh *System 7* are examples of bundled operating system software. Applications are often also included in the package. Sales aimed at a specific target, such as the medical profession, usually bundle hardware with application-specific software suited to that profession.

See also **unbundled software.**

burst mode   A method of data transmission in which information is collected and then sent in one single high-speed transmission, rather than one packet or character at a time. Systems that use *multiplexers* to serve several channels often use burst mode to service each channel in turn. Much local-area network (LAN) traffic can be considered to be burst mode transmission: long periods of inactivity punctuated by short bursts of intense activity.

bus   An electronic pathway along which signals are sent from one part of a computer to another. A PC contains several buses, each used for a different purpose:

- The *address bus* allocates memory addresses.
- The data bus carries data between the processor and memory.
- The control bus carries signals from the control unit.

See also **architecture, EISA, ISA, local bus, MCA.**

bus mastering   A technique that allows certain advanced *bus architectures* to delegate control of data transfers between the central processing unit (CPU) and associated peripheral devices to an add-in board. This technique gives *network interface cards* greater system bus access and higher data-transfer speeds.

bus network   In networking, a *topology* that allows all network *nodes* to receive the same message through the network cable at the same time; see the illustration on the following page.

See also **ring network, star network, token-ring network.**

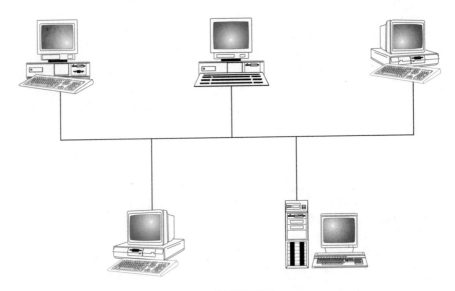

BUS NETWORK

byte Contraction of BinarY digiT Eight. A group of 8 bits, also known as an *octet*. In computer storage terms, a byte usually holds a single character, such as a number, letter, or symbol. On some older systems, a byte may only have 7 bits.

Because bytes represent a very small amount of storage, they are usually grouped into *kilobytes* (1,024 bytes), *megabytes* (1,048,576 bytes), and *gigabytes* (1,073,741,824 bytes) for convenience when describing hard-disk capacity or computer memory size.

byte-oriented protocol A *communications protocol* in which data is transmitted as a series of *bytes,* or characters. In order to distinguish the data from the control information, the protocol uses control characters that have a special meaning for the transmitting and receiving stations. Most of the common *asynchronous communications* protocols used in conjunction with modems are byte-oriented protocols.

See also **bit-oriented protocol**.

C2 A discretionary level of *operating system security* as defined by the NCSC (National Computer Security Center), requiring a user to log in to the system using a *password*.

cable modem A special cable connecting two computers so they can communicate without the need for modems.

See also **null modem**.

cabling standards National cabling standards, concerned with the performance of cables and connectors under conditions of actual use, include:

- ANSI/EIA/TIA-568-1991 Commercial Building Telecommunications Wiring.
- EIA/TIA TSB-36 Additional Cable Specifications for UTP Cables. 1991.
- EIA/TIA TSB-40 Telecommunications Systems Bulletin— Additional Transmission

Specifications for UTP Connecting Hardware. 1992.

- ANSI/EIA/TIA-568A 1995 revises the original 568 document, and adds material from TSB-36 and TSB-40.
- ANSI/EIA/TIA-569-1990 Commercial Building Standard for Telecommunications Pathways and Spaces.
- ANSI/EIA/TIA-570-1991 Residential and Light Commercial Telecommunications Wiring Standard.
- ANSI/EIA/TIA-606-1993 Administration Standard for the Telecommunications Infrastructure of Commercial Buildings.
- ANSI/EIA/TIA-607-1994 Commercial Building Grounding and Bonding Requirements for Telecommunications.

Local codes and standards may impose additional requirements.

Underwriters Laboratories (UL) tests cable and other devices to determine the conditions under which the device will function safely. Two important tests for cable performance are:

- **UL-910** tests smoke emission and flame spread for *plenum cable*.
- **UL-1666** tests smoke emission and flame spread for *riser cable*.

45

cache Pronounced "cash." A special area of memory, managed by a *cache controller*, that improves performance by storing the contents of frequently accessed memory locations and their *addresses*. When the processor references a memory address, the cache checks to see if it holds that address. If it does, the information is passed directly to the processor, so random-access memory (*RAM*) access is not necessary. A cache can speed up operations in a computer whose RAM access is slow compared with its processor speed, because cache memory is always faster than normal RAM.

There are several different types of cache:

- **Direct-mapped cache:** A location in the cache corresponds to several specific locations in memory, so when the processor calls for certain data, the cache can locate it quickly. However, since several blocks in RAM correspond to that same location in the cache, the cache may spend its time refreshing itself and calling main memory.

- **Fully associative cache:** Information from RAM may be placed in any free blocks in the cache, so that the most recently accessed data is usually present; however, the search to find that information may be slow because the cache has to index the data in order to find it.

- **Set-associative cache:** Information from RAM is kept in sets, and these sets may have multiple locations, each holding a block of data; each block may be in any of the sets, but it will only be in one location within that set. Search time is shortened, and it is less likely that frequently used data will be overwritten. A set-associative cache may use two, four, or eight sets.

A memory cache and a *disk cache* are not the same. This definition describes a memory cache, which is implemented in hardware and speeds up access to memory. A disk cache is software that improves hard-disk performance.

See also **wait state, write-back cache, write-through cache.**

cache buffer A Novell NetWare implementation of a *disk cache* used to speed up server disk accesses, thereby allowing workstations to access data more quickly. Reading data from cache memory is much faster than reading data from the hard disk.

NetWare uses cache buffers for a variety of purposes:

- For use by *NetWare Loadable Modules* (NLMs), such as local-area network (LAN) drivers,

database servers, communications servers, and print servers
- To cache each volume's *file allocation table* (FAT)
- To cache files currently in use
- To build a hash table of directory information

See also **disk cache**.

cache buffer pool   In Novell NetWare, the amount of memory available for use after the *SERVER.EXE* file has been loaded into memory.

cache controller   Pronounced "cash controller." A special-purpose processor, such as the Intel 82385, whose sole task it is to manage *cache memory*. On newer processors, such as the *Intel Pentium*, cache management is integrated directly into the processor.

cache memory   Pronounced "cash memory." A relatively small section of very fast memory (often *static RAM*) reserved for the temporary storage of the data or instructions likely to be needed next by the processor. For example, the *Intel Pentium* has an 8 kilobyte (KB) code cache as well as an 8 KB data cache.

caddy   The flat plastic container used to load a compact disc into a *CD-ROM disk drive*.

callback modem   Also known as a dialback modem. A special modem that does not answer an incoming call, but instead requires the caller to enter a code and hang up so that the modem can return the call. As long as the entered code matches a previously authorized number, the modem dials the number. Callback modems are useful in installations for which communications lines must be available for *remote users* but data must be protected from *intruders*.

caller ID   See **automatic number identification**.

call packet   A block of data that carries *addressing* information, as well as any other information needed to establish an *X.25* switched *virtual circuit*.

campus network   A network that connects *local-area networks* (LANs) from multiple departments inside a single building or set of buildings. Campus networks are

LANs because they do not include *wide-area network* (WAN) services, even though they may extend for several miles.

CAPTURE   A Novell NetWare workstation utility that redirects print jobs, allowing users to print to a network printer from within a network-unaware application. CAPTURE also allows you to redirect information to a network file, send screen displays to a network printer, and specify the number of copies to print.

See also **NPRINT, PRINTCON, PRINTDEF.**

card   A printed circuit board or *adapter* that you plug into a computer to add support for a specific piece of hardware.

See also **expansion board, expansion bus, PCMCIA.**

card services   Part of the software support needed for *PCMCIA* hardware devices in a portable computer. Card services control the use of *system interrupts*, memory, or power management.

When an application wants to access a *PCMCIA card*, it always goes through the card services software and never communicates directly with the underlying

hardware. For example, if you use a PCMCIA modem, it is the card services, not the applications program, that establishes which communications port and which interrupts and I/O addresses are in use.

See also **device driver, socket services.**

carriage return   A *control character* (ASCII 13) that signals the print head or display cursor to return to the first position of the current line.

See also **ASCII, EBCDIC, line feed.**

carrier   An analog signal of fixed amplitude and frequency that is combined with a data-carrying signal to produce an output signal suitable for transmitting data.

See also **carrier signal.**

carrier detect   See CD.

Carrier Sense Multiple Access/Collision Detection   See **CSMA/CD.**

carrier signal   A signal of chosen frequency generated to carry data, often used for long-distance transmissions. A carrier signal does not convey any information until the data is added to the signal by *modulation*, and then decoded on the receiving end by *demodulation*.

cascaded star A *network topology* in which multiple hubs or data centers are connected to each other in a succession of levels, which permits many more connections than a single level; see the accompanying illustration.

CASTOFF A Novell NetWare 3.*x* workstation utility that stops network messages from being displayed on your workstation. In NetWare 4.*x*, the *SEND* utility is used to perform this function.

See also **CASTON**.

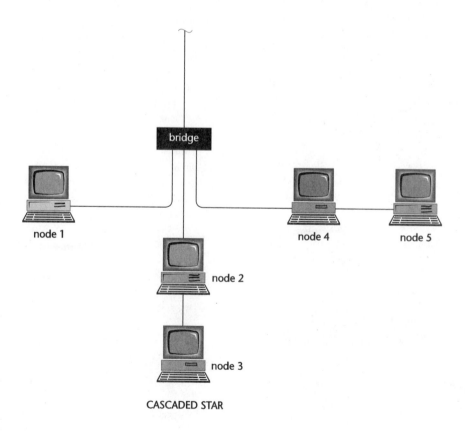

CASCADED STAR

CASTON   A Novell NetWare 3.*x* workstation utility that reverses CASTOFF and allows network messages to be displayed on your workstation once again. In NetWare 4.*x*, the function of this utility has been replaced by the *SEND* utility.

See also **CASTOFF**.

Category 1–5   The Electronics Industry Association/Telecommunications Industry Association (*EIA/TIA*) 586 cabling standards, as follows:

  • **Category 1:** For *unshielded twisted-pair* (UTP) telephone cable. This cable may be used for voice, but is not suitable for data transmissions.

  • **Category 2:** For UTP cable for use at speeds up to 4 megabits per second (Mbps). Category 2 cable is similar to IBM Cabling System Type 3 cable.

  • **Category 3:** For UTP cable for use at speeds up to 10 Mbps. Category 3 cable is the minimum requirement for *10BaseT,* and is required for *token ring*. This cable has four pairs of conductors and three twists per foot.

  • **Category 4:** For the lowest acceptable grade of UTP cable for use with 16 Mbps Token Ring.

  • **Category 5:** For 100-ohm, four-wire twisted-pair copper cable for use at speeds up to 100 Mbps

with *Ethernet* or *ATM*. This cable is low-capacitance, and shows low *crosstalk* when installed according to specifications.

See also **cabling standards, Type 1–9 cable.**

CAV   See **constant angular velocity.**

CCITT   Abbreviation for Comité Consultatif Internationale de Téléphonie et de Télégraphie. An organization based in Geneva that develops worldwide data communications standards. Three main sets of standards have been established: *CCITT Groups 1–4* standards apply to facsimile transmissions, the *CCITT V series* of standards apply to modems and error detection and correction methods, and the *CCITT X series* standards apply to *local-area networks* (LANs).

Recommendations are published every four years. Each update is identified by the color of its cover; the 1988 edition was known as the Blue Book, and the 1992 update has a white cover.

See also **ITU.**

CCITT Groups 1–4   A set of four *CCITT*-recommended standards for facsimile transmissions. Groups 1 and 2, which are no longer used, define analog facsimile transmissions. Groups 3 and 4 describe digital systems, as follows:

- **CCITT Group 3:** Specifies a 9600 bits per second (bps) modem to transmit standard images of 203 dots per inch (dpi) horizontally by 98 dpi vertically in standard mode, and 203 dpi by 198 dpi in fine mode.
- **CCITT Group 4:** Supports images up to 400 dpi for high-speed transmission over a digital data network (for example, *ISDN*), rather than over a dial-up telephone line.

CCITT V Series A set of recommended standards for data communications, including transmission speeds and operational modes, issued by *CCITT*. Each standard is assigned a number, although not in chronological order. Higher numbers do not always indicate a newer standard. A second or revised version is indicated by *bis*, and *ter* indicates a third version.

CCITT X Series A set of recommended standards issued by *CCITT* to standardize *protocols* and equipment used in public and private computer networks. The standards include transmission speeds, interfaces to

and between networks, and operation of user hardware.

CD Abbreviation for carrier detect. A signal sent from a *modem* to the attached computer to indicate that the modem is online
See also **DCD, RS-232-C.**

CDDI Abbreviation for Copper Distributed Data Interface. A version of the *FDDI* standard designed to run on shielded and *unshielded twisted-pair* cable rather than on *fiber-optic* cable.

CDPD Abbreviation for Cellular Digital Packet Data. A method used in cellular communications and wireless modems for sending data more efficiently by using any available cellular channel.

CDPD uses voice channels, but can switch to a new frequency if a voice transmission begins in the cell currently in use.

CD-I Abbreviation for Compact Disc-Interactive. A hardware and software standard disc format for data, text, audio, still video images, and animated graphics. The standard also defines methods of encoding and decoding compressed data, as well as displaying data.
See also **CD-ROM, compact disc.**

CD-R Abbreviation for CD Recordable. A type of CD device that brings *CD-ROM* publishing into the realm of the small business or home office.

From a functional point of view, a CD-R and a CD-ROM are identical; you can read CD-R discs using almost any CD-ROM drive, although the processes that create the discs are slightly different. Low-cost CD-R drives are available from several manufacturers including Kao, Kodak, Mitsui, Phillips, Ricoh, Sony, TDK, 3M, and Verbatim.

See also **erasable CD, WORM.**

CDROM A Novell *NetWare Loadable Module* (NLM) used to access a *CD-ROM* as a read-only *volume* on the *file server*. Once this NLM is loaded, users or the network administrator can mount the volume represented by the CD-ROM and access the information stored there.

CD-ROM Acronym for Compact Disc—Read-Only Memory. A high-capacity, optical storage device that uses the same technology used to make ordinary music discs to store large amounts of information. A single 4.72-inch disc can hold up to 650 megabytes.

CD-ROMs are important components of multimedia applications. They are also used to store encyclopedias, dictionaries, and other large reference works, as well as libraries of fonts and clip art for desktop publishing. CD-ROMs are increasingly replacing floppy disks as the distribution mechanism for software packages, including network operating systems and large applications, so you can load the whole operating system or package from a single compact disc.

A CD-ROM uses the *constant linear velocity data encoding scheme* to store information in a single, spiral track, divided into many equal-length segments. To read data, the CD-ROM disk drive must increase the rotational speed as the read head gets closer to the center of the disk, and decrease as the head moves back out. Typical CD-ROM data access times are in the range of 0.3 to 1.5 seconds; much slower than a hard disk.

CD-ROMs are usually considered to be *WORM* (write once, read many) devices, but several vendors (including Kodak) are working toward a format that will allow home users to add information to an existing multisession compact disc.

See also **CD-I, constant angular velocity, erasable CD, High Sierra specification.**

CD-ROM disk drive   A disk device that uses compact disc technology for information storage. Many CD-ROM disk drives also have headphone jacks, external speaker jacks, and a volume control.

CD-ROM disk drives designed for computer use are more expensive than audio CD players, because CD-ROM disk drives are manufactured to much higher tolerances. If a CD player misreads a small amount of data, the human ear probably will not detect the difference; if a CD-ROM disk drive misreads a few bytes of a program, the program will not run.

CD-ROM drives are available with the following data-transfer rates:

- **Single-speed** drives transfer data at up to 150 kilobytes per second. The earliest available drives were single speed.

- **Double-speed** drives transfer data at up to 300 kilobytes per second.

- **Quad-speed** drives have a data transfer rate of 600 kilobytes per second.

- **6X speed** drives have a data transfer rate of 900 kilobytes per second, and a disk-access time of only 140 milliseconds.

The two most popular CD-ROM drive interface cards are *SCSI* and ATAPI (AT Attachment Packet Interface). ATAPI is part of the Enhanced *IDE* specification introduced by Western Digital in 1994, and lets you plug an IDE CD-ROM directly into an IDE controller on the system's motherboard. Other CD-ROM drives may use the computer's *parallel port* or a *PCMCIA* connection.

See also **CD-ROM.**

CD-ROM Extended Architecture   Abbreviated CD-ROM/XA. An extension to the CD-ROM format, developed by Microsoft, Phillips, and Sony, that allows for the storage of audio and visual information on compact disc, so you can play the audio at the same time you view the visual data.

CD-ROM/XA is compatible with the *High Sierra specification*, also known as ISO standard 9660.

cell   Any fixed-length *packet*. For example, *Asynchronous Transfer Mode* (ATM) uses 53-byte cells.

cell relay   A form of packet transmission used in *BISDN* networks that uses a fixed-length, 53-byte cell over a *packet-switched network*. Also known as *Asynchronous Transfer Mode* (ATM).

central processing unit   Abbreviated CPU. The computing and control part of the computer. The CPU in a mainframe computer may be contained on many printed circuit boards. In a minicomputer, the CPU may be contained on several boards. The CPU in a PC is usually contained in a single, extremely powerful *microprocessor*.

Centrex   Acronym formed from CENTRal EXchange. Services provided to a company by the local telephone company. All the switching takes place at the telephone company's central office rather than at the customer site, so Centrex services are easy to expand.

Centronics parallel interface
A standard 36-pin interface used to connect a PC to a peripheral device, such as a printer, originally developed by the printer manufacturer Centronics, Inc. The standard defines eight parallel data lines, plus additional lines for status and control information.
See also **parallel port**.

Certified Novell Administrator
See **CNA**.

Certified Novell Engineer
See **CNE**.

Certified Novell Engineer Professional Association
See **CNEPA**.

Certified Novell Instructor
See **CNI**.

channel   In communications, any connecting path that carries information from a sending device to a receiving device. A channel may refer to a physical medium (for example, coaxial cable) or to a specific frequency within a larger channel.

character-based interface   An operating system or application that uses text characters rather than graphical techniques for the user interface.
See also **command line, graphical user interface, social interface**.

character code   A code that represents one specific alphanumeric or control character in a set of characters, such as the *ASCII* or the *EBCDIC* character set.

See also **Unicode**.

character mode   In IBM-compatible PCs, a *video adapter* mode in which the computer displays characters on the screen using the built-in *character set*, but does not show any graphics characters or a mouse pointer. Also known as text mode.

character set   A standard group of letters, numbers, punctuation marks, and other symbols and control characters used by a computer. Common character sets include the standard and extended *ASCII* character sets, *EBCDIC*, and *Unicode*.

See also **ASCII extended character set, ASCII standard character set**.

character string   Any group of alphanumeric characters treated as a single unit. Also known as a string.

See also **ASCII, EBCDIC**.

characters per second   Abbreviated cps. The number of characters, or *bytes*, transmitted every second during a data transfer. A measurement of the speed of operation of equipment, such as serial printers and terminals.

cheapernet wire   See **thin Ethernet**.

checksum   A method of providing information for error detection, usually calculated by summing a set of values.

The checksum is usually appended to the end of the data that it is calculated from, so that they can be compared. For example, *Xmodem*, a popular file-transfer protocol, uses a 1-byte checksum calculated by adding all the ASCII values for all 128 data bytes and ignoring any numerical overflow. The checksum is added to the end of the Xmodem data packet. This type of checksum does not always detect all errors. In later versions of the Xmodem protocol, cyclical redundancy check (CRC) is used instead for more rigorous error control.

See also **cyclical redundancy check, error detection and correction**.

chip   See **integrated circuit**.

CHKDIR   A Novell NetWare 3.*x* workstation utility that displays a

55

volume or directory's space limit, the amount of space currently in use, and the amount of free space. In NetWare 4.*x*, the function of this utility has been replaced by the *NDIR* utility.

CHKVOL A Novell NetWare 3.*x* workstation utility that displays volume information, including the total disk space allowed for a volume, the amount of space in use, the space occupied by deleted (but not purged) files, the free space, and the amount of user disk space remaining free in the volume directories. In NetWare 4.*x*, the function of this utility has been replaced by the *NDIR* utility.

CHRP Abbreviation for Common Hardware Reference Platform.

CICS See **Customer Information Control System.**

circuit

1. A communications *channel* or path between two devices capable of carrying electrical current.

2. A set of components connected together to perform a specific task.

circuit switching A temporary communications connection established as required between the sending and receiving nodes. Circuit switching is often used in modem communications over dial-up telephone lines. It is also used in some privately maintained communications networks.

See also **message switching, packet switching.**

CISC See **complex instruction set computing.**

Class A certification An *FCC certification* for computer equipment, including mainframe computers and minicomputers destined for industrial, commercial, or office use, rather than for personal use at home. The Class A commercial certification is less restrictive than the *Class B certification* for residential use, because it assumes that most residential areas are more than 30 feet away from any commercial computer equipment.

Class B certification An *FCC certification* for computer equipment, including PCs, laptops, and portables destined for use in the home rather than in a commercial setting. Class B levels of *radio frequency interference* (RFI) must be low enough so that they do not interfere with radio or television reception when there is more than one wall and 30 feet separating the computer from the receiver. Class B certification is more restrictive than the commercial *Class A certification.*

CLEAR STATION   A Novell NetWare server utility that clears the connection when a workstation *crashes* while still logged in to the server. CLEAR STATION closes all open files on the workstation and erases workstation information stored in tables on the server.

Clear to Send   See CTS.

CLIB   The Novell NetWare C-language interface library. CLIB provides services to other loadable modules so that each NetWare Loadable Module (NLM) does not need its own built-in library. CLIB is usually linked to the operating system at run time.

client   A device or application that makes use of the services provided by a server. A client typically has

only one user, whereas a server is shared by many different users.

A client may be a PC or a *workstation* on a network using services provided from the network file server, or it may be a single-user application, such as a word-processing program. Client-based applications do not allow for convenient data sharing between users, but they are immune to systemwide problems such as file-server crashes.

See also **client/server architecture, DOS client, Macintosh client, OS/2 client, Unix client, Windows client.**

client application

1. In *OLE* (object linking and embedding), the application that starts a *server application* to manipulate linked or embedded information.

2. In a *dynamic data exchange* (DDE) conversation, the application that accepts the pasted link.

client/server architecture   A computing *architecture* that distributes processing between *clients* and *servers* on the network. Clients request information from the servers. The servers store data and programs, and provide network-wide services to clients.

This arrangement exploits the available computing power by dividing an application into two distinct components: a front-end client and a back-end server.

Client/server architecture can sustain several levels of organizational complexity, including the following:

- Stand-alone (non-networked) client applications, such as local word processors.
- Applications that run on the client but request data from the server, such as spreadsheets.
- Programs that use server capabilities to share information between network users, such as electronic mail systems.
- Programs in which the physical search of records takes place on the server, while a much smaller program running on the client handles all user-interface functions, such as database applications.

Client/server computing lightens the processing load for the client PCs, but increases the load on the server. The server computers tend to have larger and faster hard-disk drives and much more memory installed than conventional PC file servers. The server may also be a minicomputer or a mainframe computer.

Clipper chip   A low-cost encryption device that the U.S. Federal Government proposes making available for public use. The chip would allow businesses to transmit encoded messages, but at the same time, allow certain government agencies to intercept and decode the messages if criminal activities were suspected. Needless to say, this proposal has generated a lot of intense discussion, particularly from civil rights groups concerned with an individual's right to privacy and other ethical issues; other potential users want access to the best available encryption systems, not just those put forward by the government.

See also **Data Encryption Standard.**

CLNP   See **Connectionless Network Protocol.**

clock   An electronic circuit that generates regularly spaced timing pulses at speeds up to millions of cycles per second. These pulses are used to synchronize the flow of information through the computer's internal communications channels.

See also **clock speed.**

clock-multiplying   A mechanism used by some Intel processors that allows the chip to process data and instructions internally at a different speed from that used by the rest of the system. For example, the Intel *80486DX2* operates at *50 megahertz* (MHz) internally, but at 25 MHz when communicating with other system components; this difference in processing speed is known as clock-doubling. The *Intel DX4* chip uses clock-tripling technology, and the *PowerPC* 601 can run at one, two, three, or four times the speed of the bus.

clock rate   See **clock speed**.

clock speed   The internal speed of a computer or processor, normally expressed in *megahertz* (MHz). Also known as clock rate.

The faster the clock speed, the faster the computer will perform a specific operation (assuming the other components in the system, such as disk drives, can keep up with the increased speed).

The Intel *8088* processor used in the original *IBM PC* had a clock speed of 4.77 Mhz—painfully slow when compared with speeds used by modern processors. For example, the Pentium

processors run at clock speeds ranging from 60 to 180 MHz.

See also **clock-multiplying, Intel OverDrive, wait state**.

clone   Hardware that is identical in function to an original. For example, an IBM clone is a PC that uses an Intel (or similar) microprocessor and functions in the same way as the IBM PC standard. A Macintosh clone functions in the same way as a computer manufactured by Apple Computer, Inc.

Although most clones do perform as intended, small internal differences can cause problems in some cases. It can be difficult to ensure consistency of components and level of operation when using a number of clones purchased over a long period of time.

See also **AMD, Cyrix, NexGen**.

closed architecture   A design that does not allow for easy, user-supplied additions. This term is often used to describe some of the early Macintosh computers, which did not allow easy expansion of the system with add-in cards. Closed architecture can also refer to a computer design whose specifications are not published or generally available, making it impossible for third-party companies to provide products that work with the computer. See also **open architecture**.

CLS A Novell NetWare server utility that clears the console screen of messages. This command is very similar to the *OFF* command.

CLTP See **Connectionless Transport Protocol**.

cluster controller An IBM or IBM-compatible device located between a group of *3270* terminals and the mainframe. The cluster controller communicates between the computer and the terminals using *SDLC* (Synchronous Data Link Control) or a *bisynchronous communications* protocol.

CLV See **constant linear velocity**.

CMIP Abbreviation for Common Management Information Protocol. The Open Systems Interconnection (OSI) management information protocol for network monitoring and control information, designated ISO 9596.

CMIP includes fault management, configuration management, performance management, and

security and accounting management. It is not widely available. See also **CMIS, SNMP**.

CMIS Abbreviation for Common Management Information Services. The Open Systems Interconnection (OSI) standard functions for network monitoring and control. See also **CMIP**.

CMOS Acronym for Complementary Metal-Oxide Semiconductor, pronounced "see-moss." A type of *integrated circuit* used in processors and for memory. CMOS devices operate at very high speeds and use little power, so they generate little heat. In the PC, battery-backed CMOS memory is used to store operating parameters, such as the *hard disk type*, when the computer is switched off.

CNA Abbreviation for Certified Novell Administrator. A Novell certification program for *network administrators* responsible for the day-to-day operation of a network.

CNE Abbreviation for Certified Novell Engineer. A Novell certification program for technicians and consultants concerned with network system design, implementation, and maintenance.

See also **Master CNE**.

CNEPA Abbreviation for Certified Novell Engineer Professional Association. An association of Certified Novell Engineers (CNEs) that provides benefits, such as workshops demonstrating how to configure and troubleshoot Novell products, as well as admission to network-related events and complementary subscriptions.

See also **CNE**.

CNI Abbreviation for Certified Novell Instructor. A Novell certification program for instructors who want to teach Novell courses.

coaxial cable Abbreviated coax, pronounced "co-ax." A high-capacity cable used in networking that contains a solid inner copper conductor surrounded by plastic insulation, and an outer braided copper or foil shield; see the accompanying illustration. Coaxial cable is used for *broadband* and *baseband* communications networks (and for cable television), because the cable is usually free from external interference and

permits high transmission rates over long distances.

See also **RG-58, RG-59, RG-62, thick Ethernet, thin Ethernet**.

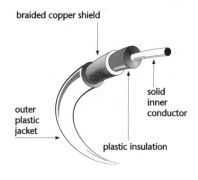

COAXIAL CABLE

codec Acronym for COder/DECoder, pronounced "coe-deck." A device that converts analog signals (such as voice or video) into a digital bit stream suitable for transmission using pulse-code modulation, and then converts those digital signals back into analog signals at the receiving end.

cold boot The computer startup process that begins when you turn on power to the computer. You are doing a cold boot when you first turn on your computer. A cold boot might also be necessary if a program or the operating system *crashes* and freezes entirely. If your keyboard is operational, a warm boot may suffice.

See also **boot, warm boot**.

collision   In networking or communications, an attempt by two nodes to send a message at exactly the same moment on the same *channel*.

See also **CSMA/CD, token-ring network**.

COLORPAL   A Novell NetWare workstation utility that sets the screen colors for NetWare menu utilities or menus created using the *NMENU* program.

COM 1–4   See **COM port**.

command interpreter   See **command processor**.

command line   Any interface between the user and the command processor that allows the user to enter commands from the keyboard for execution by the operating system.

See also **graphical user interface, shell, text mode**.

command-line argument   See **command-line switch**.

command-line switch   A parameter that alters the default mode of a command, also called a command-line argument. In many *operating systems*, a command-line switch is one or more letters or numbers preceded by the / (slash) character. In Unix, a command-line switch is called an option or a flag, and is usually a single character preceded by a hyphen (as in -r). With some commands, you can group several switches together.

See also **command line**.

command processor   The part of the *operating system* that displays the command prompt on the screen, interprets and executes all the commands and file names that you enter, and displays error messages when appropriate. Also called the command interpreter. The command processor also contains the system *environment*.

command prompt   A symbol (character or group of characters) on the screen that lets you know that the *operating system* is available and ready to receive input.

common carrier   A communications company, such as AT&T, MCI, or ITT, that provides data

and voice telecommunication services to the general public.
See also **PTT**.

Common Management Information Protocol
See **CMIP**.

communications/modem server
In a network, a server equipped with one or more modems, which can be shared by users for out-going calls.
See also **access server**.

communications parameters
Any of several settings required to allow computers to communicate successfully. In *asynchronous transmissions*, commonly used in modem communications, the settings for *baud rate*, number of *data bits*, number of *stop bits*, and *parity* parameters must all be correct.

communications protocol
1. A standard way of communicating between computers or between computers and terminals. Communications protocols vary in complexity, ranging from *Xmodem*, a simple file-transfer protocol used to transfer files from one PC to another, to the seven-layer *ISO/OSI model* used as the theoretical basis for many large, complex computer networks.

2. A hardware interface standard, such as *RS-232-C*.

communications satellite
A satellite in geostationary orbit, acting as a microwave relay station. The satellite receives signals sent from a groundstation, amplifies them, and retransmits them on a different frequency to another groundstation.
See also **downlink, propagation delay, uplink**.

compact disc
Abbreviated CD. A nonmagnetic, polished, optical disk used to store large amounts of digital information. A CD can store approximately 650 megabytes of information, equivalent to more than 1700 low-density floppy disks. This storage capacity translates into approximately 300,000 pages of text or 72 minutes of music, all on a single 4.72-inch disc.

Digital information is stored on the compact disc as a series of microscopic pits and smooth areas that have different reflective properties. A beam of laser light shines on the disc so that the reflections can be detected and converted into digital data.
See also **CD-I, CD-ROM, CD-ROM-Extended Architecture**.

63

Compact Disc-Interactive
See **CD-I.**

compatibility   The extent to which a given piece of hardware or software conforms to an accepted standard, regardless of the original manufacturer.

In hardware, compatibility is often expressed in terms of widely accepted models—for example, you might see a computer described as IBM-compatible or a modem described as Hayes-compatible. This designation implies that the device will perform in the same way as the standard device.

In software, compatibility is usually described as the ability to read data file formats created by another vendor's software, or the ability to work together and share data.

See also **plug-compatible.**

complementary metal-oxide semiconductor   See **CMOS.**

complex instruction set computing   Abbreviated CISC, pronounced "sisk." A processor that can recognize and execute more than one hundred different assembly-language, or low-level, instructions. CISC processors can be powerful, but the instructions take a high number of clock cycles to execute. This complexity is in contrast to the simplicity of reduced instruction set computing (RISC) processors, for which the number of available instructions is minimized.

See also **reduced instruction set computing.**

COM port   In DOS, the device name used to denote a serial communications port. In versions of DOS after 3.3, four COM ports are supported: COM1, COM2, COM3, and COM4. Earlier versions support only COM1 and COM2.

compressed file   A file that has been processed by a special utility so that it occupies as little hard-disk space as possible. When the file is needed, the same program decompresses the file back into its original form so that it can be read by the computer.

See also **data compression, file compression.**

computation bound   A condition in which the speed of operation of the processor actually limits the speed of program execution. The processor is limited by the number of arithmetic operations it can perform.

See also **input/output bound.**

concentrator   A *repeater* or *hub* that joins communications *channels* from several different network nodes. Concentrators are not just simple wire-concentration centers, but also provide *bridging*, *routing*, and other management functions.

concurrent   When two or more programs (processes) have access to the processor at the same time and must share the system resources, they are said to be "running concurrently." Because a computer can perform operations so quickly, the processes seem to be occurring at the same time, although actually they are not.

See also **multiprocessing, task, task-switching, thread**.

concurrent license   A software license that allows more than one person at a company to share an application over a network, providing that, at any given time, only one person is using it.

Different versions of concurrent licensing allow a fixed number of people in an office to share one copy of an application, and allow the application to be used on both desktop and portable PCs, rather than run only from the file server.

See also **application metering**.

CONFIG   A Novell NetWare server utility that displays *configuration* information. The display includes the name and internal network number of the server; the local-area network (LAN) drivers loaded; and network interface card information, such as node address, port, interrupt, frame type, network number, and the name of the protocol in use.

CONFIG.SYS   In DOS and OS/2, a special text file containing settings that control the way the workstation *operating system* works.

In DOS, the CONFIG.SYS file may contain ten to twenty lines of entries. In OS/2, it is likely to contain between seventy and one hundred lines of *configuration* information (because OS/2 is a more complex operating system than DOS). CONFIG.SYS must be located in the *root directory* of the default boot disk, normally drive C, and is read once as the system starts running.

Some applications and peripheral devices require special statements in CONFIG.SYS. Other commands in the file may specify the number of disk-read buffers or open files on your system, designate how the *disk cache* should be configured, and load any

C

special *device drivers* your system may need.

DOS 6 adds the ability to display a menu of configuration choices you can use when you start your computer. This ability allows you to create several system configurations without changing the CONFIG.SYS file each time. However, you must still *reboot* if you want to switch settings during a session.

The order of the commands in your CONFIG.SYS file may be important. If you plan to configure your system to use memory beyond the normal 640-kilobyte limit, be sure to place the commands that configure this memory at the beginning of CONFIG.SYS, before you load any device drivers that use that memory.

See also **multiple DOS configurations, NET.CFG.**

configuration   The process of establishing your own preferred setup for an application, expansion board, computer system, or network. Most modern software can establish a configuration for you automatically, although you may need to adjust that configuration to get the best results. Also, you may find that in configuring one program, you have affected the performance of another.

Configuration information is usually stored in a *configuration file* so that it can be loaded automatically next time you start your computer.

See also **AUTOEXEC.BAT, CONFIG.SYS, configuration file, NET.CFG.**

configuration file   A file, created by an application or operating system, containing configuration information specific to your own computing *environment*. Application configuration files may have a file-name extension of CFG or SET; Windows configuration files use the INI file-name extension.

If you accidentally erase an application's configuration file, the program will return to using its default settings. Although the program will continue to function, its configuration settings may not be suitable for your system.

See also **AUTOEXEC.BAT, BOOTCONF.SYS, CONFIG.SYS, NET.CFG.**

configuration management   A term covering a wide range of network administration tasks, often performed by the *network administrator*.

Configuration management includes:

• Maintaining a hardware database containing details of

routers, *bridges*, and connections, so that changes in the network can be made quickly in the event of a failure.

- Adding new *workstations* to the network as needed.

- Adding and configuring new servers and cabling systems as the network expands.

See also **DMI**.

congestion   An excessive amount of traffic on the network, causing messages to be blocked for long periods of time and adversely affecting network performance.

CONLOG   A Novell NetWare *NLM* that allows you to capture *console* messages generated during system initialization into the default file SYS:/ETC/CONSOLE.LOG, or into another file of your choosing.

connectionless   A *protocol* in which the source and destination *addresses* are included inside each *packet*, so that a direct connection or an established session between nodes is not required for communications.

Connectionless Network Protocol   Abbreviated CLNP. An *Open Systems Interconnection*

(OSI) protocol that provides the OSI Connectionless Network Service for the delivery of data. It uses *datagrams* that include addressing information to route network messages. CLNP is used for *local-area networks* (LANs) rather than *wide-area networks* (WANs). CLNP is the OSI equivalent of *IP* (Internet Protocol).

See also **Connection-Oriented Network Service**.

Connectionless Transport Protocol   Abbreviated CLTP. An *Open Systems Interconnection* (OSI) protocol that provides end-to-end transport data addressing and error correction, but does not guarantee delivery or provide any *flow control*. CLTP is the OSI equivalent of the *UDP* (User Datagram Protocol).

See also **Connection-Oriented Network Service**.

connection number   A number assigned to a workstation that attaches to a server; it may be a different number each time the workstation attaches. Connection numbers are also assigned to print servers, as well as other applications and processes that use the server connections.

CONNECTION-ORIENTED NETWORK SERVICE

Connection-Oriented Network Service   Abbreviated CONS. An *Open Systems Interconnection* (OSI) protocol that provides the service for the delivery of data. CONS is usually considered to be more efficient for *wide-area networks* (WANs) than for *local-area networks* (LANs).

See also **Connectionless Network Protocol, Connectionless Transport Protocol.**

connectivity   The degree to which any given computer or application can cooperate with other network components, purchased from other vendors, in a network environment in which resources are shared.

connect time   The period of time during which a user is logged in to the network.

console   Sometimes abbreviated cons. The monitor and keyboard from which the server or host computer activity may be monitored.

Certain *operating system* commands and utilities must be executed from the console device; they will not operate from a workstation. In some systems, the console is a virtual device that can be invoked from any workstation by a *network administrator* with the appropriate *rights* and *privileges*.

constant angular velocity   Abbreviated CAV. An unchanging speed of rotation. Hard disks use a CAV encoding scheme. The constant rate of rotation means that sectors on the disk are at the maximum density along the inside track of the disk. As the read/write heads move outwards, the sectors must spread out to cover the increased track circumference, and therefore the data-transfer rate falls off.

See also **constant linear velocity.**

constant linear velocity   Abbreviated CLV. A changing speed of rotation. CD-ROM disk drives use a CLV encoding scheme to make sure that the data density remains constant. Information on a compact disc is stored in a single, spiral track, divided into many equal-length segments. To read the data, the CD-ROM disk drive must increase the rotational speed as the read head gets closer to the center of the disc, and decrease as the head moves back out. Typical CD-ROM data access times are in the order of 0.3 to 1.5 seconds—much slower than a hard disk.

See also **constant angular velocity.**

container object   In Novell NetWare 4.*x*, an object that holds other objects in the *NDS* tree, essentially a branch in the directory structure.

See also **leaf object.**

contention   The competition between transmitting nodes for access to communications lines or network resources. The first device to gain access to a channel takes control of the channel. In the event of a *collision*, when two nodes attempt to transmit at the same time, some arbitration scheme must be invoked.

See also **CSMA/CD, token passing.**

context switching   Switching from one program to another without ending the first program. Context switching allows you to operate several programs at the same time; but it differs from true multitasking in that when you are using one program, all the other programs loaded onto your system must halt.

control character   A single ASCII character that performs a specific operation on a terminal, printer, or communications line. Control characters, such as

carriage return, line feed, bell, or escape, are usually nonprinting characters. They are grouped together as the first thirty-two characters in the ASCII character set.

See also **ASCII, EBCDIC.**

control code   A sequence of one or more characters used for hardware control, also known as setup strings or escape sequences. Control codes are used with printers, modems, and displays. Printer control codes often begin with an escape character, followed by one or more characters that the printer interprets as commands rather than text for printing.

Controlled Access Unit   Abbreviated CAU. An intelligent *MAU* (Multistation Access Unit), or multiport wiring hub for a *Token Ring* network, that allows ports to be switched on and off.

conventional memory   The amount of memory accessible by DOS in PCs using an Intel processor operating in *real mode*, normally the first 640 kilobytes (KB).

The designers of the original IBM PC made 640 KB available to the operating system and applications, and reserved the remaining space for internal system use, the

69

BIOS, and video buffers. 640 KB may not seem like much memory space now, but it was ten times the amount of memory available in other leading personal computers available at the time. Since then, applications have increased in size to the point that 640 KB is inadequate.

See also **expanded memory, extended memory, high memory area, memory management, protected mode.**

convergence   The synchronization process that a network must go through immediately after a routing change takes place on the network. Convergence time is the time required to update all the *routers* on the network with routing information changes.

See also **routing table.**

cooperative multitasking   A form of multitasking in which all running applications must work together to share system resources.

Microsoft Windows supports cooperative multitasking by maintaining a list of the active applications and the order in which they execute. When Windows transfers control to an application, other applications cannot run until that application returns control to Windows once again.

Windows' cooperative multitasking system differs from a *preemptive multitasking* system, such as that used in *OS/2* or *Windows NT*, in which the *operating system* executes each application in turn for a specific period of time (depending on priority) before switching to the next application, regardless of whether the applications themselves return control to the operating system.

See also **context switching, time-slice multitasking.**

Copeland   An advanced, 32-bit, object-oriented operating system for the Macintosh from Apple Computer. Copeland replaces the current System 7.5 operating system.

coprocessor   A secondary processor used to speed up operations by taking over a specific part of the main processor's work. The most common type of coprocessor is the math or *floating-point coprocessor*, designed to manage arithmetic calculations many times faster than does the main processor.

See also **80387, 80487.**

CPE Abbreviation for customer-premises equipment. Communications equipment, either leased or owned, used at a customer site.

cps See **characters per second**.

CPU See **central processing unit**.

crash An unexpected program halt, sometimes due to a hardware failure but most often due to a software error, from which there is no recovery. You usually need to *reboot* the computer to recover after a crash.

CRC See **cyclical redundancy check**.

critical error An error in a program that forces the program to stop until the error condition is corrected by the user. Examples of this kind of error are attempts to write to a floppy disk when there is no disk in the drive or to print to a printer that has run out of paper.

crosstalk In communications, any interference from a physically adjacent *channel* that corrupts the signal and causes transmission errors.

CSMA/CD Abbreviation for Carrier Sense Multiple Access/Collision Detection. A baseband protocol with a built-in collision-detection technique. Each *node* on the network listens first and transmits only when the line is free. If two nodes transmit at exactly the same time and a collision occurs, both nodes stop transmitting. Then, to avoid a subsequent collision, each of the two nodes waits for a different random length of time before attempting to transmit again. Ethernet and *802.3* local-area networks (LANs) use CSMA/CD access methods.

See also **collision, token passing, Token Ring network**.

CSU Abbreviation for Channel Service Unit. A device that functions as a certified safe electrical circuit, acting as a buffer between the customer's equipment and a public carrier's wide-area network (WAN). A CSU prevents faulty *CPE* (customer-premises equipment), such as *DSUs* (data service units), from affecting a public carrier's transmission systems and ensures that all signals placed on the line are appropriately timed and formed. All CSU designs must be approved and certified by the *FCC* (Federal Communications Commission).

71

Ctrl-Alt-Del   A three-key combination used in IBM-compatible computers to reset the machine and reload the *operating system*. By pressing Ctrl-Alt-Del, you initiate a warm boot, which restarts the computer without going through the power-on self tests (POSTs) normally run when the computer goes through a *cold boot*.

See also **warm boot**.

Ctrl-Break   See **Ctrl-C**.

Ctrl-C   A key combination recognized by DOS as a user-initiated interruption. Pressing Ctrl-C stops a batch file, macro, or DOS command (for example, a directory listing, a search, or a sort).

CTS   Abbreviation for Clear To Send. A hardware signal defined by the *RS-232-C* standard that indicates that the transmission can proceed.

See also **RS-232-C, RTS**.

current directory   In DOS and many other operating systems, the directory that will be searched first for any file you request, and the directory in which any new files will be stored (unless you specifically designate another directory). The current directory is not the same as the default directory, which is the directory that will be used by an application unless you specify another.

See also **period and double-period directories**.

current drive   In DOS and many other operating systems, the disk drive that is being used for reading and writing files. The current drive is not the same as the default drive, which is the drive that will be used by an application unless you specify another.

See also **drive mapping**.

cursor   A special character displayed on a monitor to indicate where the next character will appear when it is typed. In text or character mode, the cursor is usually a blinking rectangle or underline. In a *graphical user interface*, the cursor can take many shapes, depending on the current operation and its screen location.

cursor-movement keys   The keys on the keyboard that move the cursor, also called cursor-control keys. These keys include the four labeled with arrows and the Home, PgUp, End, and PgDn keys.

On full-size keyboards, cursor-movement keys are often found on the numeric keypad; laptops and notebooks often have separate cursor-movement keys.

Customer Information Control System   Abbreviated
CICS. An IBM-mainframe communications control program that manages transaction processing in IBM's *VM* and *MVS* operating systems. It also provides password security, transaction logging for backup and recovery, and an activity log that can be used to analyze session performance, as well as facilities for creating, using, and maintaining databases.

cut through   A technique used by some Ethernet hardware to speed up packet forwarding. Only the first few bytes of the packet are examined before it is forwarded or filtered. This process is much faster than looking at the whole packet, but it does allow some bad packets to be forwarded.

CX   Abbreviation for change context. A Novell NetWare 4.*x* workstation utility that displays or changes the current *NetWare Directory Services* (NDS) position, or context, and displays the *objects* in an NDS container.

cyclical redundancy check
Abbreviated CRC. A calculation method used to check the accuracy of a digital transmission over a communications link. The sending computer uses one of several formulas to calculate a value from the information contained in the data, and this value is appended to the message block before it is sent. The receiving computer performs the same calculation on the same data and should derive the same number. If the two CRCs do not match, indicating a transmission error occurred, the receiving computer asks the sending computer to retransmit the data.

This procedure is known as a redundancy check because each transmission includes extra or redundant error-checking values as well as the data itself. Common CRC patterns are 12-bit (CRC-12), 16-bit (CRC-16 and CRC-CCITT), and 32-bit (CRC-32).

Cyrix   Manufacturer of microprocessors, including clones of popular Intel chips:

- **Cx486DRX2**: A *clock-multiplying* clone of the Intel 80486 used as a replacement for an 80386 chip in an existing system. Available in three clock-doubling configurations: 20/40, 25/50, and 33/66.

73

- **Cx486SRX2:** A clock-multiplying clone of the Intel 80486 used as a replacement for an 80386 chip in an existing system. Available in four clock-doubling configurations: 16/32, 20/40, 25/50, and 33/66.
- **Cyrix 5x86:** A *pin-compatible,* clock-multiplying clone of Intel's *Pentium* processor, available in late 1995, containing 16K of on-board cache, a built-in floating-point processor, a 32-bit address bus, and a 64-bit data bus. Previously known as the M1.

See also **AMD, NexGen, P6.**

daemon Pronounced "demon." A background program that runs unattended (without user interaction), collecting information or performing operating system administration tasks. Some daemons are triggered automatically by events to perform their work; others operate at timed intervals. For example, a daemon can collect error information and store that information in a file for later analysis by another program.

DAS Abbreviation for dual-attached station. In the *Fiber Distributed Data Interface* (FDDI), a device attached to both of the dual, counter-rotating rings. *Concentrators*, *bridges*, and *routers* often use DAS connections to provide fault tolerance. In contrast, a single attached station (*SAS*) connects to only one ring.

DAT See **digital audio tape.**

data Information in a form suitable for processing by a computer, such as the digital representation of text, numbers, graphic images, or sounds. Strictly speaking, data is the plural of the Latin word datum, meaning an item of information; but the term is commonly used in both plural and singular constructions.

database A collection of related objects, including tables, forms, reports, queries, and scripts, created and organized by a database management system (*DBMS*). A database can contain information of almost any type, such as a list of magazine subscribers, personal data on the space shuttle astronauts, or a collection of graphical images and video clips.

See also **database management system, database model, table.**

database management system Abbreviated DBMS. Application software that controls the data in a database, including overall organization, storage, retrieval, security, and data integrity. A DBMS can also format reports for printed output, and import and export data from other applications using standard file formats. A data-manipulation language is also provided to support database queries.

See also **database, database model, query language**.

database model   The method used by a database management system (DBMS) to organize the structure of the database. The most common database model is the *relational database*.

See also **relational database**.

database server   Any database application that follows the *client/server architecture* model, which divides the application into two parts: a front-end running on the user's workstation and a back-end running on a server or host computer. The front-end interacts with the user and collects and displays the data. The back-end performs all the computer-intensive tasks, including data analysis, storage, and manipulation.

data bits   In *asynchronous transmissions*, the bits that actually make up the data. Usually, 7 or 8 data bits are grouped together. Each group of data bits in a transmission is preceded by a *start bit* and followed by an optional *parity* bit as well as one or more *stop bits*.

See also **communications parameters**.

Data Carrier Detect   See DCD.

data communication   The transfer of information from one computer to another over a communications link. The transfer can be occasional, continuous, or a combination of both.

data communications equipment   See DCE.

data compression   Any method of encoding *data* so that it occupies less space than it did in its original form, thus allowing that data to be stored, backed up, retrieved, or transmitted more efficiently.

Data compression is used in fax and many other forms of data transmission, CD-ROM publishing, still-image and video-image manipulation, and database management systems.

See also **Huffman coding, lossless compression, lossy compression**.

data connector (Type 1)   A connector for use with *Type 1* cable, designed by IBM for use in *Token Ring network* wiring centers.

data-encoding scheme The method used by a hard-disk controller to store information onto a hard disk or floppy disk. Common encoding schemes for the PC include the *run-length limited* (RLL) and *advanced run-length limited* (ARLL) methods.

Data Encryption Standard

Abbreviated DES. A standard method of encrypting and decrypting data, developed by the United States National Bureau of Standards. DES works by a combination of transposition and substitution. It is used by the federal government and most banks and money-transfer systems to protect all sensitive computer information.

DES has remained unbroken despite years of use. This method completely randomizes the information so that it is impossible to determine the encryption key even if some of the original text is known.

See also **encryption, PGP.**

data file A file that contains information—text, graphics, or numbers—rather than executable program code.

datagram A message unit that contains source and destination address information, as well as the data itself, which is routed through a *packet-switching network.*

data-link layer The second of seven layers of the ISO/OSI model for computer-to-computer communications. The data-link layer validates the integrity of the flow of data from one node to another by synchronizing blocks of data and controlling the flow of data.

The *Institute of Electrical and Electronic Engineers* (IEEE) has divided the data-link layer into two other layers; the *logical link control* (LLC) layer sits above the *media access control* (MAC) layer. See also **ISO/OSI model.**

data packet One unit of information transmitted as a discrete entity from one node on the network to another. More specifically, in *packet-switching networks,* a packet is a transmission unit of a fixed maximum length that contains a header, a set of data, and error control information.

data processing Abbreviated DP. Also called electronic data processing (EDP). A term used to describe work done by minicomputers and mainframe computers in a data center or business environment.

d

data protection   Techniques used by network operating systems to ensure the integrity of data on the network, including protecting data against surface defects developing on the disk and storing redundant copies of important system data, such as file indices and file allocation tables (FATs). *Disk duplexing, disk mirroring*, a well thought out *backup* scheme, and *RAID* techniques all provide different levels of data protection.

See also **diskless workstation, disk striping, disk striping with parity, fault tolerance, Hot Fix, intruder, virus.**

Data Terminal Ready
See **DTR.**

data-transfer rate

1. The speed at which a disk drive can transfer information from the drive to the processor, usually measured in megabits or megabytes per second. For example, an *SCSI* (Small Computer System Interface) drive can reach a transfer rate of up to 20 megabytes per second.

2. The rate of information exchange between two systems. For example, a PC modem may achieve 14,400 bits per second

(bps) or 28,800 bps; an Ethernet *local-area network* (LAN) may achieve 10 megabits per second (mbps); and a *Fiber Distributed Data Interface* (FDDI) system may reach 100 mbps.

dB   See **decibel.**

DB connector   Any of several types of cable connectors used for parallel or serial cables. The number following the letters DB (for data bus) indicates the number of pins that the connector usually has; a DB-25 connector can have up to twenty-five pins, and a DB-9 connector can have up to nine. In practice, not all the pins (and not all the lines in the cable) may be present in the larger connectors. If your situation demands that all the lines be present, make sure you buy the right cable. Common DB connectors include the following:

* **DB-9,** defined by the *RS-449* standard as well as the ISO (*International Standards Organization*).

* **DB-25,** a standard connector used with *RS-232-C* wiring, with twenty-five pins (thirteen on the top row and twelve on the bottom).

* **DB-37,** defined as the RS-449 primary channel connector.

DB-15, DB-19, and DB-50 connectors are also available. The accompanying illustration shows a male and female DB-25 connector.

female

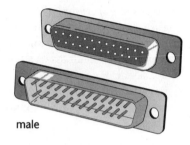

male

DB CONNECTOR

DBMS See **database management system.**

DC-2000 A quarter-inch tape minicartridge used in some tape backup systems. DC-2000 has a capacity of up to 250 megabytes when some form of *data compression* is used.
   See also **quarter-inch compatibility.**

DCB Abbreviation for disk co-processor board, a term sometimes used instead of *hard-disk controller.*

DCD Abbreviation for Data Carrier Detect. A hardware signal defined by the *RS-232-C* standard that indicates that the device, usually a modem, is on line and ready for transmission.

DCE Abbreviation for data communications equipment. In communications, any device that connects a computer or terminal to a communications channel or public network, usually a modem.
   See also **DTE.**

D-channel The data channel in *ISDN* (Integrated Services Digital Network), used for control signals and customer data. In the *Base Rate ISDN* (BRI), the D-channel operates at 16 kilobits per second (Kbps); in the *Primary Rate ISDN* (PRI), it operates at 64 Kbps.

DDCMP Abbreviation for Digital Data Communications Message Protocol. A *byte-oriented*, *link-layer* synchronous *protocol* from Digital Equipment Corporation (DEC), used as the primary data-link component of *DECnet.*

DDD Abbreviation for direct distance dialing. Use of the normal long-distance telephone system without the need for the intervention of an operator.

DDE   See **Dynamic Data Exchange**.

DDP
   Abbreviation for Datagram Delivery Protocol. A routing protocol developed by Apple Computer as a part of its AppleTalk network.

deadlock   An error condition or stalemate that occurs when two programs or devices are each waiting for a signal from the other before they can continue.

DEC   See **Digital Equipment Corporation**.

DEC Alpha   Also called the DEC Alpha AXP. A 64-bit, *RISC* (reduced instruction set computing) *microprocessor* from Digital Equipment Corporation (DEC), introduced in 1992. The Alpha is a *superscalar, superpipelined* design, which allows the processor to execute more than one instruction per clock cycle. It has an 8 kilobyte (KB) data cache, an 8 KB instruction cache, a *floating-point processor*, 64-bit registers, 64-bit data and address buses, and a 128-bit data path between the processor and memory. The internal architecture is symmetrical *multiprocessing*

(SMP) compliant, meaning that it can be used in multiprocessing configurations. Equivalent to 1.68 million transistors, the fastest Alpha runs at 200 MHz.

decibel   Abbreviated dB. One tenth of a bel, a unit of measurement common in electronics that quantifies the loudness or strength of a signal. A decibel is a relative measurement derived by comparing a measured level against a known reference.

decimal   The base-10 numbering system that uses the familiar numbers 0–9.
   See also **binary, hexadecimal**.

DECnet   A series of communications and networking products from Digital Equipment Corporation (DEC). DECnet is compatible with *Ethernet*, as well as wide-area networks (WANs) using *baseband* and *broadband* private and public communications channels. DECnet is built into the *VAX VMS* operating system.

dedicated line   A communications circuit used for one specific purpose, and not used by or

shared between other users. You
need only dial a dedicated line to
restore service after an unsched-
uled interruption. Also known as
a dedicated circuit.

See also **leased line**.

dedicated server   A computer
on the network that functions
only as a server performing specific network tasks, such as storing files, printing, or managing
external communications.

default   A standard setting, used
until an alternative is chosen. The
default server is the first server
that you log in to. The default
drive is the drive that a workstation is currently using.

default directory   A standard directory, or set of directories, used
by the operating system or by an
application. Some operating systems create several default directories when the file system is created.
For example, Novell NetWare creates the following directories when
the SYS volume is created:
SYSTEM, for the NetWare operating system files; PUBLIC, for utility
and user programs; LOGIN, for
programs allowing users to log in
to the server; and MAIL, a direc-

tory used by NetWare-compatible
electronic-mail applications.

defragmentation   The process
of reorganizing and rewriting files
so that they occupy one large area
on a hard disk rather than several
smaller areas. When a file on a
hard disk is updated, it may be
written into different areas all over
the disk. This outcome is particularly likely when the hard disk is
continuously updated over a long
period of time. This file fragmentation can lead to significant delays in
loading files, but its effect can be reversed by defragmentation.

See also **disk optimizer**.

defragmenter   Any utility that
rewrites all the parts of a fragmented
file into contiguous areas on a hard
disk. A defragmenter (such as the
DOS 6 utility DEFRAG) can
restore performance lost because
of file fragmentation.

See also **defragmentation, disk
optimizer**.

delay   In communications, a pause
in activity, representing the time
during which transmission-related
resources are unavailable for re-
laying a message.

See also **propagation delay**.

delay distortion   The distortion of a signal caused by the relative difference in speed of the various components of that signal; in particular, the distortion of the high-frequency component. Also called envelope delay.

delete   To remove a file from a disk, or to remove an item from a file. Files can be deleted using operating system commands or directly from within an application.

When a file is deleted from a disk, the file is not physically removed; although it is hidden, it is still there on the disk until it is overwritten. In certain circumstances it is possible to undelete, or recover, the original information with utilities designed for that purpose. If you find you have deleted an important file by accident, do not write any other files to that disk, so you do not overwrite the deleted file. Some network operating systems use a delete inhibit attribute to prevent accidental deletions; other operating systems rely on a read-only attribute.

See also **DELETED.SAV, FILER, SALVAGE, undelete.**

DELETED.SAV directory   A hidden Novell NetWare directory, located on each volume, used as temporary storage for deleted (but not purged) directories. Deleted files are saved in the directory from which they were originally deleted. A *network administrator* can recover and restore these files and directories with the NetWare 3.*x* utility *SALVAGE* or the NetWare 4.*x* utility *FILER.*

delimiter
1.   Any special character that separates individual items in a data set or file. For example, in a comma-delimited file, the comma is placed between each data value as the delimiter.

2.   In a *Token Ring network*, a delimiter is a bit pattern that defines the limits of a *frame* or token on the network.

demand paging   A common form of *virtual memory* management, in which pages of information are read into memory from disk only when required by the program.

See also **swapping**.

demand priority   A technique used in *100VG-nyLAN* to arbitrate access to the network and avoid *collisions*. Demand priority replaces *CSMA/CD*, which is used in slower *Ethernet* networks.

Demand priority can also prioritize specific network traffic such as video and other time-critical data, giving it a higher precedence; if multiple requests are received, the highest priority is always serviced first.

See also **Fast Ethernet.**

demodulation   In communications, the process of retrieving the data from a modulated carrier signal; the reverse of *modulation*.

See also **modem.**

departmental LAN   A *local-area network* (LAN) used by a relatively small group of people working on common tasks, that provides shared local resources, such as printers, data, and applications.

DES   See **Data Encryption Standard.**

Desktop Management Interface   See **DMI.**

desktop video   The combination of video capture hardware and application software that controls the display of video or television pictures on a desktop PC.

Desktop video is becoming increasingly important with the sharp

increase in video-conferencing applications now available.

destination address   The *address* portion of a *packet* or *datagram* that identifies the intended recipient station.

See also **source address.**

device   A general term used to describe any computer peripheral or hardware element that can send or receive data. Some examples are modems, printers, serial ports, disk drives, routers, bridges, and concentrators. Some devices require special software, or *device drivers*, to control or manage them; others have built-in intelligence.

device dependence   The requirement that a specific hardware component be present for a program to work. Device dependent software is often difficult to move or port to another computer because of its reliance on specific hardware.

See also **device independence.**

device driver   A small program that allows a computer to communicate with and control a device. Each operating system contains a standard set of device drivers for the keyboard, the monitor, and so on. When you add specialized peripheral devices, such as a CD-ROM disk drive or a network interface card, you must install the appropriate device driver so that the operating system knows how to manage the device.

device independence   The ability to produce similar results in a wide variety of environments, without requiring the presence of specific hardware. The *Unix* operating system and the PostScript page-description language are examples of device independence. Unix runs on a wide range of computers, from the PC to a Cray; PostScript is used by many different printer manufacturers.

See also **device dependence**.

device name   The name used by the operating system to identify a computer-system component. For example, LPT1 is the DOS device name for the first parallel port.

device number   A unique number assigned to a device so that it can operate on the network. Devices are identified by three numbers:

• A physical *address* set by jumpers on the adapter board.

• A device code determined by the physical address.

• A logical address determined by the order in which the drivers are loaded and by the physical address of the adapter.

DHCP   Abbreviation for Dynamic Host Configuration Protocol. A system based on *network interface card* addresses, which is used to allocate *IP* addresses and other configuration information for networked systems.

See also **TCP/IP**.

diagnostic program   A program that tests computer hardware and peripheral devices for correct operation. Some faults, known as hard faults, are relatively easy to find, and the diagnostic program will diagnose them correctly every time. Other faults, called soft faults, can be difficult to find, because they occur under specific circumstances rather than every time the memory location is tested.

Most computers run a simple set of system checks when the computer is first turned on. The PC tests are stored in *read-only memory* (ROM), and are known as *power-on self tests* (POSTs). If a POST detects an error condition, the computer will stop and display an error message on the screen.

dialback modem   See **callback modem**.

dial-in/dial-out server   See **asynchronous communications server**.

dialup line   A nondedicated communication line in which a connection is established by dialing the destination code and then broken when the call is complete.
See also **dedicated line, leased line**.

differential backup   A *backup* of a hard disk that includes only the information that has changed since the last complete backup was made.
A differential backup assumes that a *full backup* already exists, and in the event of an accident, this complete backup will be restored before the differential backup is reloaded.

digital   Describes any device that represents values in the form of binary digits.
See also **analog**.

digital audio tape   Abbreviated DAT. A method of recording information in digital form on a small audio tape cassette, originally developed by Sony and Hewlett-Packard (HP). The most common format is a 4-millimeter, helical-scan drive, which can hold more than a gigabyte of information. DATs can be used as backup media; however, like all tape devices, they are relatively slow.

Digital Equipment Corporation   Abbreviated DEC. A major manufacturer of minicomputers and mainframe computers, founded in 1957, long recognized for its high-quality computer systems. DEC's most popular product line, the VAX series, ranges from small desktop systems to large mainframes suitable for scientific and commercial processing.

dimmed command   In a *graphical user interface*, a command that is not currently available. Also known as a grayed command, because it is often displayed in light gray rather than the usual black. For example, a command to perform a network action will be dimmed until you log in to the network.

DIN connector   A connector that meets the specification of the German national standards body, Deutsche Industrie Norm (DIN). Several models of Macintosh computer use 8-pin DIN connectors as the serial port connector. On many IBM-compatible computers, a 5-pin DIN connector connects the keyboard to the system unit.

DIP   See **dual in-line package.**

DIP switch   A small switch used to select the operating mode of a device, mounted as a *dual in-line package.* DIP switches can be either sliding or rocker switches, and they are often grouped together for convenience; see the accompanying illustration. They are used in printed circuit boards, dot-matrix printers, modems, and many other peripheral devices.

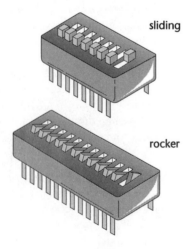

sliding

rocker

DIP SWITCH

direct distance dialing
See **DDD.**

direct distance dial network
See **public network.**

direct manipulation   In a *graphical user interface*, the process of working with objects using a mouse or other pointing device, rather than using menu selections to manipulate the objects. Using *drag-and-drop* to print a file or using the mouse to adjust the size of a window are both examples of direct manipulation.

direct memory access   Abbreviated DMA. A method of transferring information directly from a mass-storage device, such as a hard disk, into memory without the information passing through the processor. Because the processor is not involved in the transfer, DMA is usually fast.

directory   In a hierarchical file system, a convenient way of organizing and grouping files and other directories on a disk. The beginning directory is known as the *root directory,* from which all other directories must branch.

Directories inside another directory are called subdirectories.

Depending on the operating system, you can list the files in a directory in a variety of different ways: by name, by creation date and time, by file size, or by icon if you use a graphical user interface.

See also **current directory, default directory, directory, services, file allocation table, parent directory, period and double-period directories.**

directory caching   A feature of Novell NetWare that copies the *file allocation table* (FAT) and the directory entry table into the network server's memory. When file requests are made, information is retrieved from the *cache* rather than the hard disk, thus speeding up the retrieval process significantly. As the directory cache fills up, the least-used directory entries are eliminated from the cache.

directory hashing   A feature of Novell NetWare that indexes file locations on disk, thus speeding up file retrieval.

directory replication   A process that copies a master set of directories from a server, called an export server, to other specified servers or workstations, known as import computers. This process simplifies the task of maintaining and synchronizing identical sets of directories and files, because only one master copy of the data is maintained. A file is replicated when it is added to an exported directory, as well as when changes are made to the file.

directory services   A listing of all users and resources located on a network, designed to help clients locate network users and services. Some examples are the OSI's *X.500*, Novell NetWare 4.x *NetWare Directory Services* (NDS), and Banyan's *StreetTalk*.

See also **domain directory services, global directory services.**

directory structure duplication   A technique that maintains duplicate copies of the *file allocation table* (FAT) and directory entry table in separate areas of a hard disk. If the first copy is damaged or destroyed, the second copy is immediately available for use.

See also **directory verification.**

directory tree   A method of representing the hierarchical structure of the directories, subdirectories, and files on a disk. The term is often used in *graphical user interfaces*. In

d

object-oriented systems, this structure may also represent a group of objects, as in Novell NetWare 4.*x NetWare Directory Services* (NDS).

directory verification   A process that performs a consistency check on duplicate sets of *file allocation tables* (FATs) and directory entry tables to verify that they are identical. The verification occurs every time the server is started.

See also **directory structure duplication**.

disable   To turn a function off or prevent something from happening. In a *graphical user interface*, disabled menu commands are often shown in gray to indicate that they are not available.

See also **dimmed command, enable**.

DISABLE LOGIN   A Novell NetWare server utility used to prevent users from logging in to the file server, usually executed before maintenance is performed on the server. To allow users to log in again when the maintenance is complete, use *ENABLE LOGIN*.

DISABLE TTS   A Novell NetWare server utility used to turn off the *Transaction Tracking System* after an *ENABLE TTS* command has been executed.

disaster recovery   The process used to restore services after a major interruption in computing or in communications. Large events such as earthquakes or fires can interrupt networked computing activities, but so can more mundane events such as hard-disk failure or a construction worker accidentally cutting through a power or telephone line.

The whole point to disaster recovery is to plan for it before anything happens, and then follow the plan when restoring services.

See also **backup, disk duplexing, disk mirroring**.

disk cache   Pronounced "disk cash." An area of computer memory where data is temporarily stored on its way to or from a disk. When an application asks for information from the hard disk, the cache program first checks to see if that data is already in the cache memory. If it is, the disk cache program loads the information from the cache memory rather than from the hard disk. If the information is not in memory, the cache program reads the data from the disk, copies it into the cache memory for future reference, and then passes the data to the requesting application. This process is shown in the accompanying illustration.

A disk cache program can significantly speed up most disk operations. Some network operating systems also cache other often-accessed and important information, such as directories and the file allocation table (FAT).

See also **directory caching**.

disk controller   The electronic circuitry that controls and manages the operation of floppy disks or hard disks. A single disk controller may manage more than

one hard disk. Many disk controllers also manage floppy disks and compatible tape drives. In the Macintosh, the disk controller is built into the system. In IBM-compatible computers, the disk controller may be a printed circuit board inserted into the *expansion bus*, or it may be part of the hard disk drive itself, as in the case of an *Integrated Drive Electronics Interface* (IDE).

See also **Enhanced Small Device Interface, SCSI**.

disk coprocessor board   See **host bus adapter**.

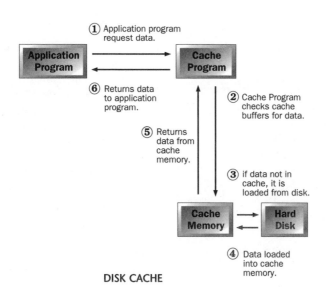

① Application program request data.

Application Program → **Cache Program**

⑥ Returns data to application program.

② Cache Program checks cache buffers for data.

⑤ Returns data from cache memory.

③ if data not in cache, it is loaded from disk.

Cache Memory → **Hard Disk**

④ Data loaded into cache memory.

DISK CACHE

disk drive   A peripheral storage device that reads and writes magnetic or optical disks. When more than one disk drive is installed on a computer, the operating system assigns each drive (or logical drive) a unique name.

Three types of disk drive are in common use: floppy disk drives, hard disk drives, and compact disc drives. Floppy disk drives accept removable 5.25-inch or 3.5-inch media. Hard disk drives, which are contained inside a protective sealed case, usually have much greater capacity and are considerably faster than floppy disk drives. Compact disc drives can be either internal or external to the system unit, and they accept compact discs loaded in special caddies.

See also **CD-ROM disk drive.**

disk duplexing   A *fault-tolerant* technique that writes the same information simultaneously onto two different hard disks. Each of the hard disks uses a different *disk controller* to provide greater redundancy. If one disk or disk controller fails, information from the other system can be used to continue operations. Disk duplexing is offered by most major network operating systems. It is designed to protect the system against a single disk failure, not multiple disk failures. Disk duplexing is no substitute for a well-planned series of disk backups.

See also **data protection, disk mirroring, RAID.**

diskless workstation   A networked computer that does not have any local disk storage capability. The computer boots and loads all its programs from the network file server. Diskless workstations are particularly valuable when sensitive information is processed; information cannot be copied from the file server onto a local disk, because the workstation does not have one.

See also **data protection, security.**

disk mirroring   A *fault-tolerant* technique that writes the same information simultaneously onto two different hard disks or two different hard-disk *partitions*, using the same *disk controller*. If one disk or partition fails, information from the other can be used to continue operations. Disk mirroring is offered by most major network operating systems. It is designed to protect the system against a single disk failure, not multiple disk failures. Disk mirroring is no substitute for a well-planned series of disk backups.

See also **data protection, disk duplexing, RAID.**

disk optimizer   A utility that re-arranges files and directories on a disk for optimum performance. By reducing or eliminating file *fragmentation* (storage in pieces in different locations on the hard disk), a disk optimizer can restore the original level of performance of your disk system. Also, it is usually easier to undelete, or recover, an unfragmented file than a frag-mented one.

Many disk optimizers will not only rewrite files as contiguous files, but will also place specific unchanging files in particular loca-tions on the disk.

See also **defragmentation.**

DISKSET   A Novell NetWare server utility that adds identifica-tion and configuration informa-tion for a new hard disk to a *host bus adapter's* EEPROM (electri-cally erasable programmable read-only memory) chip. DISKSET is used when a new disk subsystem is installed or when a hard disk is replaced on the server.

disk striping   The technique of combining a set of disk partitions located on different hard disks

into a single volume, creating a vir-tual "stripe" across the partitions that the operating system recog-nizes as a single drive; see the illus-tration on the following page. Disk striping allows multiple concurrent disk accesses and can improve per-formance considerably.

See also **disk striping with parity, RAID.**

disk striping with parity   The addition of parity information across a disk stripe so that if a disk partition fails, the data on that disk can be recreated from the information stored across the remaining partitions in the disk stripe.

See also **disk striping, RAID.**

DISMOUNT   A Novell Net-Ware server utility used to unload a volume from the server so that the disk can be repaired or re-placed. To reload the volume, use the *MOUNT* command.

DISPLAY NETWORKS   A Novell NetWare server utility that displays network information when a server is being used as a *router.* The network number of the cabling system for each avail-able network is also shown.

See also **DISPLAY SERVERS.**

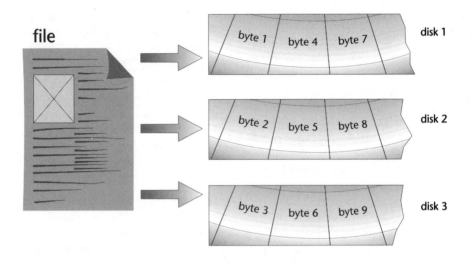

file

byte 1 byte 4 byte 7 disk 1

byte 2 byte 5 byte 8 disk 2

byte 3 byte 6 byte 9 disk 3

DISK STRIPING

DISPLAY SERVERS A Novell NetWare server utility that displays server information when a server is being used as a *router*.
See also **DISPLAY NETWORKS**.

distance vector algorithm Abbreviated DVA. A family of routing algorithms that calculate the best-path route to use for data transmission from information present in adjacent nodes on the network.

distributed computing See distributed processing.

distributed database A database managed as a single system even though it includes many clients and many servers at both local and remote sites. A distributed database requires that data redundancy is managed and controlled.

distributed processing A computer system in which processing is performed by several separate computers linked by a communications network. The term often refers to any computer system supported by a network, but more properly refers to a system in which each computer is chosen to handle a specific workload and the network supports the system as a whole. Each computer contributes to the completion of a common task by completing one or more subtasks independently of its peers, and then reports the results from these subtasks when they are complete.

See also **client/server architecture.**

DLL   See **Dynamic Link Library.**

DMA   See **direct memory access.**

DMI   Abbreviation for Desktop Management Interface. A standard *API* for identifying desktop workstation hardware and software components automatically, without intervention from the user.

At a minimum, DMI identifies the manufacturer, component name, version, serial number (if appropriate), and installation time and date of any component installed in a networked workstation. This information is designed to help network administrators resolve configuration problems quickly and easily, and to indicate when and where system upgrades should be applied. PCs, Macintosh computers, and Unix systems are all covered by DMI.

DMI is backed by Digital Equipment Corporation (DEC), IBM, Intel, Microsoft, Novell,

Sun, and more than three hundred other vendors.

DNS   Abbreviation for Domain Naming System. A distributed addressing system that resolves the *domain name* into the *IP address*. DNS is used in networks such as the *Internet* and Bitnet.

The most common high-level domains on the Internet include:

- .com: a commercial organization
- .edu: an educational establishment such as a university
- .gov: a branch of the U.S. Government
- .int: an international organization
- .mil: a branch of the U.S. military
- .net: a network
- .org: a nonprofit organization

Most countries also have unique domains named after their international abbreviation—for example, .UK for the United Kingdom and .CA for Canada.

docking station   A hardware system into which a *portable computer* fits so that it can be used as a full-fledged desktop computer. Docking stations vary from simple port replicators that allow you access to parallel and serial ports

d

and a mouse to complete systems that give you access to network connections, CD-ROMs, and even a tape backup system or *PCMCIA* ports. The portable computer and docking station are designed as two parts of the same system; you cannot swap computers and docking stations from different manufacturers or even from different models.

documentation The instructions, tutorials, specifications, troubleshooting advice, and reference guides that accompany a computer program or a piece of hardware. Documentation can be in printed or on line format. Early system documentation was often written by programmers and engineers, and was usually filled with technical jargon. Today's documentation is generally better written and easier to understand.

document management The cataloging, storage, and retrieval of documents in a networked environment. In this context, a document may be text, scanned graphics, a spreadsheet, a form, or any other unique file.

Each file is tagged with information that includes the name of the original author, document de-scription, creation date, and the name of the application used to create the document.

See also **groupware, Lotus Notes, workflow software.**

DOMAIN A Novell NetWare 4.*x* server utility used when testing newly written *NetWare Loadable Modules* (NLMs). DOMAIN lets you load the new NLM into a protected area, therefore isolating it from the core operating system and preventing an NLM that is not functioning properly from bringing down the whole network operating system.

domain A description of a single computer, a whole department, or a complete site, used for naming and administrative purposes. Top-level domains must be registered to receive mail from outside the organization; local domains have meaning only inside their own enterprise. Depending on the context, the term can have several slightly different meanings:

• In the *Internet*, a domain is part of the Domain Naming System (*DNS*).

• In Novell NetWare 4.*x*, a domain is a special area used to test new *NLMs*.

- In IBM's *SNA*, a domain represents all the terminals controlled by a specific processor.
- In *Windows NT*, a user can log in to the local computer and be authenticated to access just that one system, or can log in to a domain and be authenticated to access other servers within that domain.
- In *Lotus Notes*, a domain is one or more Notes servers that share the same Public Name and Address Book database. This database contains information about the users within the domain, including their e-mail address and other information.

See also **DOMAIN, domain name.**

domain directory services

Directory services that consist of one or more linked servers. Each domain within a network must be managed and administered separately. *Windows NT* Server and IBM's *LAN Server* both use domain directory services.

See also **global directory services.**

domain name   In the Domain Naming System (*DNS*), an easy-to-remember name that identifies a specific *Internet* host, as opposed to the numerical *IP address*.

See also **bang path.**

Domain Naming System
See **DNS.**

DOS   Acronym for Disk Operating System. An *operating system* originally developed by Microsoft for the IBM PC. DOS exists in two similar versions: *MS-DOS*, developed and marketed by Microsoft for use with IBM-compatible computers, and *PC-DOS*, supported and sold by IBM for use on computers manufactured by IBM. A third version, originally developed by Digital Research and called *DR-DOS*, is now owned by Novell and called *Novell DOS.*

DOS client   A workstation that boots DOS and gains access to the network using either a *NetWare shell* (for NetWare versions 2.x and 3.x) or the *NetWare DOS Requester* (for NetWare 4.x).

DOSGEN   A Novell NetWare workstation utility that creates a boot file called NET_DOS.SYS in the SYS:LOGIN directory on the server and then copies a workstation's boot files into this file. The workstation can boot from this file rather than from a floppy disk or local hard disk.

d

DOS prompt   A visual confirmation that *DOS* is ready to receive input from the keyboard. The default prompt includes the current drive letter followed by a greater-than symbol, as in C:>. The DOS prompt can be customized by using the PROMPT command.

See also **command line, command prompt**.

dotted decimal   See **internet address**.

DOWN   A Novell NetWare server utility that brings down the server in a way that protects data integrity. It writes all *cache buffers* to disk and closes all open files before halting the operating system.

See also **SERVER**.

downlink   The transmission of information from a satellite to an earth station.

See also **uplink**.

download

1. In communications, to transfer a file or files from one computer to another over a network or using a modem.

2. To send information, such as font information or a

PostScript file, from a computer to a printer.

downsizing   The redesign of mainframe-based business applications to applications capable of running on smaller, less expensive systems, often *local-area networks* (LANs) of PCs. *Client/server architecture* is the model most often implemented during downsizing.

When applications are moved from large computer systems to PCs, it is possible that security, integrity, and overall control will be compromised, and development and training costs can be high. However, a collection of appropriately configured PCs, networked together, can provide more than ten times the power for the same cost as a mainframe computer supporting remote terminals.

A more accurate term might be "rightsizing," to match the application requirements of the corporation to the capabilities of the hardware and software systems available.

See also **outsourcing**.

downtime   The amount of time during which a computer system is not working, because of a hardware or software failure.

downward compatibility   See
  backward compatibility.

DP   See **data processing.**

drag-and-drop   In a graphical
  user interface, to move a selected
  object onto another object with
  the mouse to initiate a process.
  For example, if you drag a document icon and drop it onto a
  word processor's icon, the program will run and the document
  will be opened. To print a file,
  you can drag the file to the
  printer icon using the mouse and
  then release the mouse button.
  You can also use drag-and-drop
  to copy a file from one disk to another, or to move a marked block
  of text to a new location inside a
  word-processed document.

DRAM   See **dynamic RAM.**

DR-DOS   A DOS-compatible operating system originally developed by Digital Research (DR),
  now owned by Novell, that runs
  on Intel processors. DR-DOS contains commands similar to those
  available in MS-DOS or PC-DOS,
  although the DR-DOS versions
  are generally more capable and
  have more *command-line switches.*

The latest version of the operating
system is called *Novell DOS.*

drive array   The group of hard
  disk drives used in one of the
  RAID (redundant array of inexpensive disks) configurations.

drive letter   A designation used
  to specify a PC disk drive. For example, the first floppy disk drive
  is usually referred to as drive A:
  and the first hard disk drive is usually referred to as drive C:.

drive mapping   The technique of
  assigning a drive letter to represent a complete directory path
  statement. Novell NetWare supports four types of drive mapping:
  • **Local drive mapping:** Maps
  drives to local hard disk and
  floppy disk drives.
  • **Network drive mapping:**
  Maps drives to volumes and directories on the network.
  • **Network search drive mapping:** Maps drives to directories
  that contain DOS applications or
  files. Search drive mappings are not
  supported on OS/2 workstations;
  use the OS/2 PATH, LIBPATH,
  and DPATH commands to
  achieve the same result.
  • **Directory map object:** Maps
  drives to directories that contain

d

frequently used files, such as applications.

See also **MAP**.

drop The location in a *multidrop line* where a tap is inserted to allow the connection of a new device.

drop cable The cable used in *thick Ethernet* to connect a network device to an *MAU* (Multistation Access Unit). The maximum cable length is 50 meters (165 feet).

DS Abbreviation for digital signal or digital service. See the accompanying illustration. There are several levels of common carrier digital transmission service:

- **DS-0:** 64 kilobits per second (Kbps).
- **DS-1:** 1.544 megabits per second (Mbps) (*T1*).
- **DS-1C:** Two DS-1 channels are *multiplexed* into a single DS-1C 3.152 Mbps channel.

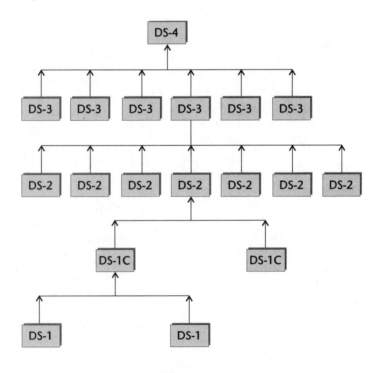

DS

- **DS-2:** Two DS-1C channels are multiplexed into one DS-2 6.312 Mbps (*T2*) channel.
- **DS-3:** Seven DS-2 channels are multiplexed into a single 44.736 Mbps (*T3*) channel.
- **DS-4:** Six DS-3 channels are multiplexed into one 274.176 Mbps (*T4*) DS-4 channel.

The higher-capacity channels are constructed by multiplexing the lower-bandwidth channels together, with some additional framing and administrative overhead.

DS-0 is also referred to as fractional T1, because it bridges the gap between 56-Kbps direct dial service (DDS) and a full T1 implementation.

DSMERGE A Novell NetWare 4.x utility used to view name and time synchronization information, to rename an NDS tree, or to merge the root structures of two separate NDS trees into one single tree.

See also **DSREPAIR, DSTRACE SET**.

DSP Abbreviation for Digital Signal Processing. An *integrated circuit* used in high-speed data manipulation. You will find DSP chips integrated into sound cards, modems, and *video conferencing* hardware where they are used in communications, image manipulation, and other data-acquisition applications.

See also **codec, desktop video**.

DSPACE A Novell NetWare 3.*x* workstation utility used to manage a server's disk space. In NetWare 4.*x*, disk-space management is provided by the *NDIR* workstation utility.

DSR Abbreviation for Data Set Ready. A hardware signal defined by the *RS-232-C* standard to indicate that the device is ready to operate.

See also **CTS**.

DSREPAIR A Novell NetWare 4.*x* server utility that finds and corrects errors in the *NetWare Directory Services* (NDS) database. DSREPAIR checks NDS *partitions* and *replicas* on the server. It also checks the file system for problems such as invalid trustee IDs, which may occur when a user is deleted from the network.

See also **DSMERGE**.

DSTRACE SET A group of SET options used on Novell NetWare 4.x servers to monitor the progress of *NetWare Directory Services* (NDS) synchronization tasks, and view any errors that occurred during the synchronization.

99

See also **DSMERGE, DSREPAIR.**

DSU   Abbreviation for Data Service Unit. A device that connects *DTE* (data terminal equipment) to digital communications lines. A DSU formats the data for transmission on the public carrier wide-area networks (WANs) and ensures that the carrier's requirements for data formats are met.
See also **CSU.**

DTE   Abbreviation for data terminal equipment. In communications, any device, such as a terminal or a computer, connected to a communications device, channel, or public network.
See also **DCE.**

DTR   Abbreviation for Data Terminal Ready. A hardware signal defined by the *RS-232-C* standard sent from a computer to a modem to indicate that the computer is ready to receive a transmission.

dual-attached station   See **DAS.**

dual homing   In *Fiber Distributed Data Interface* (FDDI), a method of cabling concentrators and stations in a tree configuration, providing an alternative route to the FDDI network should the primary connection fail. See the illustration on the next page.

dual in-line package   Abbreviated DIP. A standard housing constructed of hard plastic commonly used to hold an *integrated circuit.* The circuit's leads are connected to two parallel rows of pins designed to fit snugly into a socket; these pins may also be soldered directly to a printed circuit board.
See also **DIP switch.**

dumb terminal   A combination of keyboard and screen that has no local computing power, used to input information to a large, remote computer, often a minicomputer or a mainframe. The remote computer provides all the processing power for the system.
See also **intelligent terminal.**

duplex   In *asynchronous transmissions*, the ability to transmit and receive on the same channel at the same time; also referred to as full duplex. Half-duplex channels can transmit only or receive only.
See also **communications parameters.**

DX4   A 32-bit chip, based on the 80486, from Intel. Despite

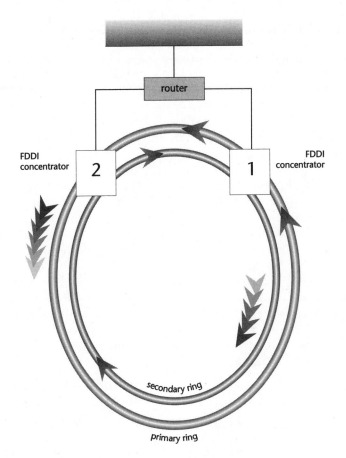

DUAL HOMING

the name, the DX4 is not a clock-quadrupled chip; it is a clock-tripled chip. For example, the 75 megahertz (MHz) version of the chip completes three CPU cycles for each cycle of the 25 MHz motherboard.

The DX4 is available in 75, 83, and 100 MHz versions, and fills the performance gap between the existing chips in the 80486 set and the Pentium processor.

See also **clock-multiplying, 80486DX, 80486DX2.**

Dynamic Data Exchange   Abbreviated DDE. A technique used for application-to-application

101

communications, available in several operating systems, including Microsoft Windows, Macintosh System 7, and OS/2.

When two or more programs that support DDE are running at the same time, they can exchange data and commands, by means of conversations. A DDE conversation is a two-way connection between two different applications, used to transmit data by each program alternately.

DDE is used for low-level communications that do not need user intervention. For example, a communications program might feed stock market information into a spreadsheet program, where that data can be displayed in a meaningful way and recalculated automatically as it changes.

DDE has largely been superseded by a more complex but more capable mechanism known as *Object Linking and Embedding* (OLE).

Dynamic Link Library
Abbreviated DLL. A program module that contains executable code and data that can be used by applications, or even by other DLLs, in performing a specific task. DLLs are used extensively in Microsoft Windows, OS/2, and in Windows NT. DLLs may have file-name extensions of .DLL, .DRV, or .FON.

The DLL is linked into the application only when the program runs, and it is unloaded again when no longer needed. If two DLL applications are running at the same time and both perform a particular function, only one copy of the code for that function is loaded, for more efficient use of limited memory. Another benefit of using dynamic linking is that the .EXE files are not as large as they would be without DLLs, because frequently used routines can be put into a DLL rather than repeated in each .EXE file that uses them. A smaller .EXE file means saved disk space and faster program loading.

dynamic RAM
Abbreviated DRAM, pronounced "dee-ram." A common type of computer memory that uses capacitors and transistors storing electrical charges to represent memory states. These capacitors lose their electrical charge, so they need to be refreshed every millisecond, during which time they cannot be read by the processor.

DRAM chips are small, simple, cheap, easy to make, and hold approximately four times as much information as a *static RAM*

(SRAM) chip of similar complexity. However, they are slower than SRAM. Processors operating at *clock speeds* of 25 megahertz (MHz) or more need DRAM with access times of faster than 80 nanoseconds, while SRAM chips can be read in as little as 10 to 20 nanoseconds.

dynamic routing   A routing technique that allows the route that a message takes to change, as the message is in transit through the network, in response to changing network conditions. Conditions forcing a route change might include unusually heavy traffic on a particular section of the network or a cable failure. Also known as dynamic adaptive routing.

d

E

802.*x*   A set of communications standards defining the physical and electrical connections in *local-area networks* (LANs), originally defined by the *Institute of Electrical and Electronics Engineers* (IEEE).

Many of the IEEE standards have also been adopted by the *International Standards Organization* (ISO), whose standards are accepted all over the world; IEEE standards 802.1 to 802.11 are now also known as ISO 8802.1 to 8802.11. You will see both designations used in networking books and magazines; it will take a while for everyone to get used to the new numbers.

802.1   An *IEEE standard* that specifies the *media-access-control* level for *bridges* linking *802.3, 802.4,* and *802.5* networks. It includes a *spanning-tree algorithm* for *Ethernet* media-access-control layer bridges, and the heterogeneous local-area network (LAN)

management specification for Ethernet and *Token Ring hubs.*

802.2   An *IEEE standard* that specifies the *logical link* sublayer of the *data-link layer* in the OSI protocol stack. The data-link layer in the OSI protocol stack is divided into the *logical link layer* and the *media access control layer.* The logical link layer provides framing, addressing, and error-control functions.

802.3   An *IEEE standard* for *CSMA/CD* (Carrier Sense Multiple Access/Collision Detection) local-area networks (LANs), including both *baseband* and *broadband networks.* The baseband version is based on the *Ethernet* network, originally developed by Xerox Corporation.

The 802.3 standard includes the following:

- **10Base2:** An implementation of the Ethernet standard on *thin Ethernet* cable, with a data-transfer rate of 10 megabits per second (Mbps), and a maximum cable-segment length of 185 meters (600 feet).

- **10Base5:** An 802.3 Ethernet standard on *thick Ethernet* cable, with a 10 Mbps data-transfer rate and a cable-segment length of up to 500 meters (1650 feet), over a *bus topology*.

- **10BaseT:** Establishes a standard for Ethernet over *unshielded twisted-pair* (UTP) wiring, the same wiring and *RJ-45* connectors used with modern telephone systems. The standard is based on a star *topology*, with each node connected to a central wiring center, with a cable-length limitation of 100 meters (330 feet).
- **1Base5:** A 1 Mbps network standard with *twisted-pair cable* based on AT&T's StarLAN.
- **10Broad36:** Defines a long-distance Ethernet with a 10 Mbps data-transfer rate and a maximum cable-segment length of 3600 meters (11,880 feet).
- **10BaseF:** Explicitly specifies *fiber-optic cable* in three different settings; 10Base-FP (fiber passive) for desktops, 10Base-FL (fiber link) for intermediate hubs and workgroups, and 10Base-FB (fiber backbone) for central facility lines between buildings.
- **100BaseVG:** A 100 Mbps Ethernet network developed by Hewlett-Packard and AT&T Microelectrics.
- **100BaseT:** A 100 Mbps Ethernet developed by Grand Junction Networks.

See also **100VG-AnyLAN.**

802.4   An *IEEE standard* for *bus topology* networks that use *token passing* to control access and network traffic, running at 10 megabits per second. *Token-bus networks* are sometimes used in manufacturing settings, but they are not often found in office-based networks.

See also **ARCnet, TOP.**

802.5   An *IEEE standard* that defines *ring networks* using *token passing* to control access and network traffic, running at 4 or 16 megabits per second. It is used by IBM's *Token Ring* network over *shielded twisted pair* (STP), *unshielded twisted pair* (UTP), or *fiber-optic cabling*. Also known as ANSI 802.1-1985.

802.6   An *IEEE standard* for *metropolitan-area networks* (MANs). It describes a Distributed Queue Dual Bus (DQDB) used for transmitting voice, video, and data over two parallel *fiber-optic cables*, with signaling rates in excess of 100 megabits per second.

802.7   An *IEEE* Technical Advisory Group (TAG) report on *broadband networks* carrying voice, data, and video traffic.

802.8   An *IEEE* Technical Advisory Group (TAG) report on the use of fiber optics in local-area networks (LANs).

802.9   An *IEEE* advisory committee on integrated data, voice, and video networking. Also known as Integrated Voice and Data (IVD) LAN.

802.10   An *IEEE* Technical Advisory Group (TAG) working on the definition of a standard security model for use over a variety of network types.

802.11   A proposed *IEEE standard* that will eventually define *wireless LANs,* incorporating pen-based computers, *PDAs*, and other portable devices.

802.12   A recent *IEEE* working group studying the 100 megabit per second Ethernet *100VG-Any-LAN* proposals from Hewlett-Packard and several other vendors.

80286   Also called the 286. A 16-bit microprocessor from *Intel*, first released in February 1982, used by IBM in the IBM PC/AT computer. Since then, it has been used in many other IBM-compatible computers.

The 80286 uses a 16-bit data word and a 16-bit data bus, with 24 bits to address memory. It has two modes:

• *Real mode* effectively limits performance to that of an 8086 microprocessor and can address 1 megabyte (MB) of memory.

• *Protected mode* prevents an application from stopping the operating system because of an error and can address 16 MB of memory.

The 80286 is equivalent to approximately 134,000 transistors, and it can execute 1.2 million instructions per second. The *floating-point processor* for the 80286 is the *80287*.

80386DX   Also called the 80386, the 386DX, and the 386. A full 32-bit microprocessor introduced by *Intel* in October 1985 and used in many IBM and IBM-compatible computers. Available in 16-, 20-, 25-, and 33-MHz versions, the 80386 has a 32-bit data word, can transfer information 32 bits at a time over the data bus, and can use 32 bits in addressing memory. It has the following modes:

• *Real mode* effectively limits performance to that of an 8086 microprocessor and can address 1 megabyte (MB) of memory.

- *Protected mode* prevents an application from stopping the operating system because of an error, and it can address 4 gigabytes (GB) of memory.
- *Virtual 8086 mode* allows the operating system to divide the 80386 into several virtual 8086 microprocessors, all running with their own 1 MB of space, and all running a separate program.

The 80386 is equivalent to about 275,000 transistors, and it can perform six million instructions per second. The *floating-point processor* for the 80386DX is the *80387*.

See also **80386SX**.

80386SX   Also called the 386SX. A lower-cost alternative to the *80386DX* microprocessor, introduced by *Intel* in 1988. Available in 16-, 20-, 25-, and 33-MHz versions, the 80386SX is an 80386DX with a 16-bit data bus. This design allows systems to be configured using cheaper 16-bit components, leading to a lower overall cost. The *floating-point processor* for the 80386SX is the *80387SX*.

80387   Also called the 387. A *floating-point processor* from *Intel*, designed for use with the *80386* family of chips. When supported by applications, a floating-point processor can speed up floating-point and transcendental math operations by ten to fifty times.

The 80387 conforms to the ANSI/IEEE 754-1985 standard for binary floating-point operations, and it is available in speeds of 16, 20, 25, and 33 megahertz (MHz).

80387SX   Also called the 387SX. A *floating-point processor* from *Intel*, designed for use with the 16-bit data bus of the *80386SX* chip only. When supported by applications, a floating-point processor can speed up floating-point and transcendental math operations by ten to fifty times.

The 80387SX conforms to the ANSI/IEEE 754-1985 standard for binary floating-point operations, and it is available only in a 16-MHz version.

80486DX   Also called the 486 or i486. A 32-bit microprocessor introduced by *Intel* in April 1989. The 80486DX represents the continuing evolution of the *80386* family of microprocessors, and it adds several notable features, including an on-board *cache*, a built-in *floating-point processor*, and a *memory management unit* (MMU), as well as certain advanced provisions for *multiprocessing*. Available in 25-, 33-, and 50-MHz versions, the 80486DX is equivalent to 1.25 million transistors, and it can perform 20 million instructions per second.

See also **DX4**.

80486DX2   Also known as the 486DX2. A 32-bit microprocessor introduced by *Intel* in 1992. It is functionally identical to, and 100 percent compatible with, the 80486DX, but with one major difference: the DX2 chip adds what Intel calls clock-doubling technology. This technology allows it to run twice as fast internally as it does with components external to the chip. For example, the DX2-50 operates at 50 MHz internally, but at 25 MHz while communicating with other system components, including memory and the other chips on the *motherboard*, thus maintaining its overall system compatibility.

Available in 50- and 66-MHz versions, the 80486DX2 contains 1.2 million transistors, and it is capable of handling 40 million instructions per second.

See also **clock-multiplying, DX4, Intel OverDrive**.

80486SL   A low-power version of *Intel's 80486DX* microprocessor, designed for use in laptop computers. In addition to having the features and performance of the 80486DX, the 80486SL provides the ability to *shadow memory*, a lower operating voltage of 3.3 volts (the 80486DX uses 5 volts), and features designed to stop certain system components when the computer is not in use in order to conserve and prolong battery life.

80486SX   Also called the 486SX. A 32-bit microprocessor introduced by *Intel* in April 1991 as a lower-cost alternative to the *80486DX*. The 80486SX can be described as an 80486DX with the *floating-point processor* circuitry disabled. Available in 16-, 20-, and 25-MHz versions, the 80486SX contains the equivalent of 1.185 million transistors, and it can execute 16.5 million instructions per second.

See also **80487**.

80487   Also called the 487. A *floating-point processor* from *Intel*, designed for use with the *80486SX* chip. When supported by application programs, a floating-point processor can speed up floating-point and transcendental math operations by ten to fifty times.

The 80487 is essentially an 80486 with the floating-point circuitry still enabled. When an 80487 is added into the coprocessor socket of a *motherboard* running the 80486SX, it effectively becomes the main processor, shutting down the 80486SX and taking over all operations.

The 80487 conforms to the ANSI/IEEE 754-1985 standard for binary floating-point operations.

See also **80486DX**.

E   See **exa-**.

EBCDIC   Acronym for Extended Binary Coded Decimal Interchange Code, pronounced "eb-se-dic." EBCDIC is the *character set* commonly used on large IBM mainframe computers, most IBM minicomputers, and computers from many other manufacturers. It is an 8-bit code, allowing 256 different characters (see Table A.4 in the appendix). Unlike with *ASCII*, the placement of the letters of the alphabet in EBCDIC is discontinuous. Also, there is no direct character-to-character match when converting from EBCDIC to ASCII; some characters exist in one set but not in the other.

echo

1. A transmitted signal that is reflected back to the sender strongly enough so that it can be distinguished from the original signal, often encountered on long-distance telephone lines and satellite links.

2. A form of repetition, used as a mechanism in testing network nodes, in which each receiving station on the network echoes a message back to the main server or host computer.

echo cancellation   A mechanism used to control echoes on communications links such as satellite links. The modem checks for a delayed duplication of the original signal and adds a reversed version of this transmission to the channel on which it receives information. This process effectively removes the echo without affecting the incoming signal. Echo cancellation is a part of the CCITT V.32 standard for 9600 bit-per-second modems.

ECNE   See **Master CNE**.

EDIT   A Novell NetWare server NLM used to create or edit text files of up to 8 kilobytes (KB) in size. Existing files can be extended an additional 4KB.

EDP   Abbreviation for electronic data processing. See **data processing.**

EEMS   See **Enhanced Expanded Memory Specification.**

effective rights   In Novell NetWare, any rights an object can use to look at or change a specific directory, file, or other object. Effective rights are recalculated every time an object attempts such an operation.

See also **Inherited Rights Mask, rights, trustee rights.**

EGP   Abbreviation for External Gateway Protocol. A *routing protocol* used to exchange network availability information among organizational networks. EGP indicates whether a given network is reachable, but it does not evaluate that information or make routing or priority decisions.

See also **BGP.**

EIA   Abbreviation for Electronic Industries Association. A trade association representing American manufacturers in standards organizations. The EIA has published and formalized several important standards, including RS-232-C, RS-422, RS-423, RS-449, RS-485, and RS-530. Standards having to do with communications are produced jointly with the Telecommunications Industry Association.

See also EIA/TIA 586.

EIA/TIA 586   A standard, jointly defined by the Electronic Industries Association and the Telecommunications Industry Association (EIA/TIA), for telecommunications wiring used in commercial buildings.

The standard is designed to:

• Specify a generic wiring system for all commercial buildings.

• Define media types, as well as connections and terminations.

• Provide a basis for interoperation between competing products and services in wiring, design, installation, and management.

• Allow for the wiring of a building before the definition of the products that will use that wiring, and allow for elegant future expansion.

EIA/TIA 586 applies to all *unshielded twisted-pair* wiring that

111

works with *Ethernet, Token Ring, ISDN,* and other networking systems.

See also **cabling standards, Category 1-5.**

EISA   Acronym for Extended Industry Standard Architecture, pronounced "ee-sah." A PC *bus* standard that extends the traditional AT-bus to 32 bits and allows more than one processor to share the bus.

EISA was developed by the so-called Gang of Nine (AST Research, Compaq Computer Corporation, Epson, Hewlett-Packard, NEC, Olivetti, Tandy, Wyse Technology, and Zenith Data Systems) in reply to IBM's introduction of its proprietary *MCA* (Microchannel Architecture). EISA maintains compatibility with the earlier *ISA* (Industry Standard Architecture), and it also provides for additional features introduced by IBM in the MCA standard. EISA accepts ISA *expansion cards*, and so, unlike MCA, is compatible with earlier systems.

See also **local bus, PCI, PCMCIA.**

electromagnetic interference

Abbreviated EMI. Any electro-magnetic radiation released by an electronic device that disrupts the operation or performance of another device. EMI is produced by many sources commonly found in an office environment, including fluorescent lights, photocopiers, and motors such as those used in elevators. EMI is also produced by natural atmospheric or solar activity.

See also **Class A certification, Class B certification, FCC, radio-frequency interference.**

electronic data interchange

Abbreviated EDI. A method of electronically exchanging business documents, including bills of materials, purchase orders, and invoices. Customers and suppliers can establish an EDI network by means of *Open Systems Interconnect* (OSI) standards, or by using proprietary products. Widely accepted standards include ANSI X.12, ISO 9735, and CCITT X.435.

electronic data processing

See **data processing.**

electronic mail   See e-mail.

elevator seeking   A feature of

Novell NetWare that allows the server read-write head to access files in the direction that the head is already traveling across the disk, rather than in the order in which they were requested. This feature allows the drive heads to operate continuously, and thus improves disk performance and minimizes disk-head seek times.

ELF See **extremely low-frequency emission.**

ELS NetWare Abbreviation for Entry Level System NetWare, an early version of NetWare for small networks, discontinued in 1991 but still widely used.

e-mail The use of a network to transmit text messages, memos, and reports, also called electronic mail. Users can send a message to one or more individuals, to a predefined group, or to all users on the system. When you receive a message, you can read, print, forward, answer, or delete it.

An e-mail system may be implemented on a *peer-to-peer network*, a *client/server architecture*, a mainframe computer, or on a dialup service, such as CompuServe, GEnie, or MCI Mail. E-mail is by far the most popular *Internet* application, with well over 80 percent of Internet users taking advantage of the service.

E-mail has several advantages over conventional mail systems, including:

• E-mail is fast—very fast when compared to conventional mail.

• If something exists on your computer as a file—text, graphical images, even program files and video segments—you can usually send it as e-mail.

The problems associated with e-mail are similar to those associated with online communications in general: security, privacy (always assume that your e-mail is not private), and the legal status of documents exchanged electronically.

See also **CCITT X Series, mailbox, MIME, voice mail.**

e-mail address The addressing information required for an *e-mail* message to reach the correct recipient.

See also **bang path, mailbox.**

EMI See **electromagnetic interference.**

EMM See **expanded memory manager.**

EMS   See Expanded Memory Specification.

emulator   A device built to work exactly like another device—hardware, software, or a combination of both. For example, a *terminal emulation* program lets a PC pretend to be a terminal attached to a mainframe computer or to an online service by providing the control codes that the remote system expects to receive.

enable   To turn a function on or allow something to happen. When a function is enabled, it is available for use. In a *graphical user interface*, enabled menu commands are often shown in black type.

See also **disable**.

ENABLE LOGIN   A Novell NetWare server utility used to re-enable a login after it has been disabled with the *DISABLE LOGIN* command.

ENABLE TTS   A Novell NetWare server utility used to reestablish the *Transaction Tracking System* (TTS) after it has been disabled with the *DISABLE TTS* command.

Encapsulated PostScript   Abbreviated EPS. The file format of the PostScript page-description language. The EPS standard is device independent, so that images can easily be transferred between different applications, and they can be sized and output to different printers without any loss of image quality or distortion.

The EPS file contains the PostScript commands needed to recreate the image, but the image itself cannot be displayed on a monitor unless the file also contains an optional preview image stored in TIFF or PICT format.

The EPS file can only be printed on a PostScript-compatible laser printer, and the printer itself determines the final printing resolution; a laser printer might be capable of 300 dots per inch (dpi), whereas a Linotronic printer is capable of 2450 dpi.

encapsulation   The process of inserting the *frame* header and data from a higher-level *protocol* into the data frame of a lower-level protocol.

See also **tunneling**.

encryption   The process of encoding information in an attempt to make it secure from unauthorized access. The reverse of this process is known as decryption.

There are two main encryption schemes in common use:

- **Private (Symmetrical) Key Schemes:** An encryption algorithm based on a private *encryption key* known to both the sender and the recipient of the information. The encrypted message is unreadable, and can be transmitted over non-secure systems.

- **Public (Asymmetrical) Key Schemes:** An encryption scheme based on using the two halves of a long bit sequence as encryption keys. Either half of the bit sequence can be used to encrypt the data, but the other half is required to decrypt the data.

See also **Clipper chip, Data Encryption Standard, PGP, ROT13.**

encryption key   A unique and secret number used to encrypt data to protect it from unauthorized access.

See also **Clipper chip, Data Encryption Standard, PGP, ROT-13.**

ENDCAP   A Novell NetWare 3.*x* workstation utility that frees a workstation's printer port after the *CAPTURE* command was used to send information to a

printer or file. In NetWare 4.*x*, this function is performed by an option of the CAPTURE command.

end node   A networked node such as a PC that can only send and receive information for its own use; it cannot route or forward information to another node.

end-of-file   Abbreviated EOF. A special code placed after the last *byte* in a file that indicates to the operating system that no more data follows. An end-of-file code is needed because disk space is assigned to a file in blocks, and the file may not always terminate at the end of a block. In the *ASCII* system, an EOF is represented by the decimal value 26, or by the Ctrl-Z *control character*.

end-of-text   Abbreviated ETX. A character used in computer communications to indicate the end of a text file. In the *ASCII* system, an ETX is represented by the decimal value 3, or by the Ctrl-C *control character*. A different symbol, *end-of-transmission* (EOT, ASCII 4, or Ctrl-D), is used to indicate the end of a complete transmission.

e

end-of-transmission   Abbreviated EOT. A character used in computer communications to indicate the end of a transmission. In the *ASCII* system, an EOT is represented by the decimal value 4, or by the Ctrl-D *control character*.

end user   Often refers to people who use an application to produce their own results on their own computer or workstation. During the mainframe computer era, end users were people who received output from the computer and used that output in their work. They rarely, if ever, actually saw the computer, much less learned to use it themselves. Today, end users often write macros to automate complex or repetitive tasks, and sometimes write procedures using command languages.

Enhanced Expanded Memory Specification   Abbreviated EEMS. A revised version of the original Lotus-Intel-Microsoft *Expanded Memory Specification* (LIM EMS) that lets DOS applications use more than 640 kilobytes of memory space.

See also **memory management**.

Enhanced Small Device Interface   Abbreviated ESDI. A popular hard disk, floppy disk, and tape drive interface standard, capable of a data-transfer rate of 10 to 20 megabits per second. ESDI is most often used with large hard disks.

See **also hard-disk interface, IDE, SCSI, ST506 Interface.**

enterprise   A term used to encompass an entire business group, organization, or corporation, including all local, remote, and satellite offices.

Enterprise Network Services   Abbreviated ENS. A software product based on Banyan Systems' *StreetTalk* Directory Service for *VINES* that brings *global directory service* features to other networks. ENS includes StreetTalk Directory Assistance, the Banyan Security Service, and Banyan Network Management.

Specific versions of ENS are available for Novell NetWare, SCO UNIX, and HP-UX, so that servers running those operating systems can interoperate and share management in a network with VINES servers.

enterprise network   A network that connects every computer in every location of a business group, organization, or corporation, and runs the company's *mission-critical applications*.

In many cases an *enterprise* network will include several different types of computers running different operating systems and attached to different kinds of networks.

envelope delay   See **delay distortion**.

environment

1. The complete set of hardware and software resources made available to any user of a system.

2. The operating system that a program needs in order to execute. For example, a program may be said to be running in the Unix environment.

3. In DOS, an area of memory used to store system-wide information, such as the path and details of the *command prompt*. Users or applications place values in the environment by using the SET command.

EOF   See **end-of-file**.

EOT   See **end-of-transmission**.

EPS   See **Encapsulated PostScript**.

equalization   The process of balancing a circuit by reducing frequency and phase distortion, so that it passes all expected frequencies with equal efficiency.

erasable CD   A standard format that allows users to store and revise large amounts of data on a normal compact disc. The standard is supported by Sony, Phillips, IBM, Hewlett-Packard, and other leading companies. One of the major advantages of this new standard is that it is completely compatible with existing compact discs, and makers of *CD-ROM disk drives* only have to make minor manufacturing changes to existing drives to meet the standard.

See also **archive, backup, CD-R, CD-ROM**.

error   The difference between the expected and the actual. In computing, the way that the operating system reports unexpected, unusual, impossible, or illegal events is by displaying an error number or *error message*. Errors range from trivial, such as an attempt to write a file to a disk drive that

117

does not contain a disk, to fatal, such as when a serious operating system bug renders the system useless.

In communications, errors are often caused by line noise and signal distortion. *Parity* or *cyclical redundancy check* (CRC) information is often added as overhead to the data stream, and techniques such as *error detection and correction* are employed to detect and correct as many errors as possible.

See also **attenuation, crosstalk, error handling, error message, error rate, NEXT, parity error.**

error detection and correction

Abbreviated EDAC. A mechanism used to determine whether transmission errors have occurred, and if so, to correct those errors. Some programs or transmission *protocols* simply request a retransmission of the affected block of data if an error is detected. More complex protocols attempt to both detect and determine at the receiving end what the correct transmission should have been.

See also **checksum, cyclical redundancy check, forward error correction, Hamming code, MNP.**

error handling   The way that a
program copes with errors that occur as the program is running.

Good error handling manages unexpected events or wrongly entered data gracefully, usually by opening a dialog box to prompt the user to take the appropriate action or enter the correct information. Badly written programs may just stop the computer when the wrong data is entered or when an unanticipated disk error occurs.

error message   A message from
the program or the operating system that contains information about a condition that requires some human intervention to solve. Error messages can indicate relatively trivial problems, such as a disk drive that does not contain a disk, as well as fatal problems, such as when a serious operating system bug renders the system useless and requires a system *reboot.*

error rate   In communications,
the ratio between the number of bits received incorrectly and the total number of bits in the transmission, also known as bit error rate *(BER).* Some methods for determining error rate use larger or logical units, such as *blocks, packets,* or *frames.* In these cases, the measurement of error rate is expressed in terms of the number of units found to be in error out of the total number of units transmitted.

escape sequence A sequence of characters, beginning with Escape (ASCII 27) and followed by one or more other characters, that performs a specific function. Escape sequences are often used to control printers or monitors, where they are treated as commands and acted upon rather than processed as characters that should be printed or displayed.

ESDI See **Enhanced Small Device Interface.**

Ethernet A popular network *protocol* and cabling scheme with a transfer rate of 10 megabits per second, originally developed by Xerox in 1976. Ethernet uses a bus *topology* and network nodes are connected by either thick or thin *coaxial cable*, *fiber-optic cable*, or *twisted-pair cable*. Ethernet uses *CSMA/CD* (Carrier Sense Multiple Access/Collision Detection) to prevent network failures or *collisions* when two devices try to access the network at exactly the same time.

The original DIX (Digital Equipment, Intel, Xerox), or Blue Book, standard has evolved into the slightly more complex IEEE *802.3* standard, and the ISO's 8802.3 specification.

The advantages of Ethernet include:

- Easy to install at a moderate cost.
- Technology is available from many sources and is very well known.
- Offers a variety of cabling options.
- Works very well in networks with only occasional heavy *traffic*.

And the disadvantages include:

- Heavy traffic can slow down the network.
- A break in the main cable can bring down large parts of the network, and troubleshooting a bus topology can prove difficult.

See also **ARCnet, CDDI, demand priority, Fast Ethernet, FDDI, 100VG-AnyLAN.**

Ethernet address See hardware address.

Ethernet packet A variable-length unit in which information is transmitted on an *Ethernet* network. An Ethernet packet consists of a *synchronization* preamble, a *destination address*, a *source address*, a type code indicator, a data field that can vary from 46 to 1500 bytes, and a *cyclical redundancy check* (CRC) that provides a statistically derived value used to confirm the accuracy of the data. See the accompanying illustration of an IEEE *802.3* Ethernet packet.

exa- Abbreviated E. A prefix meaning one quintillion or 10^{18}. In computing, the prefix means 1,152,921,504,606,846,976, or the power of 2 closest to one quintillion (10^{60}).

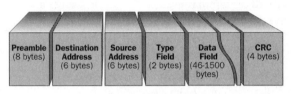

| Preamble (8 bytes) | Destination Address (6 bytes) | Source Address (6 bytes) | Type Field (2 bytes) | Data Field (46-1500 bytes) | CRC (4 bytes) |

ETHERNET PACKET

EtherTalk An implementation of the *Ethernet local-area network* (LAN) developed for Apple computers, designed to work with the *AppleShare* network operating system. EtherTalk operates over *coaxial cable* at the Ethernet transfer rate of 10 megabits per second, much faster than the 230.4 kilobits per second rate available with *AppleTalk*. Each networked Macintosh computer must be supplied with a special *EtherTalk* network interface card.

ETX See **end-of-text**.

even parity See **parity**.

exabyte Abbreviated EB. 1 quadrillion kilobytes, or 1,152,921,504,606,846,976 bytes.

EXIT A Novell NetWare server command used to return to the DOS *partition* after the *DOWN* command. If DOS has been removed from the server to conserve memory, this command *reboots* the server.

expandability The ability of a system to accommodate expansion. In hardware, this may include the addition of more memory, more or larger disk drives, and new adapters. In software, expandability may include the ability of a network to add users, nodes, or connections to other networks.

expanded memory   A DOS mechanism by which applications can access more than the 640 kilobytes (KB) of memory normally available to them. The architecture of the early Intel processors restricted the original IBM PC to accessing 1 MB of memory, 640 KB of which was available for applications; the remaining 384 KB was reserved for system use, the *BIOS*, and the video system. At that time, 640 KB was more than ten times the amount of memory available in other personal computers. However, as both applications and DOS grew, they began to run out of room.

The *Expanded Memory Specification* LIM 4.0 is the standard method of accessing expanded memory. This specification lets programs running on any of the Intel 8086 family of processors access as much as 32 MB of expanded memory. The *expanded memory manager* (EMM) creates a block of addresses into which data (held in memory above the 1 MB limit) is swapped in and out as needed by the program. In other words, a 64 KB segment of addressable memory creates a small window through which segments of expanded memory can be seen, but only one segment at a time.

See also **conventional memory, memory management**.

expanded memory manager   Abbreviated EMM. A *device driver* that supports the software portion of the *Expanded Memory Specification* (EMS) in an IBM-compatible computer.

See also **memory management**.

Expanded Memory Specification   Abbreviated EMS. The original version of the Lotus-Intel-Microsoft Expanded Memory Specification (LIM EMS), which lets DOS applications use more than 640 kilobytes of memory space.

See also **Enhanced Expanded Memory Specification, expanded memory, memory management**.

expansion board   See **adapter**.

expansion bus   An extension of the main computer bus that includes *expansion slots* for use by compatible adapters, such as memory boards, video adapters, hard-disk controllers, and *SCSI* interface cards.

expansion slot   One of the connectors on the expansion bus that

e

gives an *adapter* access to the system bus. You can install as many additional adapters as there are expansion slots inside your computer.

For portable computers, an expansion slot is often supplied by a *PCMCIA* connection designed to accept a *PC Card*.

expansion unit   An external housing available with certain portable computers designed to contain additional *expansion slots* and maintain a connection to the main expansion bus in the computer's system unit.

extended ASCII character set
See **ASCII extended character set.**

Extended Binary Coded Decimal Interchange Code
See **EBCDIC.**

Extended Industry Standard Architecture   See **EISA.**

extended LAN   A term used to describe a network that consists of a series of *local-area networks* (LANs) connected by *bridges*.

extended memory   Memory beyond 1 megabyte (MB) on computers using the Intel *80286* and later processors, not configured for *expanded memory*. PCs based on the early Intel processors could access only 1 MB of memory, of which 640 kilobytes (KB) was available for applications, and the remaining 384 KB was reserved for DOS, the BIOS, and video settings.

Later processors can access more memory, but it was the *80386* with its ability to address 4 gigabytes of memory that really made extended memory usable. Also, the Microsoft Windows memory manager HIMEM.SYS lets Windows use all of the extended memory installed in a computer.

Extended memory is particularly valuable when using *OS/2*, which can take full advantage of its benefits.

See also **conventional memory, Extended Memory Specification, memory management.**

extended memory manager   A *device driver* that supports the software portion of the *Extended Memory Specification* in an IBM-compatible computer.

See also **memory management.**

Extended Memory Specification
Abbreviated XMS. A standard developed by Microsoft, Intel, Lotus, and AST Research that has become the preferred way of accessing extended memory in the PC. DOS and Microsoft Windows include the extended memory device driver HIMEM.SYS, and this command or an equivalent must be present in your *CONFIG.SYS* file before you can access extended memory.

See also **conventional memory, expanded memory, memory management**.

external command
A DOS command that is a separate program, usually stored in the DOS directory. FORMAT, BACKUP, and FDISK are examples of external commands.

See also **internal command**.

External Gateway Protocol
See **EGP**.

external modem
A stand-alone modem, separate from the computer and connected to it by a serial cable. LEDs on the front of the chassis indicate the current modem status. An external modem can be used with different computers at different times and also with different types of computers.

external reference
In Novell NetWare 4.x, a pointer to a *NetWare Directory Services* (NDS) object that is not located on the current server.

extremely low-frequency emission
Abbreviated ELF. Radiation emitted by a computer monitor and other common electrical appliances. ELF emissions fall into the range of 5 to 2000 hertz, and decline with the square of the distance from the source. Emissions are not constant around a monitor; they are higher from the sides and rear and weakest from the front of the screen. Low-emission models are available, and laptop computers with an LCD display do not emit any ELF fields.

See also **electromagnetic interference, radio-frequency interference, very low-frequency emission**.

486 See 80486DX.

486DX2 See 80486DX2.

486SX See 80486SX.

487 See 80487.

facsimile See **fax**.

4B/5B encoding A data-translation scheme used in *FDDI* in which every group of four bits is represented by a five-bit symbol, which is then encoded using a standard method, usually NRZI (non-return to zero inverted).

fading In both electrical and wireless systems, a decrease in a signal's strength. Fading may be due to physical obstructions of the transmitter or receiver, distance from the source of the transmission, or some form of external interference from other signals or from atmospheric conditions.

fail-safe system Any computer system that is designed to keep operating, without losing data, when part of the system seriously malfunctions or fails completely.

fail-soft system Any computer system that is designed to fail gracefully, with the minimum amount of data or program destruction, when part of the system malfunctions. Fail-soft systems close down nonessential functions and operate at a reduced capacity until the problem has been resolved.

fake root A subdirectory that functions as the *root directory*. Fake roots can be useful with network applications that must be installed in the root directory. You can install the application in a subdirectory, and then map a fake root on the file server to the subdirectory containing the application.

FAQ Abbreviation for frequently asked questions, pronounced "fack." A *USENET* document that contains answers to questions that new users often ask when they first subscribe to a *newsgroup*. The FAQ contains answers to common questions that the seasoned users have grown tired of answering. New users should look for and read the FAQ before posting their question, just in case the FAQ contains the answer.

FAQs are posted to the newsgroup on a regular basis, weekly or monthly, and some grow so large that they are divided into sections; the designation 1/4 indicates that the section being viewed is the first of a total of four sections.

Fast Ethernet A term applied to the IEEE *802.3* Higher Speed Ethernet Study Group proposals, which were originally developed by Grand Junction Networks, 3Com, SynOptics, Intel, and others. Also known as 100BaseT.

Fast Ethernet modifies the existing Ethernet standard to allow speeds of 10 or 100 megabits per second, or both, and uses *CSMA/CD* access method.

The official standard defines three *physical-layer* specifications for different cabling types:

- **100BaseTX** for two-pair *Category 5 unshielded twisted-pair*.

- **100BaseT4** for four-pair Category 3, 4, or 5 unshielded twisted-pair.
- **100BaseFX** for *fiber-optic cable*.

See also **100VG-AnyLAN, 10/100**.

FAT See **file allocation table**.

fatal error An operating system or application program error from which there is no recovery without reloading the program or *rebooting* the operating system.

fault management One of the five basic types of network management defined by the *International Standards Organization* (ISO) and *CCITT*. Fault management is used in the detection, isolation, and correction of faults on the network.

fault tolerance A design method that ensures continued system operation in the event of individual failures by providing redundant elements. At the component level, the design includes redundant chips and circuits and the capability to bypass faults automatically. At the computer-system level, any elements that are likely to fail, such as processors and large disk drives, are replicated.

Fault-tolerant operations often require backup or *UPS* (uninterruptible power supply) power systems in the event of a main power failure. In some cases, the entire computer system is duplicated in a remote location to protect against vandalism, acts of war, or natural disaster.

See also **data protection, disk duplexing, disk mirroring, RAID, System Fault Tolerance.**

fax   Abbreviation for facsimile. The electronic transmission of copies of documents for reproduction at a remote location. The term fax can be used as a verb for the process, and as a noun for the machine that does the work and also for the item that is actually transmitted.

The sending fax machine scans a paper image and converts the image into a form suitable for transmission over a telephone line. The receiving fax machine decodes and prints a copy of the original image. Each fax machine includes a scanner, modem, and printer.

Originally, facsimile machines were rotating drums (CCITT Groups 1 and 2), then came modems (CCITT Group 3), and

eventually they will be completely digital (CCITT Group 4).

See also **CCITT Groups 1–4, fax modem.**

fax board   See **fax modem.**

fax modem   An adapter that fits into a PC *expansion slot* providing many of the capabilities of a full-sized fax machine, but at a fraction of the cost. Some *external modems* also have fax capabilities.

The advantages of a fax modem include ease of use and convenience; the main disadvantage is that the material you want to fax must be in digital form in the computer. Unless you have access to a scanner, you cannot fax handwritten notes, line art, or certain kinds of graphics. Most faxes sent directly from a PC using a fax modem are text files.

There are three main classes of fax modem:

- **SendFax:** originally developed by Sierra Semiconductor, these fax modems are send-only, and date from the days when a single-function fax modem was much cheaper than one that could both send and receive.
- **Class 1:** an early fax-modem standard that specified that most of the processing of the fax

127

document should be performed by the application software.

• **Class 2:** a more recent standard that shifts the task of preparing the fax document to the fax modem itself. In this standard, the modem hardware manages all data-compression and error-correction functions. Most Class 2 modems use an interim version of the standard from August 1990, but the standard was revised further, with the final version gaining approval in November 1992. Fax modems that support the first version are described as Class 2 modems, while those that support the later standard are known as Class 2.0 modems. The Intel SatisFAXtion fax modems follow another standard, called CAS (Communications Application Specification).

fax server   A server that offers *fax* sending and receiving services to users on the network.

FCC   Abbreviation for Federal Communications Commission. A United States government regulatory body for radio, television, all interstate telecommunications services, and all international services that originate inside the United States. All computer equipment must be certified by

the FCC before it can be offered for sale in the United States. The certification ensures that the equipment meets the legal limits for conductive and radio frequency interference, which could otherwise interfere with commercial broadcasts.

See also **FCC certification**.

FCC certification   Approval by the *FCC* (Federal Communications Commission) that a specific computer model meets its standards for *radio frequency interference* (RFI) emissions. There are two levels of certification: *Class A certification* for computers used in commercial settings, such as mainframes and minicomputers, and the more stringent *Class B certification*, for computers used in the home and in home offices, such as PCs, laptops, and portables.

See also **extremely low-frequency emission, very low-frequency emission**.

FCONSOLE   A Novell NetWare 3.*x* workstation utility that allows a network administrator to manage the file server from a workstation. A network administrator can log in to or out of a server, broadcast messages to other users, examine or change server information, and bring down the file server. In NetWare 4.*x*, these functions are provided by the *MONITOR* command.

FDDI   Abbreviation for Fiber Distributed Data Interface. The *ANSI* X3T9.5 specification for fiber-optic networks transmitting at a speed of up to 100 megabits per second (Mbps) over a dual, counter rotating, *token-ring* topology. See the accompanying illustration.

FDDI's 100 Mbps speed is close to the internal speed of most computers, which makes it a good choice to serve as a super *backbone* linking two or more LANs, or as a fiber-optic bus connecting high-performance engineering workstations. FDDI is suited to systems that require the transfer of large amounts of information, such as medical imaging, three-dimensional seismic processing, and oil reservoir simulation. The FDDI-II version of the standard is designed for networks transmitting real-time full-motion video (or other information that cannot tolerate any delays), and requires that all nodes on the network use

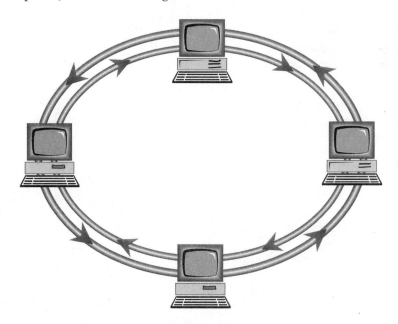

FIBER DISTRIBUTED DATA INTERFACE

FDDI-II; otherwise the network automatically reverts to FDDI.

An FDDI network using *multimode fiber-optic cable* can include as many as five hundred stations up to 2 kilometers (1.25 miles) apart; with *single-mode fiber,* run length increases up to 60 kilometers (37.2 miles) between stations. This type of network can also run over shielded and unshielded twisted-pair cabling (when it is known as *CDDI*, or Copper Distributed Data Interface) for shorter distances.

FDM   See **frequency-division multiplexing.**

Federal Communications Commission   See **FCC.**

female connector   Any cable connector with receptacles designed to receive the pins on the male connector; see the accompanying illustration.

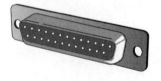

FEMALE CONNECTOR

Fiber Distributed Data Interface   See **FDDI.**

fiber-optic cable   A transmission technology that sends pulses of light along specially manufactured optical fibers. Each fiber consists of a core, thinner than a human hair, surrounded by a sheath with a much lower refractive index; see the accompanying illustration. Light signals introduced at one end of the cable are conducted along the cable as the signals are reflected from the sheath.

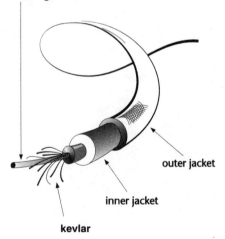

optical fiber
surrounded by
cladding

outer jacket

inner jacket

kevlar

FIBER-OPTIC CABLE

Fiber-optic cable is lighter and smaller than traditional copper cable, is immune to electrical interference, offers better security, and has better signal-transmitting qualities. However, it is more expensive than traditional cables and is more difficult to repair. Fiber-optic cable is often used for high-speed *backbones*, but as prices drop, we may even see fiber-optic cable running to the desktop.

See also **multimode fiber, single-mode fiber.**

file   A named collection of information that appears to the user as a single entity and is stored on disk. A file can contain a program or part of a program, just data, or a user-created document. Files may actually be fragmented or stored in many different places across the disk. The operating system manages the task of locating all the pieces when a request is made to read the file.

file allocation table   Abbreviated FAT, pronounced "fat." A table, maintained by the operating systems, that lists all the blocks of disk space available on a disk. The FAT includes the location of each block, as well as whether it is in use, available for use, or damaged in some way and

therefore unavailable. Because files are not necessarily stored in consecutive blocks on a disk, the FAT also keeps track of which pieces belong to which file.

OS/2 supports a compatible version of the DOS FAT, sometimes known as the SuperFAT, which adds 32-bit capabilities to increase speed, access to OS/2 extended attributes, and a free-space bitmap.

See also **file fragmentation, High-Performance File System.**

file and record locking   A method of controlling file access in a *multiuser* environment, where there is always a possibility that two users will attempt to update the same file at the same time but with different information. The first user to access the file locks out all the other users, preventing them from opening the file. After the file is updated and closed again, the next user can gain access.

File locking is a simple way to prevent simultaneous updates, but it can seriously degrade system performance if many users attempt to access the same files time after time. To prevent this slowdown, many *database management systems* use *record locking* instead. Record locking limits

131

access to individual records within the database file.

file compression A technique that shrinks program or data files so that they occupy less disk space. The file must then be extracted or decompressed before use. Some types of files, such as word processor documents, can be compressed by 50 percent or more. Recompressing an already compressed file usually makes the file slightly larger because of the compression overhead.

Novell NetWare 4.*x* provides a form of configurable compression, managed internally by the operating system. Certain files flagged "Immediate Compress" are compressed immediately; other files are automatically compressed when they have not been accessed for a specified amount of time. Files are decompressed the next time they are accessed by a user.

See also **file-compression program**.

file-compression program An application that compresses files so that they take up less space on the disk. Some file-compression programs are individual, stand-alone applications; others are built into the operating system.

NetWare, Novell DOS 7, PC-DOS 7, and MS-DOS 6 contain file-compression facilities built into the operating system, and similar features are available in programs such as Stacker from Stac Electronics.

One type of file-compression program compresses one or more files at a time. The utilities PKZIP (for DOS and OS/2) and StuffIt (for the Macintosh) operate that way. Another type compresses all the files on a specific disk, disk *partition*, or *volume*. Stacker and the DoubleSpace program released as part of DOS are examples of this type of file-compression program.

Many of the stand-alone file-compression programs, such as PKZIP, LHArc, and Stuffit, are shareware.

Utility packages, such as PC Tools from Central Point Software, also contain file-compression programs.

See also **file compression**.

file-conversion program An application that converts a file from one format to another. The conversion may be between the formats of two applications that use the same operating system (such as two DOS or Microsoft Windows word processors) or between the formats of applications from different operating systems. Applications are also available that convert a graphical image from one *file format* to another.

Many of the applications that change a Macintosh file into an IBM-compatible file, or vice versa, consist of two programs running simultaneously on two physically connected computers. MacLink Plus from Data Viz and LapLink Mac from Travelling Software are two examples of this type of file-conversion program.

See also **file-transfer program**.

file format   A file structure that defines the way information is stored in the file and how the file appears on the screen or on the printer. The simplest file format is a plain *ASCII file*. Some of the more complex formats are DCA (Document Content Architecture) and RTF (Rich Text Format), which include control information for use by a printer; TIFF (Tagged Image File Format) and EPS (Encapsulated PostScript), which hold graphics information; and DBF (Xbase database file) and DB (Paradox file), which are database formats. Word processing programs, such as Microsoft

Word and WordPerfect, also create files in special text formats.

file fragmentation   Storage of files in pieces scattered on a disk. As files grow on a hard disk, they can be divided into several small pieces. By fragmenting files, the operating system makes reasonable use of the disk space available. The problem with file fragmentation is that the disk heads must move to different locations on the disk to read or write to a fragmented file. This process takes more time than reading the file as a single piece. To speed up file operations, you can use a *disk optimizer* or *defragmenter*.

file indexing   A technique used in Novell NetWare to speed up accesses to large files by indexing *file allocation table* (FAT) entries.

file locking   See **file and record locking**.

file name   The name of a file on a disk used so that both you and the operating system can find the file again. Every file in a directory must have a unique name, but files in different directories can share the same name.

133

In DOS, file and directory names have two parts. They can have up to eight characters in the name, and up to three characters in the optional file-name extension, separated from the name by a period. Many applications take over the extension part of the file name, using specific groups of characters to designate a particular file type.

In the Macintosh operating system, file names can be up to thirty-one characters and can contain any character except a colon (:), which is used to separate elements of a path name.

In the OS/2 *High-Performance File System* (HPFS), files can have names of 254 characters, including many characters that are illegal in DOS file names, such as spaces. The Windows NT File System (*NTFS*) allows 255-character file names and also provides some degree of security by including *permissions* when sharing files.

file-name extension　In the *file allocation table* (FAT) file system, an optional three-character suffix added to the end of a file name and separated from the name by a period.

FILER　A Novell NetWare 4.x menu utility used to manage the NetWare file system. Almost any

task related to the file system can be performed using FILER. Administrators can view information about files, directories, and volumes; modify and view attributes, rights, and trustee assignments for files and directories; search for files and directories; copy files, and recover and purge deleted files. In NetWare 3.x, these last two functions are found in the *SALVAGE* and *PURGE* commands.

file recovery　The process of recovering deleted or damaged files from a disk. A file can be deleted accidentally, or can become inaccessible when part of the file's control information is lost. In many operating systems, a deleted file still exists on disk until the space it occupies is overwritten with something else or until the file is purged.

See also **undelete**.

file server　A networked computer used to store files for access by other client computers on the network. On larger networks, the file server runs a special *network operating system*. On smaller installations, the file server may run a PC operating system supplemented by *peer-to-peer networking* software.

See also **client, server**.

file sharing The sharing of files over a network, or between several applications running on the same workstation. Shared files can be read, reviewed, and updated by more than one individual. Access to the file or files is often regulated by *password protection*, account or security clearance, or file locking to prevent simultaneous changes by multiple users.

See also **file and record locking**.

filespec A contraction of FILE SPECification, commonly used to denote the complete drive letter, path name, directory name, and file name needed to access a specific file.

file system In an operating system, the structure by which files are organized, stored, and named. Some file systems are built-in components of the operating system; others are installable. For example, OS/2, Unix, and Windows NT support several different file systems, including the *file allocation table* (FAT) file system, *High-Performance File System* (HPFS), and the NT File System (*NTFS*). Other, installable file systems allow for CD-ROM support.

file-transfer program An application used to move a file from a computer of one type to a computer of another type. The file format itself may also be changed during this transfer.

Many of the applications that change a Macintosh file into an IBM-compatible file, or vice versa, consist of two programs running simultaneously on two physically connected computers. MacLink Plus from Data Viz and LapLink Mac from Travelling Software are two file-transfer programs that also offer a wide variety of popular file-format conversions.

See also **file-conversion program, FTP, Gopher, Kermit, Xmodem, Ymodem, Zmodem.**

File Transfer Protocol See FTP.

file transfer protocol A method of transferring information from one computer to another, over a modem and a telephone line or over a network. The protocol divides the information into smaller units, and each unit is processed in sequence. The transfer protocol also handles *error detection and correction*.

See also **asynchronous transmission, FTP, Gopher, Kermit, Xmodem, Ymodem, Zmodem.**

f

135

FILTCFG   A Novell NetWare 4.*x* *NLM* that allows you to set up and configure filters for *IPX*, *TCP/IP*, or *AppleTalk* protocols.

filtering

1. The mechanism that prevents certain source and destination addresses from crossing a *bridge* or *router* onto another part of the network.

2. The process of automatically selecting specific frequencies and discarding others.

finger   A *Unix* utility found on many *Internet* systems that displays information about a specific user, including full name, login time, and location.

Finger may also display the contents of the user's .plan or .profile file, and there are those who exploit this in novel ways to display such varied information as instructions for using a university's Coke-vending machine, posting sports scores, and listing earthquake activity.

fire phasers   A Novell NetWare login script command that makes a noise using the workstation's speaker. The sound is supposed to resemble the phasers on the USS Enterprise. With fire phasers, you can have the computer emit up to nine sounds or blasts.

firewall   A barrier established by a *router,* or by special software running on a dedicated computer system, that only allows one-way traffic—outward from the protected network. A firewall is a device commonly used to protect networks from unwelcome *intruders.*

See **data protection.**

firmware   Any software stored in a form of read-only memory—OM, EPROM (erasable programmable read-only memory), or EEPROM (electrically erasable programmable read-only memory)—that maintains its contents when power is removed.

FLAG   A Novell NetWare workstation utility used to view or modify file or directory *attributes.*

FLAGDIR   A Novell NetWare 3.*x* workstation utility used to view or modify directory or subdirectory *attributes.* In NetWare 4.*x*, this function is provided by the *FLAG* workstation utility.

flame   A deliberately insulting *e-mail* message or post to a *USENET newsgroup*, often containing a personal attack on the writer of an earlier post.
See also **flame bait, flame war.**

flame bait   An insulting or outrageous e-mail post to a *USENET newsgroup* specifically designed to provoke other users into flaming the originator.
See also **flame, flame war.**

flame war   In a *USENET newsgroup*, a prolonged series of *flames*, which may have begun as a creative exchange of views but which quickly descended into personal attacks and crude name-calling.
See also **flame bait.**

flash memory   A special form of read-only memory (*ROM*) that can be erased at signal levels commonly found inside the PC. This ability allows the contents to be reprogrammed without removing the chips from the computer. Also, once flash memory has been programmed, you can remove the *expansion board* it is mounted on and plug it into another computer without loss of information.
See also **PC Card, PCMCIA slot.**

floating-point processor   A special-purpose, secondary processor designed to perform floating-point calculations much faster than the main processor. Many processors, such as the *80386*, have matched companion floating-point processors. However, a modern trend in processor design is to integrate the floating-point unit into the main processor, as in the *80486* and *Pentium*.

flow control

1. In communications, control of the rate at which information is exchanged between two computers over a transmission channel. Flow control is needed when one of the devices cannot receive the information at the same rate as it can be sent, usually because some processing is required on the receiving end before the next transmission unit can be accepted. Flow control can be implemented either in hardware or in software.

2. In networking, control of the flow of data throughout the network, ensuring that network segments are not congested. A router controls data flow, by routing around any trouble spots.
See also **handshaking.**

f

footprint   The amount of desktop space or floor space occupied by a computer or display terminal.

foreground   In an operating system, a process that runs in the foreground is running at a higher level of priority than is a background task. Only *multitasking* operating systems support true foreground and background processing; however, some application programs can mimic it. For example, many word processors will print a document while still accepting input from the keyboard.

See also **background**.

formatting   The process of *initializing* a new, blank floppy disk or hard disk so that it can be used to store information.

form feed   Abbreviated FF. A printer command that advances the paper in the printer to the top of the next page. The form feed button on the printer performs this function. An application can also issue the command. In the ASCII character set, a form feed has the decimal value of 12.

forward error correction   A technique used to control errors that insert extra or redundant bits into the data stream. The receiving device uses the redundant bits to detect and, if possible, correct the errors in the data.

See also **error detection and correction**.

forwarding   The process of passing a packet on to an intermediate or final destination. Forwarding takes place in network bridges, routers, and gateways.

four-wire circuit   A transmission system in which two *half-duplex* circuits, consisting of two wires each, are combined to create one *full-duplex* circuit.

fractional T1   One portion of a *T1* circuit. A T1 circuit has a capacity of 1.544 megabits per second (Mbps), the equivalent of twenty-four 64 kilobit per second (Kbps) channels. Customers can lease as many of these 64 Kbps channels as they need; they are not required to lease the entire 1.544 Mbps circuit.

fragmentation   See **file fragmentation**.

frame   A block of data suitable for transmission as a single unit, also referred to as a packet or block. Some media can support multiple frame formats.

frame relay   A *CCITT* standard for a *packet-switching* protocol, running at speeds of up to 2 megabits per second, that also provides for *bandwidth on demand*. Frame relay is less robust than *X.25* but provides better efficiency and higher throughput.

Frame relay is available from many companies, including AT&T, CompuServe, Sprint, WilTel, and the Bell companies.

See also **Asynchronous Transfer Mode, BISDN, cell relay.**

framing   The process of dividing data up for transmission into groups of bits, and adding a header as well as a checksum to form a frame. In asynchronous communications, framing is the process of inserting *start bits* and *stop bits* before and after the data to be transmitted.

free memory   An area of memory not currently in use. Often refers to the memory space remaining for applications to use after the operating system and the system device drivers have been loaded.

frequency-division multiplexing   Abbreviated FDM. A method of sharing a transmission channel by dividing the *bandwidth* into several parallel paths, defined and separated by guard bands of different frequencies. All signals are carried simultaneously.

FDM is used in *analog* transmissions, such as in communications over a telephone line or on a *baseband network*.

See also **statistical multiplexing, time-division multiplexing.**

frequently asked questions   See **FAQ.**

front-end application   An application running on a networked workstation that works in conjunction with a back-end system running on the server. Examples are e-mail and database programs.

See also **client/server architecture.**

front-end processor   A specialized processor that manipulates data before passing it on to the main processor. In large computer-to-computer communications systems, a front-end processor is often used to manage all aspects of communications, leaving the main computer free to handle the data processing.

See also **back-end processor.**

Frye Utilities   A package of network management utilities from Frye Computer Systems that includes hardware and software inventory, NetWare server monitoring, traffic monitoring, application metering, and software distribution.

FTAM   Abbreviation for File Transfer, Access, and Management. The *Open Systems Interconnection* (OSI) protocol for transferring and remotely accessing files on different makes and models of computers that are also using FTAM.

FTP   Abbreviation for File Transfer Protocol. The *TCP/IP* protocol used to log in to a network, list files and directories, and transfer files. FTP supports a range of file types and formats, including *ASCII, EBCDIC,* and *binary files.*

See also **anonymous FTP, Gopher, TELNET.**

full backup   A *backup* that includes all files on a hard disk or set of hard disks. A network administrator must decide how

often to perform a full backup, balancing the need for security against the time taken for the backup.

See also **differential backup, incremental backup.**

full-duplex   Abbreviated FDX. The capability for simultaneous transmission in two directions, so that devices can be sending and receiving data at the same time.

See also **four-wire circuit, half-duplex.**

full-page display   Any monitor capable of displaying a whole page of text. Full-page display is useful for graphical art and desktop publishing applications.

function keys   The set of programmable keys on the keyboard that can perform special tasks assigned by the current application. Most keyboards have ten or twelve function keys (F1-F10 or F1-F12), some of which are used by an application as shortcut keys. For example, many programs use F1 to gain access to the Help system. In some programs, the use of function keys is so complex that special plastic key overlays are provided as guides for users.

140

G   Abbreviation for *giga-*, meaning 1 billion, or 10^9.
   See also **gigabyte**.

gateway   A shared connection between a local-area network (LAN) and a larger system, such as a mainframe computer or a large *packet-switching network*, whose *communications protocols* are different. Usually slower than a *bridge* or *router*, a gateway is a combination of hardware and software with its own processor and memory used to perform protocol conversions.
   See also **brouter**.

gateway server   A communications server that provides access between networks that use different access protocols.

gauge   A measurement of the physical size of a cable. Under the American Wire Gauge (AWG) standards, higher numbers indicate thinner cable.
   See also **cabling standards**.

GB   See **gigabyte**.

gender changer   A special intermediary connector for use with two cables that both have only male connectors or only female connectors; see the accompanying illustration.

male to male

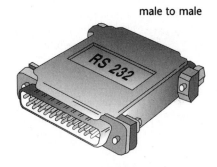

GENDER CHANGER

geostationary   Also known as geosynchronous. The type of orbit required to keep a communications satellite in a fixed position relative to the earth. The satellite's angular rate and direction of rotation are matched to those of the earth, and the satellite orbits the earth every 24 hours at about 36,000 kilometers (22,350 miles).

Three satellites in geostationary orbit can cover 95 percent of the earth's surface (the remaining 5 percent is above the Arctic Circle).

geosynchronous   See **geostationary.**

giga-   A prefix meaning 1 billion, or 10^9.
See also **gigabyte.**

gigabit   Abbreviated Gbit. Usually 1,073,824 binary digits or *bits* of data. Sometimes used as equivalent to one billion bits.
See also **kilobit, megabit.**

gigabyte   Abbreviated GB. Strictly speaking, one billion bytes; however, in computing, in which bytes are most often counted in powers of 2, a gigabyte becomes 2^{30}, or 1,073,741,824 bytes.

global directory services   Directory services that view the entire network as a single entity. A global directory system allows the network administrator to define all network resources—users, printers, and servers—at one time.
Banyan's *StreetTalk* and Novell's *NetWare Directory*

Services (NDS) are examples of global directory services.
See also **domain directory services.**

global group   In *Windows NT Server*, *user accounts* granted server and workstation rights in their own and other *domains* whose security systems allow access. Global groups are a means of providing *rights* and *permissions* to resources inside and outside the domain to a group of users within a single domain.

global login   A mechanism that lets users log in to the network, rather than repeatedly logging in to individual servers.

global network   An international network that spans all departments, offices, and subsidiaries of the corporation. Global networks bring their own set of problems, including those of different time zones, languages, established standards, and *PTT* (Postal Telephone and Telegraph) companies.

Gopher   A popular *client/server* application that presents *Internet* resources as a series of menus, shielding the user from the underlying mechanical details of *IP* addresses and different access methods.

Gopher menus may contain documents you can view or download, searches you can perform, or additional menu selections. When you choose one of these items, Gopher does whatever is necessary to obtain the resource you requested, either by downloading a document or by jumping to the selected Gopher server and presenting its top-level menu.

Gopher clients are available for most popular operating systems, including the Macintosh, DOS, Windows, and Unix.

See also **Gopherspace.**

Gopherspace   A collective term used to describe all the *Internet* resources accessible using *Gopher*. Gopher is so good at hiding the mechanical details of the Internet that this term was coined to represent all the resources reachable using Gopher.

GOSIP   Acronym for Government OSI Profile. A suite of standards intended for use in government projects and based on the *Open Systems Interconnection* (OSI) reference model. Some measure of GOSIP compliance is required for government networking purchases. Both United States and United Kingdom GOSIPs exist.

grace login   Allows a user to finish logging in using an expired *password* without changing it. You can set the number of grace logins a user is allowed.

GRANT   A Novell NetWare 3.*x* utility that assigns users rights to access or use directories and files. You can also grant rights using the *FILER* menu utility.

See also **RIGHTS.**

graphical user interface   Abbreviated GUI, pronounced "gooey." A graphics-based user interface that allows users to select files, programs, or commands by pointing to pictorial representations on the screen rather than by typing long, complex commands from a command prompt.

Applications execute in windows, using a consistent set of pull-down menus, dialog boxes, and other graphical elements, such as scroll bars and icons. This consistency among interface elements is a major benefit for the user, because as soon as you learn how to use the interface in one program, you can use it in all

143

other programs running in the same environment.

The use of graphical elements in a user interface was pioneered at Xerox Corporation's Palo Alto Research Center (PARC) in the early 1970s. Unfortunately, at that time the hardware needed to support such a user interface was well beyond the reach of most users. In 1979, Steve Jobs of Apple Computer visited PARC and recognized the importance of the user-interface work being done; this visit led to the development of the interface for the ill-fated Apple Lisa computer, and eventually to the Apple Macintosh series of computers. Since then, GUIs have emerged for most computing environments, including the Macintosh System 7, Microsoft Windows and Windows NT, Unix, and the OS/2 Desktop.

See also **character-based interface, social interface, X Window.**

graphics accelerator board A specialized *expansion board* containing a *graphics coprocessor* as well as all the other circuitry found on a video adapter. Transferring most of the graphics processing tasks from the main processor to the graphics accelerator board improves system performance considerably,

particularly for Microsoft Windows users.

See also **S3 86C9xx.**

graphics coprocessor A fixed-function graphics chip, designed to speed up the processing and display of high-resolution images. Popular graphics coprocessors include the *S3 86C9xx* accelerator chips.

graphics mode A video adapter mode in which everything displayed on the screen is created pixel by pixel. Text mode, by contrast, uses ready-made characters from a built-in character set.

grayed command See **dimmed command.**

group A set of network users who have been assigned to a network user group so that they all have the same level of *security* in the same directories.

group object In Novell NetWare, an object that contains a list of user object names.

groupware Network software designed for use by a group of people all working on the same project or using the same data. Groupware can range from relatively simple programs designed to do one thing well (such as For-Comment from Broderbund Software), to enhanced e-mail products (such as WordPerfect Office or Banyan Intelligent Messaging Service), all the way to total

operating environments, offering applications program development capabilities (such as *Lotus Notes* or DEC TeamLink).

See also **workflow software, workgroup.**

GUI   See **graphical user interface.**

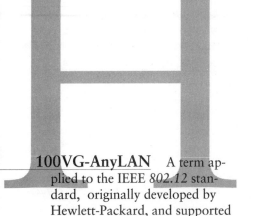

100VG-AnyLAN A term applied to the IEEE *802.12* standard, originally developed by Hewlett-Packard, and supported by Novell, Microsoft, AT&T, and others.

100VG-AnyLAN modifies the existing *Ethernet* standard to allow speeds of 10 or 100 megabits per second (Mbps), and uses the *demand priority* access method; it can also be an upgrade path from 16 Mbps *Token Ring* networks.

100VG-AnyLAN runs over four-pair *Category 3*, *4*, and *5 unshielded twisted-pair* wiring, and up to five repeaters are allowed between *end nodes*.

See also **Fast Ethernet, 10/100.**

hacker In the programming community, where the term originated, this term describes a person who pursues knowledge of computer systems for its own sake—someone willing to "hack through" the steps of putting together a working program. More recently, in popular culture at large, the term has come to mean a person who breaks into other people's computers with malicious intent (what programmers call a "cracker"). Many countries now treat convicted hackers in the same way that they treat conventional breaking-and-entering criminals.

See also **intruder.**

half-duplex Abbreviated HDX. In *asynchronous transmissions*, the ability to transmit on the same channel in two directions, but only in one direction at a time.

See also **communications parameters, duplex, full-duplex.**

Hamming code A *forward-error correction* technique used to detect and correct single-bit errors during transmission. The Hamming code adds three verification bits to the end of each four bits of data. The receiving device performs a similar process to ensure that the four data bits were received correctly and to detect any missing bits.

See also **error detection and correction.**

hand-held computer   A portable computer that is small enough to be held in one hand.

handshaking   The exchange of *control codes* or particular characters to maintain and coordinate data flow between two devices, so that data is only transmitted when the receiving device is ready to accept the data.

Handshaking can be implemented in either hardware or software, and it occurs between a variety of devices. For example, the data flow might be from one computer to another computer, or from a computer to a peripheral device, such as a modem or printer.

See also **flow control, XON/XOFF**.

hard-coded   A description of software written in a way that does not allow for flexibility or future expansion. For example, program variables may be placed in the code rather than supplied as input from the user.

See also **hard-wired**.

hard disk   The part of a hard disk drive that stores data, rather than the mechanism for reading and writing to it.

hard-disk controller   An *expansion board* that contains the necessary circuitry to control and coordinate a *hard disk drive*. Many hard-disk controllers are capable of managing more than one hard disk, as well as floppy disks and tape drives. On some PCs, the hard-disk controller is built into the *motherboard*, and in the case of an *Integrated Drive Electronics* hard disk, the controlling circuitry is mounted on the drive itself, eliminating the need for a separate controller.

hard disk drive   A storage device that uses a set of rotating, magnetically coated disks called *platters* to store data or programs. In everyday use, the terms hard disk, hard disk drive, and hard drive are used interchangeably, because the disk and the drive mechanism are a single unit.

A typical hard disk platter rotates at up to 3600 revolutions per minute, and the read/write heads float on a cushion of air from 10 to 25 millionths of an inch thick, so that the heads never come into contact with the recording surface. The whole unit is hermetically sealed to prevent airborne contaminants from entering and interfering with these close tolerances.

Hard disks range in storage capacity from a few tens of megabytes to several terabytes. The more storage space on the disk, the more important your backup strategy becomes. Hard disks are reliable, but they do fail, and usually at the most inconvenient moment.

See also **high-capacity storage system, mini hard disk, RAID, SLED.**

hard-disk interface   A standard way of accessing the data stored on a hard disk. Several different hard-disk interface standards have evolved over time, including the *ST506 Interface, Enhanced Small Device Interface* (ESDI), *Integrated Drive Electronics Interface* (IDE), and *SCSI* (Small Computer System Interface).

See also **PCMCIA.**

hard-disk type   A number stored in a PC's *CMOS* RAM memory area that defines certain hard-disk characteristics, such as the number of read/write heads and the number of cylinders on the disk. This number is not accessible directly from the operating system. Some PCs require a special *configuration program* to access the hard-disk type; others permit

access via the computer's built-in ROM *BIOS* setup program.

hard reset   A system reset made by pressing the computer's reset button, or by turning the power off and then on again. A hard reset is used only when the system has crashed so badly that pressing Ctrl-Alt-Del *to reboot* does not work.

hardware   All the physical electronic components of a computer system, including peripheral devices, printed-circuit boards, displays, and printers. If you can stub your toe on it, it must be hardware.

See also **firmware, liveware, software.**

hardware address   The address assigned to a *network interface card* by the original manufacturer, or if the interface card is configurable, by the network administrator. This address identifies the local device address to the rest of the network and allows messages to find the correct destination. Also known as the physical address, *media-access-control* (MAC) address, or *Ethernet address*.

h

hardware dependence   The requirement that a specific hardware component be present for a program to work. Hardware-dependent software is often difficult to move or port to another computer.

See also **hardware independence**.

hardware independence   The ability to produce similar results in a wide variety of environments, without requiring the presence of specific hardware. The Unix operating system and the PostScript page-description language are both examples of hardware independence. Unix runs on a wide range of computers, from the PC to a Cray; PostScript is used by many printer manufacturers.

See also **hardware dependence**.

hardware interrupt   An *interrupt* or request for service generated by a hardware device, such as a keystroke from the keyboard or a tick from the clock. Because the processor may receive several such signals simultaneously, hardware interrupts are usually assigned a priority level and processed according to that priority.

See also **interrupt request, software interrupt**.

hard-wired   Describes a system designed in a way that does not allow for flexibility or future expansion. May also refer to a device that is connected directly to the network, such as a printer.

See also **hard-coded**.

Hayes-compatible modem
Any modem that recognizes the commands in the industry-standard *AT command set*, originally defined by Hayes Microcomputer Products, Inc.

HBA   See **host bus adapter**.

HCSS   See **high-capacity storage system**.

HDLC   Abbreviation for High-level Data Link Control. An international protocol defined by *ISO* (International Standards Organization), included in CCITT *X.25 packet-switching networks*. HDLC is a *bit-oriented*, synchronous protocol that provides error correction at the *data-link layer*. In HDLC, messages are transmitted in variable-length units known as *frames*; see the accompanying illustration.

See also **SDLC**.

flag	address	control	data	frame check sequence	flag

HDLC

heartbeat An *Ethernet* signal quality test function. This signal proves that a component is working, and is capable of detecting *collisions*. Also known as signal quality error or SQE.

HELP A Novell NetWare utility that provides information about *NetWare Loadable Modules* (NLMs) and other server or workstation utilities. HELP displays a brief description of the command, an example showing how to use it, and the complete command syntax. A similar help command is also available in some versions of DOS and in OS/2.

hertz Abbreviated Hz. A unit of frequency measurement; 1 hertz equals one cycle per second.
See also **megahertz**.

heterogeneous network

A network that consists of workstations, servers, network interface cards, operating systems, and applications from many different vendors, all working together as a single unit. The network may also use different media and different *protocols* over different network links.
See also **enterprise network, homogeneous network**.

Hewlett-Packard Company

Abbreviated HP. A major manufacturer of hand-held calculators, personal computers, minicomputers, mainframes, scientific and medical equipment, test and measurement equipment, laser printers, plotters, and software.

Founded by William Hewlett and David Packard in 1939 in a garage, the company is now headquartered in Palo Alto, California. HP has a widely diversified product line of more than 10,000 items, and it has a well-earned reputation for building rugged and reliable equipment.

HP is a recognized leader in local-area network (LAN) technology, and made the original proposal that became known as *100VG-AnyLAN*.

h

hexadecimal   Abbreviated hex. The base-16 numbering system that uses the digits 0 to 9, followed by the letters A to F, which are equivalent to the decimal numbers 10 through 15.

Hex is a convenient way to represent the binary numbers computers use internally, because it fits neatly into the 8-bit byte. All the sixteen hex digits 0 to F can be represented in four bits, and two hex digits (one digit for each set of four bits) can be stored in a single byte. This means that one byte can contain any one of 256 different hex numbers, from 0 through FF.

See also **binary, decimal.**

HFSCD   A Novell NetWare 4.x *NLM* that provides support for Apple's Hierarchical File System (HFS) format for CD-ROM. The HFS allows users to store both files and directories inside other directories; an earlier file system, Macintosh File System or MFS, only allowed a flat file system without subdirectories. HFSCD allows users to access files and applications from a Macintosh-compatible CD-ROM attached to the server.

See also **HFSCDCON.**

HFSCDCON   A Novell NetWare 4.x *NLM* used to configure the *HFSCD* module.

hidden file   In many operating systems, any file that has the hidden attribute set, which indicates to the operating system that information about the file should not appear in normal directory listings. There may also be further restrictions on a hidden file, and users may not be able to delete, copy, or display the contents of such a file.

high-capacity storage system   Abbreviated HCSS. A data-storage system that extends the storage capacity of a Novell NetWare 4.*x* server by integrating an optical-disk library, or *jukebox*, into the NetWare file system. Network users and applications can access files and directories on the jukebox with the same NetWare commands and function calls used to access files from a hard disk. The most frequently used HCSS files may be *cached* temporarily on the server hard disk to speed up access times. HCSS can also access a magnetic tape system.

See also **archive.**

high-end   An expensive, full-featured product from the top of a company's product list.
See also **low-end**.

High-level Data Link Control
See HDLC.

high-level language   Any machine-independent programming language that uses English-like syntax in which each statement corresponds to many assembly language instructions. High-level languages free programmers from dealing with the underlying machine architecture and allow them to concentrate on the logic of the problem at hand.
See also **low-level language**.

high memory area   Abbreviated HMA. In an IBM-compatible computer, the first 64 kilobytes (KB) of *extended memory* above the 1 megabyte (MB) limit of 8086 and 8088 addresses. Programs that conform to the *Extended Memory Specification* (EMS) can use this memory as an extension of *conventional memory*. However, only one program, such as DOS, Microsoft Windows, or an application, can use or control HMA at a time. If DOS is loaded into the HMA,

approximately 50 KB more conventional memory becomes available for use by applications.
See also **expanded memory, extended memory, memory management**.

High-Performance File System
Abbreviated HPFS. A file system available in *OS/2* and *Windows NT* that supports the following:

• Long, mixed-case file names of up to 255 characters

• Up to 64 kilobytes of extended *attributes* per file

• Faster disk access with an advanced *disk cache* for caching files and directory information

• Highly contiguous file allocation that eliminates *file fragmentation*

• Hard disks of up to 64 gigabytes in size

DOS does not recognize the HPFS file structure, and it cannot be used on a floppy disk.

High Sierra specification   A specification for CD-ROM data that served as the basis for the *ISO* (International Standards Organization) 9660 standard. It is called High Sierra because it was defined at a meeting held near Lake Tahoe in November 1985.

h

HMA   See **high memory area.**

home page   On the *Internet World Wide Web*, an initial starting page. A home page may be prepared by an individual or by a corporation, and is a convenient jumping-off point to other Web pages or Internet resources.

See also **HTML, HTTP, SGML, URL.**

homogeneous network   A network that consists of one type of workstation, server, network interface card, and operating system, with a limited number of applications, all purchased from a single vendor. All nodes use the same protocol and the same control procedures.

See also **enterprise network, heterogeneous network.**

hooked vector   An intercepted *interrupt* vector that now points to a replacement *interrupt service routine* (ISR) rather than to the original service routine. Because DOS interrupts are always channeled through the same *interrupt vector table*, it is relatively easy for *terminate-and-stay-resident* (TSR) programs to alter these vectors to gain control of parts of the computer.

hop count   In *routing*, the number of links that must be crossed to get from any given source node to any given destination node. In Novell NetWare, the destination network can be no more than 16 hops (servers or routers) from the source. Hop count is often used as a metric for evaluating a route for a least-cost routing algorithm.

host   The central or controlling computer in a networked or *distributed processing* environment, providing services that other computers or terminals can access via the network.

host bus adapter   A board acting as an interface between the processor and the hard-disk controller in a network server, used by Novell NetWare to relieve the main processor of data-storage and retrieval tasks. Also known as a disk coprocessor board (DCB).

Hot Fix   A Novell NetWare feature that marks defective disk blocks dynamically so that they will not be used by the operating system. Data is redirected from any faulty blocks to a small portion of disk space set aside as the Hot Fix redirection area. It then marks the defective area as bad, and the server will not attempt to store data there again. By default, 2 percent of a disk partition is set aside as the Hot Fix redirection area.

HotJava An interactive *Internet World Wide Web* browser from Sun Microsystems.

HotJava is the player for programs written in Java, a programming language designed to create small executable programs that can be downloaded quickly and can run in a small amount of memory.

Using Java, you can create interactive Web sites that can download programs to other computers. These programs can display animation and perform other tasks; they can also cooperate with other programs on the Web.

See also **HTML, HTTP, SGML.**

HP See **Hewlett-Packard Company.**

HPFS See **High-Performance File System.**

HSM Abbreviation for Hierarchical Storage Management. A combination of several different types of file-storage systems, managed by intelligent software.

In HSM, data is moved from one type of storage to another depending on how frequently the data is accessed; active data is held on hard disks, less frequently used data is held in near-line storage such as an optical disk system, and data used only infrequently is stored in a tape backup.

See also **archive, high-capacity storage system, jukebox.**

HTML Abbreviation for Hypertext Markup Language. A standard *hypertext* language used to create *World Wide Web* pages and other hypertext documents.

When you access an HTML document, you will see a mixture of text, graphics, and links to other documents. If you select a link, the related document will open automatically, no matter where that document is located. Hypertext documents often have the file-name extension .html.

See also **home page, HTTP, SGML, URL.**

HTTP Abbreviation for Hypertext Transport Protocol. The protocol used to manage the links

155

between one *hypertext* document and another.

HTTP is the mechanism that opens the related document when you select a hypertext link, no matter where that related document happens to be.

See also **home page, HTML, SGML, URL.**

hub   A device used to extend a network so that additional workstations can be attached. There are two main types of hub:

• *Active hubs* amplify transmission signals to extend cable length and ports.

• *Passive hubs* split the transmission signal, allowing additional workstations to be added, usually at a loss of distance.

In some *star networks*, a hub is the central controlling device.

Huffman coding   In data compression, a method of encoding data on the basis of the relative frequency of the individual elements. Huffman coding is often used with text files, where the coding is based on the frequency of occurrence of each letter, because it is a *lossless compression* method. Huffman coding is used in fax transmissions.

See also **data compression, lossy compression.**

hypermedia   A term used to describe non-sequential applications that have interactive, *hypertext* linkages between different multimedia elements of graphics, sound, text, animation, and video.

If an application relies heavily on text-based information, it is known as hypertext; however, if full-motion video, animation, graphics, and sound are used, it is considered to be hypermedia.

hypertext   A method of presenting information so that it can be viewed by the user in a non-sequential way, regardless of how the topics were originally organized.

Hypertext was designed to make a computer respond to the nonlinear way that humans think and access information—by association, rather than the linear organization of film, books, and speech.

In a hypertext application, you can browse through the information with considerable flexibility, choosing to follow a new path each time you access the information. When you click on a highlighted word, you activate a link to another hypertext document, which may be located on the same *Internet* host or can be on a completely different system thousands of miles away. These links depend on the care that the document originator used when assembling the document; unfortunately, many links turn into dead ends.

See also home page, HTML, HTTP, SGML, World Wide Web.

Hz   See **hertz.**

h

I

i486 See 80486.

IAC See **Inter-Application Communication.**

IBM See **International Business Machines Corporation.**

IBM cabling systems See **Type 1-9 cable.**

IBM 3270 A general name for a family of IBM system components—printers, terminals, and terminal cluster controllers—that can be used with a mainframe computer by an *SNA* (Systems Network Architecture) link. *Terminal-emulation* software that emulates a 3270 terminal is available for both DOS and Microsoft Windows, as well as for OS/2.

IBM-compatible computer
Originally, any personal computer compatible with the IBM line of personal computers. With the launch of IBM's PS/2 line of computers containing the proprietary *MCA* (Microchannel Architecture), which replaced the AT bus, two incompatible standards emerged, and so the term became misleading. It is becoming more common to use the term "industry-standard computer" when referring to a computer that uses the AT or ISA bus, and the term "DOS computer" to describe any PC that runs DOS and is based on one of the Intel family of chips.

IBM PC A series of personal computers based on the Intel 8088 processor, introduced by IBM in mid-1981. The original IBM PC had 16 kilobytes (KB) of memory, expandable to 64 KB on the *motherboard*, and a monochrome video adapter incapable of displaying bitmapped graphics. The floppy disk drive held 160 KB of data and programs. The original model did not have a hard disk; that came later with the release of the IBM PC/XT.

By using an *open architecture* in the PC, IBM opened the way for third-party vendors, who quickly began manufacturing add-on components, such as video adapters, memory boards,

159

and other hardware and software items in support of the system.

IBM did not develop the operating system used in the PC; it commissioned Microsoft to do the job. This operating system, which was based on an earlier system, CP/M, came to be known as MS DOS.

In recent years, IBM has concentrated on providing cost-effective systems to compete with Compaq, Packard-Bell, and the other clone makers, and on innovative products such as the *IBM ThinkPad* 701C, also known as the "Butterfly" because of its expanding keyboard.

See also **IBM-compatible computer, IBM PC/AT, IBM PC/XT, IBM PS/2.**

IBM PC/AT   A series of personal computers based on the Intel 80286 processor, introduced by IBM in 1984. The AT represented a significant performance increase over previous computers, up to 75 percent faster than the PC/XT, and the AT bus standard is used in many clones or IBM-compatible computers.

See also **IBM PC, IBM PC/XT, IBM PS/2.**

IBM PC/XT   A series of personal computers based on the Intel 8088 processor, introduced by IBM in 1983. The PC/XT was the first IBM personal computer to offer a built-in hard disk and the capability to expand memory up to 640 kilobytes on the *motherboard*. The original PC/XT used an Intel 8088 running at a *clock speed* of 4.77 megahertz (MHz)—very slow compared with today's 66 and 100 MHz clock speeds.

See also **IBM PC, IBM PC/AT, IBM PS/2.**

IBM PS/2   A series of personal computers, using several different Intel processors, introduced by IBM in 1987. The main difference between the PS/2 line and earlier IBM personal computers was a major change to the internal bus. Previous computers used the AT bus, also known as *ISA* (Industry Standard Architecture), but IBM used the proprietary *MCA* (Microchannel Architecture) in the PS/2 line instead. MCA expansion boards will not work in an ISA computer.

See also **IBM PC, IBM PC/AT, IBM PC/XT.**

IBM RS/6000   A set of seven or nine separate 32-bit chips used in IBM's line of *reduced instruction set computing* (RISC) workstations. With up to 7.4 million transistors, the RS/6000 uses a *superscalar* design with four separate 16-kilobyte data-cache units and an 8-kilobyte instruction cache. The joint venture announced between IBM, Apple, and Motorola in late 1991 specified the development of a single-chip version of the RS/6000 architecture called the *PowerPC*.

IBM ThinkPad   A series of innovative and popular notebook computers from IBM.

The ThinkPad first introduced the touch-sensitive dual-button pointing stick (called a Track-Point), the pencil-eraser-like device, found between the G, H, and B keys, that is now found on many different portable computers and that replaces the mouse.

The ThinkPad 701C, also known as "the Butterfly," introduced another innovative concept, that of the expanding keyboard. When the 701C case is closed, the TrackWrite keyboard is completely concealed inside the case; the right half sits above the left. When the case is opened, the two parts of the full-sized keyboard automatically unfold and overhang the edges of the case. The 701C, based on the *Intel DX2 50* MHz processor, also contains an internal 14,400 bps fax/data modem with built-in speaker phone and digital answering machine, infrared wireless file transfer, and two *PCMCIA* Type I or Type II *PC cards* or one Type III card.

IC   See **integrated circuit**.

ICMP   Abbreviation for Internet Control Message Protocol. That portion of *TCP/IP* that provides the functions used for *network-layer* management and control.

icon   In a *graphical user interface*, a small screen image representing a specific element that the user can manipulate in some way, selected by moving a mouse or other pointing device.

An icon may represent an application, a document, embedded and linked objects, a hard disk drive, or several programs collected together in a group icon.

See also **social interface**.

IDE   See **Integrated Drive Electronics**.

IEEE See **Institute of Electrical and Electronics Engineers.**

IEEE standards The *Institute of Electrical and Electronics Engineers* (IEEE), acting as a coordinating body, has established a number of telecommunications standards, including Group 802 as follows:

- **IEEE 802.1D:** An access-control standard for *bridges* linking 802.3, 802.4, and 802.5 networks.
- **IEEE 802.2:** A standard that specifies the *data-link layer* for use with 802.3, 802.4, and 802.5 networks.
- **IEEE 802.3 1Base5:** A standard matching the AT&T Star-LAN product with a 1 megabit per second data transfer rate and a cable-segment length of up to 500 meters.
- **IEEE 802.3 10Base2:** An implementation of the *Ethernet* standard on *thin Ethernet* cable with a data transfer rate of 10 megabits per second, and a maximum cable-segment length of 185 meters (600 feet).
- **IEEE 802.3 10Base-T:** Establishes a standard for Ethernet over unshielded twisted-pair wiring: the same wiring and *RJ45* connectors used with modern telephone systems. The standard is based on a star topology, with each node connected to a central wiring center, with a cable-length limitation of 100 meters (325 feet).
- **IEEE 802.3 10Broad36:** Defines a long-distance Ethernet with a 10 megabit per second data rate, and a maximum cable-segment length of 3600 meters.
- **IEEE 802.4:** Defines bus topology networks that use token passing to control access and network traffic, running at 10 megabits per second.
- **IEEE 802.5:** Defines *ring networks* that use token passing to control access and network traffic, running at 4 or 16 megabits per second. It is used by IBM's *Token Ring* network.
- **IEEE 802.6:** Defines an emerging standard for *metropolitan area networks* (MANs) transmitting voice, video, and data over two parallel *fiber-optic cables*, using signaling rates of up to 155 megabits per second.
- **IEEE 802.7:** The Broadband Technical Advisory Committee provides advice on broadband techniques to other IEEE subcommittees.
- **IEEE 802.8:** The Fiber-Optic Technical Advisory Committee provides advice on fiber-optic technology to other IEEE subcommittees.
- **IEEE 802.9:** The Integrated Data and Voice Networks group

is presently working to integrate data, voice, and video to 802 LANs and ISDN.

- **IEEE 802.10:** The Network Security Technical Advisory Group is developing a standard definition of a network security model.
- **IEEE 802.11:** The Wireless Networking group is developing standards for wireless networks.
- **IEEE 802.12:** The Demand Priority group is working on standards for the 100 megabits per second Ethernet standard.

You will also see many of these standards referred to by their ISO reference numbers; IEEE standards 802.1 through 802.11 are also known as ISO standards 8802.1 through 8802.11.

imaging   The process of capturing, storing, cataloging, displaying, and printing graphical information, as well as the scanning of paper documents for archival storage.

Network users can store and then retrieve imaged documents from large, centralized image-storage systems, using applications such as *Lotus Notes* or other groupware.

See also **document management, high-capacity storage system, optical character recognition.**

impedance   An electrical property of a cable that combines capacitance (the ability to store an electrical charge), inductance (the ability to store energy in the form of a magnetic field), and resistance (the ability to impede or resist the flow of electric current), measured in ohms. Impedance can be described as the apparent resistance to the flow of alternating current at a given frequency. Mismatches in impedance along a cable cause distortions and reflections. Each transmission *protocol* and network *topology* specifies its own standards for impedance.

incremental backup   A backup of a hard disk that consists of only those files created or modified since the last backup was performed.

See also **differential backup, full backup.**

Industry Standard Architecture
See **ISA.**

INETCFG   A Novell NetWare 4.*x* *NLM* used to set up and configure *AppleTalk, IP,* and *IPX* protocols.

infrared transmission   A method of wireless transmission that uses part of the infrared spectrum to transmit and receive signals. Infrared transmissions take advantage of a frequency range just below that of visible light, and they require a line-of-sight connection between transmitter and receiver.

See also **mobile computing, wireless communications.**

Inherited Rights Filter   Abbreviated IHF. In NetWare 4.*x*, the mechanism that controls the rights a user can inherit from parent directories and container objects.

Inheritance allows an assignment applied at one point to apply to everything below that point in the file and directory structure. The IHF for any file, directory, or object is a part of NetWare's access control information.

See also **FILER, Inherited Rights Mask, NETADMIN, RIGHTS.**

Inherited Rights Mask   Abbreviated IRM. In NetWare 3.*x*, the mechanism that controls the rights a user can inherit. By default, IRM allows all rights to be inherited. Both files and directories have individual IRM controls.

See also **ALLOW, FILER, Inherited Rights Filter.**

initialize   In the Macintosh, the process of preparing a new, blank floppy or hard disk for use. Initializing completely obliterates any information previously stored on the disk. In DOS systems, this process is known as formatting the disk.

See also **formatting.**

INITIALIZE SYSTEM   A Novell NetWare 4.*x* server utility used for multiprotocol router configuration. This utility executes all the commands in the NET.CFG file, and is usually run from the *AUTOEXEC.NCF* file.

in-place migration method   In Novell NetWare, a method of upgrading an existing NetWare 4.01, 4.02, or 3.1*x* server to NetWare 4.1.

See also **across-the-wire migration.**

input/output   Abbreviated I/O. The transfer of data between the computer and its peripheral devices, disk drives, terminals, and printers.

input/output bound   Abbreviated I/O bound. A condition in which the speed of operation of the input/output port limits the speed of program execution. Getting the data into and out of the computer is more time-consuming than processing that same data.
See also **computation bound.**

INSTALL   A Novell NetWare server utility used for managing, maintaining, and updating NetWare servers. INSTALL can be used for the following tasks:
• Creating, deleting, and managing hard-disk partitions and NetWare volumes on the server.
• Installing NetWare and other additional products, and updating the license or registration disk.
• Adding, removing, checking, and unmirroring hard disks.
• Changing server startup and configuration files.
See also **DSREPAIR, MIGRATE, VREPAIR.**

install   To configure and prepare hardware or software for operation. Many application packages have their own installation programs, which copy all the required files from the original distribution floppy disks into appropriate directories on your hard disk, and then help to configure the program to your own operating requirements. Microsoft Windows programs are installed by a program called SETUP.
If you are upgrading to NetWare 4.*x* from 3.*x*, INSTALL offers two migration options: *across-the-wire migration* and *in-place migration*. If you are upgrading from NetWare 2.*x*, you must first upgrade to 3.*x*, and then to NetWare 4.*x*.

installable file system   Abbreviated IFS. A file system that is loaded dynamically by the operating system when it is needed. Different file systems can be installed to support specific needs, in just the same way as device drivers are loaded to support specific hardware.

installation program   A program whose sole function is to install (and sometimes configure) another program. The program guides the user through what might otherwise be a rather complex set of choices, copying the correct files into the right directories, decompressing them if necessary, and asking for the next disk when appropriate. An installation program may also ask for a person's name and a company name

165

so that the startup screen can be customized.

Some older IBM-compatible installation programs may change the CONFIG.SYS or AUTO-EXEC.BAT files without letting you know; others will ask permission and add their statements to the end of the existing commands.

See also **AUTOEXEC.BAT, CONFIG.SYS.**

Institute of Electrical and Electronics Engineers

Abbreviated IEEE, pronounced "eye-triple-ee." A membership organization, founded in 1963, including engineers, students, and scientists. IEEE also acts as a coordinating body for computing and communications standards, particularly the IEEE *802.x* standards for the physical and data-link layers of local-area networks (LANs), following the *ISO/OSI model.*

instruction set

instruction set   The set of machine-language instructions that a processor recognizes and can execute. An instruction set for *reduced instruction set computing* (RISC) may only contain a few instructions; a computer that uses *complex instruction set computing* (CISC) may be able to recognize several hundred instructions.

INT 14   Abbreviation for Interrupt 14, the PC interrupt used to reroute messages from the serial port to the network interface card, used by some *terminal-emulation* programs.

integrated circuit   Abbreviated IC, also known as a chip. A small semiconductor circuit that contains many electronic components.

Integrated Drive Electronics

Abbreviated IDE. A popular hard-disk interface standard, used for disks in the range of 40 megabytes to 1.2 gigabytes, requiring medium to fast data-transfer rates. The electronic control circuitry is located on the drive itself, thus eliminating the need for a separate hard-disk controller card.

See also **Enhanced Small Device Interface, SCSI, ST506 Interface.**

Integrated Services Digital Network   See ISDN.

integrated software   Application software that combines the functions of several different major applications, such as a spreadsheet, a database, a word processor, and a communications program, into a single package.

Integrated software provides a consistent user interface in all the modules, and allows the user to transfer data from one part of the system to another quickly and easily. It is also usually inexpensive. Unfortunately, integrated software packages do not usually offer all the complex features available with their stand-alone counterparts.

Examples of integrated software are Microsoft Works from Microsoft and ClarisWorks from Claris.

See also **software suite.**

Intel Corporation   A major manufacturer of microprocessors, including those used in IBM-compatible personal computers, founded in 1968. Intel has developed a wide range of processors and board-level products, used in applications as varied as personal computers, automobiles, robots, and supercomputers, as well as the multibus architecture used in many industrial and proprietary applications. Intel also manufactures modems, fax modems, memory chips, flash memory products, and other peripheral devices.

From twelve employees and $3000 revenue in 1968, Intel has grown to thirty-two thousand employees worldwide, generating more than $11.5 billion in annual revenue. The name Intel is a contraction of Integrated Electronics.

intelligent hub   See **smart hub.**

intelligent terminal   A terminal connected to a large computer, often a mainframe, that has some level of local computing power and can perform certain operations independently from the remote computer, but does not usually have any local disk-storage capacity.

See also **dumb terminal.**

Intel OverDrive   The original Intel OverDrive was designed as a user-installable upgrade to an *80386SX* or *80386DX*-based computer, while the Pentium OverDrive chip is designed as a replacement for a 486-based system.

OverDrive chips boost system performance by using the same *clock-multiplying* technology found in the Intel 80486DX-2 and *DX4* chips. Once installed, an OverDrive processor can increase application performance by an estimated 40 to 70 percent.

167

INTER-APPLICATION COMMUNICATION

Inter-Application Communication
Abbreviated IAC. In Macintosh System 7, a feature of the System software that allows independent applications to share and exchange information. IAC takes two main forms:

- **Publish-and-subscribe:** Allows users to create documents made of components created by multiple applications.

- **Apple events:** Let one application control another. For example, two programs can share common data, and one program can request that the other perform some action.

IAC is often referred to as program linking in the System 7 manuals.

See also **Dynamic Data Exchange**.

interface
The point at which a connection is made between two hardware devices, between a user and a program or operating system, or between two applications.

In hardware, an interface describes the logical and physical connections used, as in *RS-232-C*, and is often considered to be synonymous with the term *port*.

A user interface consists of the means by which a program communicates with the user, including a command line, menus, dialog boxes, online help systems, and

so on. User interfaces can be classified as character-based, menu-driven, or graphical.

Software interfaces are *Application Program Interfaces* (APIs) and consist of the codes and messages used by programs to communicate behind the scenes.

See also **graphical user interface, social interface**.

interface standard
Any standard way of connecting two devices or elements that have different functions. Many different interface standards are used for personal computers. These include *SCSI, Integrated Drive Electronics* (IDE), and the *Enhanced Small Device Interface* (ESDI) for hard disks; *RS-232-C* and the *Centronics parallel interface* for serial devices and parallel printers; and the *ISO/OSI model* for local-area network (LAN) communications over a network.

interleaved memory
A method of speeding up access by dividing *dynamic RAM* (DRAM) into two (or more) separate banks.

DRAM requires that its contents be updated at least every thousandth of a second, and while this update is taking place, it cannot be read by the processor. Interleaved memory divides available memory into banks so that the processor can read from one bank while the other is cycling, and so does not have to wait. Because interleaved memory does not require special hardware, it is one of the most cost-effective ways of speeding up system operation.

See also **SRAM, wait state.**

INTERLNK A DOS command, first introduced in MS DOS 6, that starts the INTERLNK program. INTERLNK connects two computers using their parallel or serial ports and allows the computers to share disks and printer ports.

To use INTERLNK, you must have DOS 6 on one computer and DOS 3.3 or later on the other, and you must use a three-wire serial cable, a seven-wire null-modem cable, or a bidirectional parallel cable to complete the connection. Also, the INTERLNK.EXE device driver must be added to the *CONFIG.SYS* file.

INTERLNK redirects drives in the order specified (the first server drive is redirected to the first client drive, and so on). However, INTERLNK does not redirect CD-ROM drives or network drives. You should not use the following DOS commands with the IN-TERLNK server: CHKDSK, DEFRAG, DISKCOMP, DISK-COPY, FDISK, FORMAT, SYS, UNDELETE, or UNFORMAT.

See also **INTERSVR.**

internal command Any DOS command that is not a separate program and is always available to the user. DIR, COPY, and TYPE are examples of internal commands.

See also **external command.**

internal modem A modem that plugs into the *expansion bus* of a personal computer, or into the *PCMCIA* connector of a laptop computer.

See also **external modem.**

International Business Machines Corporation Abbreviated IBM, also known as "Big Blue." Once the world's largest computer company, IBM has suffered a reversal of fortune recently. Known originally for its huge range of mainframe computers, IBM introduced the IBM PC, which quickly emerged as an industry standard. Since its introduction in 1981, the PC has seen many changes, and an enormous number of companies worldwide now manufacture or market

169

hardware, software, and peripheral devices for IBM-compatible computers.

IBM also has a huge research effort, and has introduced many innovative products, including the small, touch-sensitive TrackPoint, which replaces the mouse on many portable computers, the ThinkPad 701C with its expanding full-sized keyboard, and OS/2, IBM's multitasking, 32-bit operating system for Intel-based computers.

See also **IBM PC, IBM PC/AT, IBM PC/XT, IBM PS/1, IBM PS/2, IBM ThinkPad.**

International Standards Organization
Abbreviated ISO. An international standard-making body, based in Geneva, that establishes global standards for communications and information exchange. *ANSI* is the United States member of ISO.

The seven-layer International Organization for Standardization's Open Systems Interconnection (ISO/OSI) model for computer-to-computer communications is one of the ISO's most widely accepted recommendations.

See also **ISO/OSI model.**

Internet
The world's largest computer network, consisting of more than two million computers supporting over twenty million users in hundreds of different countries. The Internet is growing at a phenomenal rate—between 10 and 15 percent per month—so any size estimates are quickly out-of-date.

The Internet was originally established to meet the research needs of the U.S. Defense industry, but it has grown into a huge global network serving universities, academic researchers, commercial interests, and government agencies, both in the U.S. and overseas. The Internet uses *TCP/IP* protocols, and many of the Internet *hosts* run the *Unix* operating system.

See also **e-mail, FTP, Gopher, Gopherspace, Internet address, TELNET, USENET, World Wide Web.**

internet
Abbreviation for internetwork. Two or more networks using different networking protocols, connected by means of a *router*. Users on an internetwork can access the resources of all connected networks.

Internet address
An address on the Internet. An Internet address takes the form *someone@abc.def.xyz*, where *someone* is a user's name or part of a user's name, *@abc* is the network computer of the user, and *def* is the name of the host organization. The last three letters

denote the kind of institution the user belongs to: edu for educational, com for commercial, gov for government, mil for the military, org for miscellaneous organizations, and net for Internet administrative organizations.

See also **domain**.

internet address   In a Novell NetWare environment, a software address consisting of a 4-byte network address and a 6-byte node address. A node's internet address denotes both the network that the workstation is located on and the physical address of the device. The standard address form is known as dotted decimal, as in 199.2.207.9.

Internet Architecture Board

Abbreviated IAB. The coordinating committee for management of the *Internet*. IAB has two main subcommittees:

- **The Internet Engineering Task Force:** (IETF) specifies protocols and recommends Internet standards.
- **The Internet Research Task Force:** (IRTF) researches new technologies and refers them to the IETF.

Previously, the abbreviation stood for Internet Activities Board.

Internet Control Message Protocol   See **ICMP**.

Internet Engineering Task Force   See **Internet Architecture Board**.

Internet Packet Exchange
See **IPX**.

Internet Research Task Force
See **Internet Architecture Board**.

interoperability   The ability to run application programs from different vendors across local-, wide-, and metropolitan-area networks, giving users access to data and applications across *heterogeneous networks*. A network user need not know anything about the operating system or the configuration of the network hardware to be able to access data from the file server.

Interoperability is boosted by the increasing availability of products that conform to open standards rather than to specific proprietary protocols. The products work in accordance with national and internationally accepted standards.

See also **internet**.

interprocess communication

Abbreviated IPC. A term that describes all the methods used to pass information between two programs running on the same computer in a multitasking operating system, or between two programs running on a network, including *pipes*, *shared memory*, *queues*, *Dynamic Data Exchange* (DDE), and *Object Linking and Embedding* (OLE).

See also **Inter-Application Communication.**

interrupt

A signal to the processor generated by a device under its control, such as the system clock, that interrupts normal processing. An interrupt indicates that an event requiring the processor's attention has occurred, causing the processor to suspend and save its current activity, and then branch to an *interrupt service routine* (ISR).

In the PC, interrupts are often divided into three classes: internal hardware, external hardware, and software interrupts. The Intel 80*x*86 family of processors supports 256 prioritized interrupts, of which the first 64 are reserved for use by the system hardware or by DOS.

See also **interrupt request.**

Interrupt 14   See INT 14.

interrupt controller

A chip used to process and prioritize hardware *interrupts*. In IBM-compatible computers, the Intel 8259A Programmable Interrupt Controller responds to each hardware interrupt, assigns a priority, and forwards it to the main processor.

See also **interrupt request.**

interrupt handler

Special software invoked when an *interrupt* occurs. Each type of interrupt, such as a clock tick or a keystroke, is processed by its own specific interrupt handler. A table, called the *interrupt vector table*, maintains a list of addresses for these specific interrupt handlers.

See also **hooked vector.**

interrupt request

Abbreviated IRQ. Hardware lines that carry a signal from a device to the processor. A hardware *interrupt* signals that an event has taken place that requires the processor's attention. The interrupt may come from the keyboard, the network interface card, or the system's disk drives.

IBM PC and PC/XT computers have one interrupt controller chip and eight IRQs from 0 to 7. IBM

PC/AT computers and computers with MCA (Microchannel Architecture) have two chips tied together and fifteen IRQs. See the accompanying list for the devices associated with IRQs 0 through 15. Note that IRQ 2 is used in AT-class machines for access to the second interrupt controller chip that manages IRQs 8 through 15.

Interrupt Request (IRQ)	Device
0	Timer
1	Keyboard
2	Cascade
3	COM2
4	COM1
5	Hard disk
6	Floppy disk
7	LPT1
8	Clock
9	PC network
10-12	Unused
13	Coprocessor
14	Hard disk
15	Unused

INTERRUPT REQUEST

Any PC with an ISA (*Industry Standard Architecture*) bus has a limited number of possible hardware interrupts, and interrupt conflicts, in which two expansion cards are configured to use the same interrupt, are often common when setting up new systems or adding new nodes to the network. The easiest way to resolve IRQ conflicts is to reduce the number of cards in the PC to the minimum, and then add cards back in one at a time until the one that is causing the conflict is found. Then assign alternative addresses until the problem is solved.

See also **interrupt controller.**

interrupt service routine Abbreviated ISR. When an *interrupt* occurs, the processor suspends and saves its current activity, and then branches to an ISR. This routine processes the interrupt, whether it was generated by the system clock, a keystroke, or a mouse click. When the ISR is complete, it returns control to the suspended process.

interrupt vector table A list of addresses for specific software routines known as interrupt handlers. In a DOS computer, the interrupt vector table consists of 256 pointers located in the first megabyte of memory.

See also **hooked vector, interrupt handler.**

INTERSVR A DOS command first introduced with MS DOS 6 that starts the server program used to transfer files between computers using the *INTERLNK* program. The INTERLNK.EXE

173

device driver must be installed by *CONFIG.SYS* before this command can be used.
See also **INTERLNK.**

intruder   An unauthorized user of a computer system, usually a person with malicious intent.
See also **firewall, hacker.**

inverted backbone   A network *architecture* in which the wiring *hub* and *routers* become the center of the network, and all the network segments attach to this hub.
See also **backbone.**

I/O   See **input/output.**

IP   Abbreviation for Internet Protocol. The *TCP/IP session-layer* protocol that regulates packet forwarding by tracking internet addresses, routing outgoing messages, and recognizing incoming messages.

IPX   Abbreviation for Internet Packet Exchange. Part of Novell NetWare's *protocol stack*, used to transfer data between the server and workstations on the network. IPX packets are *encapsulated* and carried by the *packets* used in

Ethernet and the *frames* used in *Token Ring* networks.
See also **SPX.**

IPXCON   A Novell NetWare 4.x *NLM* used to monitor and troubleshoot IPX routers and network segments in an IPX internetwork.
See also **IPXPING.**

IPX external network number A hexadecimal number used to identify a network cable segment, assigned when the NetWare *IPX* protocol is bound to a network interface board in the server. An IPX external network number can have from one to eight digits (1 to FFFFFFFE).

IPX internal network number A hexadecimal number that identifies a NetWare server. Each server on the network must have a unique IPX internal network number. The number can have from one to eight digits (1 to FFFFFFFE) and is assigned to the server during NetWare installation.

IPXODI   Abbreviation for Internet Packet Exchange Open Datalink Interface. In recent versions of Novell NetWare, the requirement to generate a unique *DOS client* protocol file

(IPX.COM) for each workstation has been replaced by three new components: the *link-support layer*, the *multiple-link interface driver* (MLID) or network interface card device driver, and the *Open Datalink Interface* (ODI) version of the *IPX* (Internet Packet Exchange).

This approach has two major benefits: the ability to bind two different protocols to a single network interface card, and the ability to load and unload individual drivers as required. In earlier NetWare versions, the only way to remove the IPX driver was to reboot the workstation.

IPXPING   A Novell NetWare 4.*x* *NLM* used to send an IPX *ping* packet to a node or a workstation. IPXPING is only used as a troubleshooting aid.

IPXS   A Novell NetWare server *NetWare Loadable Module* (NLM) that supports the standard NetWare *IPX* protocol. IPXS must be the first NLM loaded onto the server. Because other modules depend on IPXS being present, it should be loaded automatically when the server first boots.

IrDA   Abbreviation for Infrared Data Association. A trade association of computer and telecommunications hardware and software suppliers, including Hewlett-Packard, Apple Computer, AST, Compaq, Dell, IBM, Intel, Motorola, Novell, and others.

IrDA is concerned with standards definitions for products that use *wireless communications*.

IRQ   See **interrupt request**.

ISA   Abbreviation for Industry Standard Architecture. The 16-bit bus design first used in IBM's PC/AT computer in 1984. ISA has a bus speed of 8 megahertz, and a maximum throughput of 8 megabytes per second. *EISA* (Extended Industry Standard Architecture) is a 32-bit extension to this standard bus.

See also **local bus, MCA, PCI local bus, VL bus**.

ISDN   Abbreviation for Integrated Services Digital Network. A *CCITT* standard for a worldwide digital communications network intended to replace all current systems with a completely digital, synchronous, full-duplex transmission system. Computers and other devices connect to

ISDN via simple, standardized interfaces. When complete, ISDN systems will be capable of transmitting voice, video, and data, all on the same line—something that currently takes three connections to achieve.

See also **Basic Rate ISDN, BISDN, Primary Rate ISDN.**

ISO See **International Standards Organization.**

isochronous service A method of transmitting real time data using preallocated bandwidth on a communications link, allowing time-synchronized transmissions with very little delay. Isochronous service is required for real time data such as synchronized voice and video, where delays in packet delivery would be unacceptable.

Asynchronous Transfer Mode (ATM) can provide isochronous service because its cells are always the same size, so it is possible to guarantee accurate and timely delivery of *packets*. Other networks can provide isochronous service by using a priority scheme to dedicate bandwidth to video traffic.

ISO/OSI model Abbreviation for International Standards Organization/Open System Interconnection model. A networking reference model defined by the ISO that divides computer-to-computer communications into seven connected layers; see the illustration on the opposite page. Such layers are known as a *protocol stack.*

Each successively higher layer builds on the functions of the layers below, as follows:

• **Application layer 7:** The highest level of the model. It defines the manner in which applications interact with the network, including database management, e-mail, and terminal-emulation programs.

• **Presentation layer 6:** Defines the way in which data is formatted, presented, converted, and encoded.

• **Session layer 5:** Coordinates communications and maintains the session for as long as it is needed, performing security, logging, and administrative functions.

• **Transport layer 4:** Defines protocols for structuring messages and supervises the validity of the transmission by performing some error checking.

• **Network layer 3:** Defines protocols for data routing to ensure that the information arrives at the correct destination node.

- **Data-link layer 2:** Validates the integrity of the flow of data from one node to another by synchronizing blocks of data and controlling the flow of data.

- **Physical layer 1:** Defines the mechanism for communicating with the transmission medium and interface hardware.

ISR See **interrupt service routine.**

ITU Abbreviation for International Telecommunications Union. The United Nations umbrella organization that develops and standardizes telecommunications worldwide. The ITU also contains the *CCITT*, the International Frequency Registration Board (IFRB), and the Consultative Committee on International Radio (CCIR). In popular usage, CCITT standards are being referred to as ITU standards.

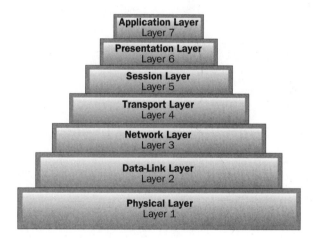

ISO/OSI MODEL

J

jabber A continuous and meaningless transmission generated by a network device, usually the result of a user error or a hardware malfunction.

jitter A type of distortion found on *analog* communications lines that results in data-transmission errors.

job A unit of work done by a computer, usually in a mainframe environment. A job can be the one-time execution of a single file or the execution of a whole series of programs to accomplish a complex task.

jukebox A high-capacity storage device that uses an autochanger mechanism to mount or dismount optical disks automatically. A jukebox typically contains one to four disks and a mechanism that picks up disks from a bay and loads them into the drives as they are needed.

See also **high-capacity storage system, HSM.**

jumper A small plastic and metal connector that completes a *circuit*, usually to select one option from a set of several user-definable options. Jumpers are often used to select one particular hardware *configuration* from a choice of configurations.

K See **kilo-**.

Kb See **kilobit**.

KB See **kilobyte**.

Kbit See **kilobit**.

Kbps See **kilobits per second**.

Kbyte See **kilobyte**.

Kermit A file-transfer protocol developed at Columbia University and placed in the public domain, used to transfer files between PCs and mainframe computers over standard telephone lines.

Data is transmitted in variable-length blocks up to ninety-six characters long, and each block is checked for transmission errors. Kermit detects transmission errors and initiates repeat transmissions automatically.

See also **Xmodem, Ymodem, Zmodem**.

kernel The most fundamental part of an operating system. The kernel stays resident in memory at all times, often hidden from the user, and manages system memory, the file system, and disk operations.

See also **mach, microkernel, shell**.

KEYB A Novell NetWare server utility that enables server keyboard types other than the standard United States English keyboard. Seventeen types are supported: United States English, British English, French, German, Italian, Spanish, Portuguese, Belgian, Canadian French, Danish, Norwegian, Swedish, Latin American, Dutch, Swiss German, Swiss French, and Russian.

See also **LANGUAGE**.

keyboard buffer A small amount of system memory used to store the most recently typed keys, also known as the type-ahead buffer. Some utilities let you collect a number of keystrokes or commands and edit or reissue them.

keyboard template   A plastic card that fits over certain keys (usually the function keys) on the keyboard as a reminder of how to use them. These templates are specific to an application, and they can be useful for new or occasional users.

key combination   In menu-driven and graphical user interfaces, some menu commands can be executed by certain combinations of keystrokes, also known as shortcut keystrokes. By using key combinations, users can bypass the menus, and thus speed up operations.

key redefinition   The ability of a computer program to assign different functions to specific keys.

keystroke   The action of pressing and then releasing a key on the keyboard to initiate some action or enter a character.

keyword   Any of the words, sometimes known as reserved words, that make up the vocabulary of a particular programming language or set of operating system commands and utilities.

kilo-   A prefix indicating 1000 in the metric system. Because computing is based on powers of 2, kilo usually means 2^{10}, or 1024. To differentiate between these two uses, a lowercase k is used to indicate 1000 (as in kHz), and an uppercase K is used to indicate 1024 (as in KB).
See also **mega-**.

kilobaud   One thousand *baud*. A unit of measurement of the transmission capacity of a communications channel.
See also **baud**.

kilobit   Abbreviated Kb or Kbit. 1024 bits (binary digits).
See also **gigabit, megabit**.

kilobits per second   Abbreviated Kbps. The number of *bits*, or binary digits, transmitted every second, measured in multiples of 1024 bits per second. Used as an indicator of communications transmission rates.
See also **megabits per second**.

kilobyte   Abbreviated K, KB, or Kbyte. 1024 bytes.
See also **exabyte, gigabyte, megabyte, petabyte, terabyte**.

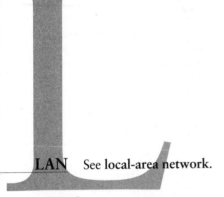

LAN See **local-area network**.

LANalyzer A hardware/software combination product from Network Communications Corp. used to troubleshoot and monitor performance and activity on *Ethernet* and *Token Ring* local-area networks (LANs).

The LANalyzer hardware includes an on-board processor and a 2-megabyte buffer for packet capturing. The package can decode most of the LAN protocols in common use, including Net-Ware, *TCP/IP, DECnet, Banyan, Network File System* (NFS), *AppleTalk Filing Protocol* (AFP), *Open Systems Interconnection* (OSI), *SNA* (Systems Network Architecture), *NetBEUI, Xerox Network Services* (XNS), and *SMB* (Server Message Block).

LANalyzer for Windows A Microsoft Windows-based software product from Novell used to troubleshoot and monitor network performance and activity. The LANalyzer main screen is a dashboard of gauges displaying real-time statistics, including local-area network (LAN) utilization, packets per second, and errors per second. User-specified alarms can also be set on these gauges.

LAN-aware An application that contains mechanisms for *file and record locking* to prevent multiple simultaneous access when used on a network. The term is often applied in a broader sense, to any application capable of running in a networked environment.

See also **mail-enabled**.

LANDesk Manager A package of network management utilities from Intel Corporation that includes hardware and software inventory, NetWare server monitoring, client monitoring and control, network traffic monitoring, virus protection, remote access, remote control, and print-queue management.

LANDesk Manager also includes a Desktop Management Interface (*DMI*) remote management console and DMI desktop agents or service layers for DOS and Windows clients.

LAN Distance
A remote access software package from IBM that lets network users log in from their PC or portable computer when they are away from the office.

LANGUAGE
A Novell NetWare 4.*x* server utility used to set the language for the server operating system, operating system message files, and *NetWare Loadable Modules* (NLMs). The default is English, but NetWare supports seventeen other languages for the operating system.

See also **KEYB**.

LANLord
A package of network management utilities from Symantec Corporation that includes hardware and software inventory, client monitoring and control, traffic monitoring, application metering, and virus protection. This package also includes automatic task scheduling, alerting, and report generation.

LAN Manager
A network operating system, developed by Microsoft and 3Com, that runs on *80386* and *80486* computers. The file-server software is a version of OS/2; client PCs can be OS/2, DOS, Unix, or Macintosh. *Disk mirroring, disk duplexing*, and UPS (uninterruptible power supply) monitoring functions are available. The network operating system supports *IPX/SPX*, *TCP/IP*, and *NetBEUI*. The illustration on the following page shows the LAN Manager architecture.

See also **Windows NT, Windows NT 3.5 Server.**

LANRover E Plus
A remote access package from Shiva Corporation that lets network users log in from their PC or portable computer when they are away from the office.

LAN Server
An IBM network operating system, based on a version of OS/2, that runs on *80386* and later Intel processors, as well as on the *PowerPC*. LAN Server supports Microsoft Windows, DOS, OS/2, and Macintosh clients, and *AppleTalk, IPX/SPX*,

Layer 7: application layer	redirector	named pipes
Layer 6: presentation layer		

Layer 5: session layer	Server Message Block (SMB)

Layer 4: transport layer	NetBIOS	
Layer 3: network layer	NetBIOS Extended User Interface (Net BEUI)	Transmission Control Protocol Internet Protocol (TCP/IP)

Layer 2: data-link layer	Network Driver Interface Specification (NDIS)

Layer 1: physical layer	network interface card and cabling

LAN MANAGER

TCP/IP, and *NetBIOS* protocols. LAN Server supports *domain directory services* and encrypted passwords, but does not include C-2 level certification.

LANtastic   A popular *peer-to-peer network* operating system, from Artisoft Inc., that runs with DOS, OS/2, or Microsoft Windows and supports Microsoft Windows, DOS, OS/2, Macintosh, and Unix clients.

The network can be run with all stations sharing files with all other stations, or for enhanced performance, with one PC acting as a dedicated file server. This server PC can be returned to a DOS machine easily, and LANtastic can be removed from memory when it is not being used. LANtastic supports an unlimited number of users, includes built-in CD-ROM, network e-mail, and network fax support, scheduling and network management, file-level security, and can connect easily into the NetWare environment.

LAN WorkGroup   Novell's *TCP/IP* client software that is located and managed centrally from the NetWare file server. The system also includes file-transfer and printer-redirection programs for both DOS and Windows. The LAN WorkGroup differs from its stand-alone counterpart, Lan Workplace, in that it can be managed from the file server. IP addresses can be assigned as needed allowing for the cost savings of concurrent licensing.

See also **LAN WorkPlace**.

LAN WorkPlace   Novell's *TCP/IP* client software, for DOS and Windows systems, that resides on the client system.

See also **LAN WorkGroup**.

LAP   Abbreviation for Link Access Procedure. The link-level protocol specified by the CCITT X.1 recommendation used for communications between *DCE* (data communications equipment) and *DTE* (date terminal equipment).

See also **LAP-B**.

LAP-B   Abbreviation for Link Access Procedure-Balanced. A common CCITT *bit-oriented*, *data-link layer* protocol used to link terminals and computers to *packet-switched networks*. It is equivalent to the *HDLC* (High-level Data Link Control) asynchronous balanced mode, in which a station can start a transmission without receiving permission from a control station.

LapLink   A popular communications package, from Traveling Software, used to transfer and synchronize files between a laptop computer and a desktop or networked computer.

laptop computer   A small, portable computer that is light enough to carry comfortably, with a flat screen and keyboard that fold together. Laptop computers are battery-operated. Advances in battery technology allow laptop computers to run for many hours between charges. Laptop computers often have a thin, backlit or sidelit *liquid-crystal display* (LCD) screen. Some models can mate with a *docking station* to perform as a full-sized desktop system back at the office, and many new laptop computers allow direct connection to the network with PCMCIA network interface cards. In some laptop computers, a set of business applications are built into ROM (read-only memory).

See also **mobile computing, notebook computer, palmtop computer, PCMCIA, wireless communications.**

LASTDRIVE   A DOS *CONFIG.SYS* command used to specify the maximum number of drives you can access on your system, often set by networking software.

LCD   See **liquid-crystal display.**

LCD monitor   A monitor that uses *liquid-crystal display* (LCD) technology. Many laptop and notebook computers use LCD monitors because of their low power requirements.

leaf object   In Novell NetWare 4.x, an NDS object that cannot contain any other objects; also

known as a non-container object. Leaf objects can be printers, servers, print queues, or even users.

See also **container object.**

leased line   A communications *circuit* or telephone line reserved for the permanent use of a specific customer, also called a private line.

See also **dedicated line.**

legacy systems   Computing systems that have been in use for a long time, either in the corporation (as in the case of mainframe computers), or in the home and small office (as in the case of older PCs). The problems of *backward compatibility* with legacy systems is always a thorny one, because they often perform essential functions that cannot be disrupted.

See also **legacy wiring.**

legacy wiring   Preinstalled wiring that may or may not be suitable for use with a network.

See also **legacy systems.**

level 2 cache   A secondary static RAM *cache* located between the primary cache and the rest of the system. A level 2 cache is often larger than the primary cache, and it is usually slower. In Intel's *P6 processor*, the level 2 cache will be implemented as a part of the package that holds the CPU.

See also **memory cache.**

light-wave communications

Usually refers to communications using *fiber-optic cables* and light generated by light-emitting diodes (LEDs) or lasers.

LIM EMS   See **Expanded Memory Specification.**

line adapter   In communications, a device that converts a digital signal into a form suitable for transmission over a communications channel such as a modem.

line analyzer   Any device that monitors and displays information about a transmission on a communications channel. A line analyzer is used for troubleshooting and load monitoring.

line driver   In communications, a hardware device used to extend the transmission distance between computers that are connected using *leased lines*. A line is required at each end of the line for digital communications.

line feed   Abbreviated LF. A printer command that advances the paper in the printer by one line, leaving the print head in the same position. In the *ASCII character set*, a line feed that has a decimal value of 10.

See also **ASCII, EBCDIC, carriage return.**

line-of-business application

See **mission-critical application.**

line-of-sight   An unobstructed path between the transmitter and receiver. Laser, microwave, and infrared transmissions all require a clear line-of-sight.

See also **wireless communications.**

line-sharing device   A small electronic device that allows a fax machine and a telephone answering machine to share the same phone line. The device answers the call and listens for the characteristic high-pitched fax carrier signal. If this signal is detected, the call is routed to the fax machine; if it is not present, the call is sent to a telephone or answering machine instead.

line speed   In communications, the transmission speed that a line

will reliably support for any given grade of service.

link level   Part of the CCITT's *X.25* standard that defines the link protocol. *LAP* (Link Access Procedure) and *LAP-B* (Link Access Procedure-Balanced) are the link access protocols recommended by CCITT.

link-state routing algorithm
A routing algorithm in which each *router* broadcasts information about the state of the links to all other nodes on the *internetwork*. This algorithm reduces routing loops but has greater memory requirements than the *distance vector algorithm*.

link-support layer   Abbreviated LSL. An implementation of the *Open Datalink Interface* (ODI) that works between the NetWare server's local-area network (LAN) drivers and communications protocols, such as *IPX* or *TCP/IP*, allowing network interface cards to service one or more *protocol stacks*. LSL is also used on workstations.

See also **multiple-link interface driver, ODINSUP**.

LIP   Abbreviation for Large Internet Packet. A mechanism that allows the Novell NetWare *internetwork* packet size to be increased from the default 576 bytes, thus increasing throughput over *bridges* and *routers*.-liquid crystal display

liquid-crystal display   Abbreviated LCD. A display technology common in portable computers that uses electric current to align crystals in a special liquid. The rod-shaped crystals are contained between two parallel, transparent electrodes. When current is applied, the electrodes change their orientation, creating a dark area. Many LCD screens are also backlit or sidelit to increase visibility and reduce eyestrain.

LIST DEVICES   A Novell NetWare server utility that lists all the hardware devices attached to the server, including tape drives, disks, optical disks, and other storage devices.

LISTDIR   A Novell NetWare 3.*x* workstation utility that displays information about a directory, including a list of subdirectories and the creation date, Inherited Rights Mask, and your effective rights for each of these subdirectories. In NetWare 4.*x*, this function is provided by the NDIR command.

listserver Abbreviated listserv. An automatic mailing system on the *Internet*.

Rather than sending *e-mail* on a particular topic to a long list of people, you send it instead to a special e-mail address, where a program automatically distributes the e-mail to all the people who subscribe to the *mailing list*.

Several programs have been written to automate a mailing list; you may also encounter mailserv, majordomo, or almanac.

Mailing lists are usually devoted to a specific subject, rather than to general interest communications.

See also **newsgroup, USENET**.

liveware A slang term for the people who use computers, as distinct from hardware, firmware, or software.

LLC See **logical link control**.

LOAD A Novell NetWare server utility used with all *loadable modules* to link them to the NetWare operating system. This command can be used from the console

prompt as needed or in one of the server startup (.NCF) files to load modules automatically every time the server is booted.

See also **MODULES, UN-LOAD**.

loadable module In Novell NetWare, a program that can be loaded and unloaded from the server or workstation while the operating system is running. Two common types of loadable module are *NetWare Loadable Modules* (NLMs) (servers) and *Virtual Loadable Modules* (VLMs)(workstations).

load balancing A technique that distributes network traffic along parallel paths to make the most efficient use of the available *bandwidth* while providing redundancy at the same time. Load balancing will automatically move a user's job from a heavily loaded network resource to a less loaded resource.

load sharing The ability of two or more remote *bridges* to share their load in a parallel configuration. If a bridge fails, traffic is routed to the next parallel bridge.

local-area network Abbreviated LAN. A group of computers and associated peripheral devices connected by a communications channel, capable of sharing files and other resources between several users.

See also **file server, metropolitan-area network, peer-to-peer network, wide-area network, zero-slot LAN.**

local bus   A PC bus specification that allows peripheral devices to exchange data at a rate faster than the 8 megabytes per second allowed by the *ISA* (Industry Standard Architecture) and the 32 megabytes per second allowed by the *EISA* (Extended Industry Standard Architecture) definition.

Local bus can achieve a maximum data rate of 133 megabytes per second with a 33 MHz bus speed, 148 megabytes per second with a 40 MHz bus, or 267 megabytes per second with a 50 MHz bus. Local bus capability must be built into the system's *motherboard* right from the start; it is not possible to convert an ISA-, EISA-, or MCA-based computer into a local-bus system.

To date, the *VESA* (Video Electronics Standards Association) video cards have been the main peripheral to benefit from local bus use, although Intel's *PCI*

(Peripheral Component Interconnect) local bus is gaining popularity.

local disk   In networking, a disk attached to a workstation rather than to the file server.

local drive   A drive lacated on your workstation or PC, rather than a drive available to you over the network.

See also **network drive.**

local group   In *Windows NT 3.5 Server,* a group granted *rights* and *permissions* to just the resources on the servers of its own *domain.*

See also **global group.**

local loop   That part of a communications circuit that connects subscriber equipment to equipment in a local telephone exchange.

local printer   In networking, a printer attached to a workstation rather than to the file server or a print server.

LocalTalk   The *shielded, twisted-pair* (STP) wiring and connectors available from Apple for connecting Macintosh computers using the built-in AppleTalk network hardware.

1

locked file   A file that you can open and read, but not write to, delete, or change in any way.

logical drive   The internal division of a large hard disk into smaller units. One single physical drive may be organized into several logical drives for convenience. DOS supports up to twenty-three logical drives on a system. On a single floppy disk system, the disk drive might function as both logical drive A and logical drive B.

logical link control   Abbreviated LLC. The upper component of the *data-link layer* that provides data repackaging functions for operations between different network types.

The *media access control* is the lower component that gives access to the transmission media itself.

logical unit   See LU.

LOGIN   A Novell NetWare workstation utility that lets a user log in to the server and run *login scripts*.

See also **ATTACH, LOGOUT**.

log in   To establish a connection to a computer system or online information service before using it, also known as log on. Many systems require the entry of an identification number or a password before the system can be accessed.

See also **C2, logout, password protection**.

LOGIN directory   In Novell NetWare 4.*x*, the SYS:LOGIN directory, created during the network installation, that contains the *LOGIN* and *NLIST* utilities used to log in to and view a list of currently available NetWare servers. NetWare 3.*x* has *SLIST* instead. For NetWare users running OS/2, the LOGIN directory is SYS:LOGIN\OS2.

login script   A small file or macro that executes the same set of instructions every time a user logs in to a computer system or network. Login scripts can map drives, display messages, set environment variables, and run programs, and are critical for proper configuration of each user's network environment.

A communications script may send the user-identification information to an online information service each time a subscriber dials up the service.

See also **script**.

log off   See **log out**.

log on   See **log in**.

LOGOUT   A Novell NetWare utility used to log out of the network, or to disconnect from a specific server while remaining attached to all other connections.

See also **LOGIN**.

log out   To relinquish a session and sign off a computer system by sending a terminating message. Also known as log off. The computer may respond with its own message, indicating the resources consumed during the session or the period between log in and log out. Logging out of a computer is not the same as shutting down or turning off the computer.

See also **log in**.

long-haul modem   A modem or other communications device that can transmit information over long distances.

See also **short-haul modem**.

loopback   A troubleshooting test in which a signal is transmitted from a source to a destination and then back to the source again so that the signal can be measured and evaluated or the data contained in the signal can be examined for accuracy and completeness.

lossless compression   Any data-compression method that compresses a file by rearranging or recoding the data that it contains in a more compact fashion. With lossless compression, there is no loss of original data when the file is decompressed. Lossless compression methods are used on program files and on images such as medical x-rays, when data loss cannot be tolerated.

Many lossless compression programs use a method known as the Lempel-Ziv algorithm, which searches a file for redundant strings of data and converts them to smaller tokens. When the compressed file is decompressed, this process is reversed.

See also **lossy compression**.

lossy compression   Any data-compression method that compresses a file by discarding any data that the compression mechanism decides is not needed. Original data is lost when the file is decompressed. Lossy compression methods may be used for shrinking audio or image files, when absolute accuracy is not required and the loss of data will not be noticed; however, this technique is unsuitable for more critical applications in which data loss cannot be tolerated, such as with medical images or program files.

See also **lossless compression**.

Lotus Notes
A popular *groupware* product from Lotus Development Corporation.

Lotus Notes is the defining force behind the entire groupware market, and is the target that all other developers aim for. Notes contains a very flexible database that can contain a wide variety of data types with none of the restrictions that normally apply, such as fixed field lengths. A Notes field can contain text, scanned images, OLE embedded objects, even *hypertext* links to other Notes documents. This database is closely linked with an e-mail system that allows users to forward any document in any Notes database to any other Notes database; a user can send e-mail to the database, and an application can even send e-mail to an individual user. Notes can also maintain multiple copies of the database, perhaps on the LAN or on remote workstations, and can synchronize these copies using background dial-up modem connections, IPX/SPX, or TCP/IP.

Notes is supported by a large number of networks, including AppleTalk, Banyan VINES, IBM APPC, Novell NetWare, TCP/IP, and X.25.

See also **workflow software**.

Lotus SmartSuite
A popular *software suite* from Lotus Development Corporation. SmartSuite consists of the 1-2-3 spreadsheet, WordPro word processor (previously known as Ami Pro), Approach database, Freelance Graphics, and the Organizer *personal information manager*.

SmartSuite is also available in a version called NotesSuite, which is integrated with *Lotus Notes* for *groupware* applications.

low-end
Describes any inexpensive product, from the bottom of a company's product list, that includes a reduced set of capabilities.

See also **high-end**.

low-level language   In programming, a language close to *machine language*. All assembly languages are considered to be low-level languages.

See also **high-level language**.

LPT*x* ports   In DOS, the device name used to denote a parallel communications port, often used with a printer. DOS supports three parallel ports: LPT1, LPT2, and LPT3. OS/2 adds support for network ports LPT4 through LPT9.

LSL   See **link-support layer**.

LU   Abbreviation for logical unit. A suite of protocols developed by IBM to control communications in an *SNA* (Systems Network Architecture) network, as follows:

- **LU0:** Uses SNA transmission control and flow-control layers.

- **LU1, LU2, and LU3:** Control host sessions.
- **LU4:** Supports peer-to-peer and host-to-device communications between peripheral nodes.
- **LU6.2:** The peer-to-peer protocol of APPC. It also features comprehensive end-to-end error processing and a very generalized *Application Program Interface* (API).
- **LU7:** Data Stream terminals used on AS/400 systems.

See also **APPC, PU**.

LU6.2   See LU.

luggable computer   Slang term for an early portable computer, designed in the mid-1980s, that was just barely transportable. Fortunately, luggable computers disappeared quickly when the modern generation of small, light, and powerful laptop and notebook computers appeared.

M See **mega-**.

rather than a conventional monolithic kernel.

The microkernel is designed to manage only the most fundamental operating system operations, including interrupts, task scheduling, messaging, and virtual memory; other modules can be added as necessary for file management, network support, and other tasks.

m See **milli-**.

MAC See **media access control**.

MacBinary In the Macintosh, a *file transfer protocol* that ensures a proper transfer of Macintosh files over a modem. Most Macintosh communications programs support sending and receiving files in MacBinary, but the protocol is not often supported in other environments.

Mach An operating system created from scratch at Carnegie-Mellon University, designed to support advanced features such as *multiprocessing* and *multitasking*.

Mach has its roots in the Unix world, and was originally based on BSD 4.4; however, its most notable feature is that it employs a relatively small *microkernel*

machine code See **machine language**.

machine language The native *binary* language used internally by the computer; also known as machine code. Machine language is difficult for humans to read and understand. Programmers create applications using high-level languages, which are translated into a form that the computer can understand by an assembler, a compiler, or an interpreter. Whichever method is used, the result is machine language.

Macintosh Abbreviated Mac. A range of personal computers introduced in 1984 by Apple Computer, Inc. featuring a popular and easy-to-use *graphical user interface*. The computer is based on the Motorola *68000* series of microprocessors and uses a proprietary operating system to simulate the user's desktop on the screen.

The original Mac was a portable, self-contained unit with a small monochrome screen, 128 kilobytes (KB) of memory, two serial ports, extended sound capabilities, and a single 400 KB, 3.5-inch floppy disk. The computer was an instant success, and users quickly began to demand more power and additional features. Apple released many new models over the years, expanding the range to include Macs based on the 68020, 68030, and 68040 processors, adding color, more memory, a built-in *SCSI* interface, a 32-bit bus, and larger and faster hard disks.

Introduced in 1991, the Power-Book series of notebook computers offers both power and convenience in a very small package, posing a real challenge to the DOS-based laptops. The Power-Book Duo is a practical solution to the problem of one computer for the desktop and another that fits into a briefcase for use while traveling. The Duo can dock into a larger desktop *docking station* with a full-sized keyboard and color display. Configuration is automatic, including printer, network, and file-server connections. See also **Power Mac.**

Macintosh client   Any Macintosh computer attached to a network. A Macintosh client can store and retrieve information from a NetWare server running NetWare for Macintosh modules and can run executable Macintosh network files.

Macintosh File System   Abbreviated MFS. In the Macintosh, an older system that stored files in a flat structure rather than the hierarchical system used in more recent versions. All current Macintosh models can read disks created using MFS.

macro   A stored group of keystrokes or instructions that can automate a complex or repetitive sequence of application commands. Many of the major spreadsheet, word processing, and database programs let users create and edit macros to speed up operations. Some macros can incorporate control structures, such as DO/WHILE loops and IF/THEN branching statements. See also **login script, script.**

MAGAZINE   A Novell Net-
Ware server utility used when a
media magazine is inserted or removed from a server.
See also **MEDIA**.

mail-aware application   Any
application with the ability to
send and receive e-mail. Applications in the *document management, groupware*, and *workflow*
categories all use e-mail to interconnect users and help with the
flow of inoformation. This integration of e-mail is made possible
in part by API's such as Microsoft's
Messaging API, and Novell's *Message Handling Service*.
Sometimes known as a message-
enabled application.

mailbox   In e-mail systems, an
area of hard-disk space used to
store e-mail messages until users
can access them. An on-screen
message often tells users that they
have mail.

MAIL directory   The SYS:MAIL
directory used by Novell NetWare-
compatible mail applications.
This directory may also be used
to store user print information
and login scripts.

mail-enabled application
Any application that includes an
e-mail function but that also provides additional services, such as
contact-management software,
intelligent mail handling, and
workflow automation. Also
known as message-enabled
application.
See also **groupware, Lotus
Notes, workflow software**.

mainframe computer   A large,
fast, *multiuser* computer system,
often utilizing multiple processors, designed to manage large
amounts of data and complex
computing tasks. Mainframes are
normally installed in large corporations, universities, or military
installations and can support hundreds, even thousands, of users.
The feature that distinguishes
mainframe computers from other
types is that they perform all processing at one central location;
the terminals accessed by users
have no local computing power of
their own.
See also **dumb terminal, minicomputer**.

maintenance release   A software upgrade that corrects minor
bugs or adds a few small features.

m

This type of release is usually distinguished from a major release by an increase in only the decimal portion of the version number; for example, from 3.1 to 3.11 rather than from 3.1 to 4.0.

MAKEUSER   A Novell NetWare 3.*x* workstation utility that automates the process of creating or deleting users and *user accounts*. In NetWare 4.*x*, this function is performed by the *UIMPORT* workstation utility.

male connector   Any cable connector with pins designed to engage the sockets on the female connector; see the accompanying illustration.

See also **female connector**.

MALE CONNECTOR

MAN   See **metropolitan-area network**.

MANAGE   An application included with *Banyan VINES*

network operating system that is used for network administration.

Use MANAGE to set up user profiles, *access rights*, *groups*, *security attributes*, and file and printing services.

Management Information System   Abbreviated MIS. A computer-based information system that integrates data from all the departments that it serves to provide company management with the information it needs to make timely decisions, keep track of progress, and solve problems.

Manchester encoding   In communications, a method used to encode data and timing signals in the same transmitted data stream. The signal state during the first half of the bit period indicates its data value (1 is high; 0 is low). A transition to the opposite state in the middle of the bit period acts as the timing signal.

MAP   A Novell NetWare workstation utility that lets users create, view, or change network drive mappings. There are three types of drive mappings:

- Local drive mapping refers to a local hard disk, such as a disk in a workstation.

- Network drive mapping refers to a directory in the NetWare file system.
- Search drive mapping refers to a directory that the DOS operating system will search when requested files are not found in the current directory.

map   In *DOS clients* and *OS/2 clients*, to assign a drive letter to a directory path on a volume. For example, if drive F: is mapped to the directory SYS:ACCTS \PAYABLE, users can access that directory each time they change to drive F:.

Manufacturing Automation Protocol   See **MAP**

MAP   Abbreviated Manufacturing Automation Protocol. A protocol that was originally developed by General Motors and was designed for use in a manufacturing environment.
See also **TOP**.

MAPI   See **Messaging API**.

mark parity   See **parity**.

Master CNE   A Novell certification program for CNEs who want

to focus on the support of enterprise-wide networks. The Master CNE program is viewed by many as the advanced degree of NetWare certification, because candidates must demonstrate proficiency in specialized networking technologies, as well as an in-depth knowledge of the NetWare operating system.
See also **CNA, CNI**.

MATHLIB   A Novell NetWare server *NetWare Loadable Module* (NLM) that links a server's math coprocessor to the network operating system. This NLM should be loaded automatically every time the server starts up.
See also **MATHLIBC**.

MATHLIBC   A Novell NetWare server *NetWare Loadable Module* (NLM) that provides a library of math functions for those servers that do not have a math coprocessor installed. This NLM should be loaded automatically every time the server starts up.
See also **MATHLIB**.

MAU   Abbreviation for Multistation Access Unit, sometimes abbreviated MSAU. A multiport wiring hub for *Token Ring networks* that can connect up to

m

eight lobes to a ring network. IBM refers to a MAU that can be managed remotely as a *Controlled Access Unit*.

MB   See **megabyte**.

Mb   See **megabit**.

MBONE   Abbreviation for Multicast Backbone. An experimental method of transmitting digital video over the *Internet* in real time.

The *TCP/IP* protocols used for Internet transmissions are unsuitable for real time audio or video; they were designed to deliver text and other files reliably, but with some delay. MBONE requires the creation of another backbone service with special hardware and software to accommodate video and audio transmissions; the existing Internet hardware cannot manage time-critical transmissions.

Mbps   See **megabits per second**.

MCA   Abbreviation for Microchannel Architecture. A 32-bit, proprietary *expansion bus*, first introduced by IBM in 1987 for the *IBM PS/2* range of computers and also used in the *IBM RS/6000* series.

MCA was designed for *multiprocessing*. It allows expansion boards to identify themselves, thus eliminating many of the conflicts that arose through the use of manual settings in the original bus. The MCA bus can also be driven independently by multiple bus master processors.

MCA is physically and electronically incompatible with expansion boards that follow the earlier 16-bit AT bus standard: the boards are about 50 percent smaller and the bus depends on more proprietary integrated circuits.

See also **EISA, ISA, local bus, PCI local bus**.

mean time between failures

Abbreviated MTBF. The statistically derived average length of time for which a system component operates before failing. MTBF is expressed in thousands or tens of thousands of hours, also called power-on hours or POH.

See also **mean time to repair**.

mean time to repair   Abbreviated MTTR. The average length of time that it takes to repair a failed component.

See also **mean time between failures.**

MEDIA   A Novell NetWare server utility used at the console prompt after a prompt to insert or remove media from the server.

See also **MAGAZINE.**

media access control   Abbreviated MAC. The lower component of the *data-link layer* that governs access to the transmission media. The *logical link control* layer is the upper component of the data-link layer. MAC is used in *CSMA/CD* and *token-ring* local-area networks (LANs) as well as in other types of networks.

Media Control Interface
Abbreviated MCI. A standard interface used for controlling *multimedia* files and devices. Each device has its own device driver that implements a standard set of MCI functions, such as stop, play, and record.

media filter   A device used to convert the output signal from a *Token Ring* adapter board to work with a specific type of wiring. For example, a media filter can link 16-megabits per second Token Ring network interface cards with *unshielded twisted-pair* (UTP) wiring, thus saving the expense of additional cable runs.

medium attachment unit   Abbreviated MAU. A transceiver that attaches to the *AUI* (Attachment Unit Interface) port on an Ethernet adapter and provides electrical and mechanical attachments to *fiber-optic cable*, *twisted-pair cable* (TP), or other media types.

meg   A common abbreviation for megabyte.

mega-   Abbreviated M. A prefix meaning one million in the metric system. Because computing is based on powers of 2, mega usually means 2^{20} or 1,048,576; the power of 2 closest to one million.

megabit   Abbreviated Mbit. Usually 1,048,576 binary digits or bits of data. Often used as equivalent to 1 million bits.

See also **bit, megabits per second.**

m

203

megabits per second Abbreviated Mbps. A measurement of the amount of information moving across a network or communications link in one second, measured in multiples of 1,048,576 bits.

megabyte Abbreviated MB. Usually 1,048,576 bytes. Megabytes are the unit of measurement for computer memory or hard-disk capacity.

megahertz Abbreviated MHz. One million cycles per second. A processor's *clock speed* is often expressed in megahertz. The original IBM PC operated an 8088 running at 4.77 MHz; the more modern Pentium processor runs at 120 MHz; and the MIPS R4400 runs internally at 150 MHz.

MEMORY A Novell NetWare server utility that displays the amount of server *memory* available to the network operating system.

memory The primary *RAM* (random-access memory) installed in the computer. The operating system copies applications from disk into memory, where all program execution and data processing takes place, and then writes the results back to disk. The amount of memory installed in the computer can determine the size and number of programs that it can run, as well as the size of the largest data file.

See also **dynamic RAM, static RAM, swapping, virtual memory.**

memory address The exact location in memory that stores a particular data item or program instruction.

memory board A printed circuit board containing memory chips. When all the sockets on a memory board are filled, and the board contains the maximum amount of memory that it can manage, it is said to be "fully populated."

memory cache An area of high-speed memory on the processor that stores commonly used code or data obtained from slower memory, eliminating the need to access the system's main memory to fetch instructions.

The Intel 82385 cache controller chip was used with fast *static RAM* on some systems to increase performance, but more modern processors include cache-management functions on the main processor.

The Intel 80486 contains a single 8-kilobyte (KB) cache to manage both data and instruction caching. The Pentium contains two separate 8 KB caches, one each for data and instructions.

See also **cache, level 2 cache.**

memory chip   A chip that holds data or program instructions. A memory chip may hold its contents temporarily, as in the case of *RAM* (random-access memory), or permanently, as in the case of *ROM* (read-only memory).

memory management   The way in which the computer handles memory. In a DOS-based PC, you may find the following kinds of memory:

- *Conventional memory*: The area of memory below 640 kilobytes (KB).
- *Upper memory*: The 384 KB of memory between 640 KB and 1 megabyte (MB); also known as reserved memory. This space is used by system hardware such as the video adapter. Unused portions of upper memory are known as upper memory blocks (UMBs). On an 80386 (or later) processor, UMBs can be used for device

drivers or terminate-and-stay-resident (TSR) programs.

- *Extended memory*: The memory above 1 MB on 80386 (or later) processors. Extended memory needs an extended memory manager, such as HIMEM.SYS.
- *High memory area*: The first 64 KB of extended memory.
- *Expanded memory*: Memory other than conventional memory that can be used by certain DOS applications. Expanded memory requires an expanded memory manager.

Many of the design decisions made in the original PC, and in early versions of DOS, define these apparently random memory boundaries.

memory management unit   Abbreviated MMU. The part of the processor that manages the mapping of virtual *memory addresses* to actual physical addresses. In some systems, such as those based on early Intel or Motorola processors, the MMU was a separate chip; however, in most modern processors, the MMU is integrated into the central processing unit (CPU) chip itself.

memory map   The organization and allocation of memory in a computer. A memory map will give an indication of the amount of memory used by the operating system, as well as the amount remaining for use by applications.

memory-resident program

See **terminate-and-stay-resident program**.

mesh network
A network *topology* in which every device is connected by a cable to every other device on the network. Multiple links to each device are used to provide network link redundancy; see the accompanying illustration.

message channel
A form of *interprocess communication* found in *multitasking* operating systems. Interprocess communications allow two programs running in the same computer to share information.

See also **pipe, queue, semaphore**.

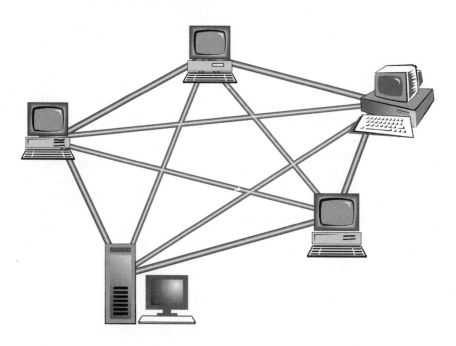

MESH NETWORK

Message Handling Service

Abbreviated MHS. A popular protocol for *e-mail* storage, management, and exchange, originally created by Action Technologies, and then licensed by Novell. MHS can collect, route, and deliver e-mail and other files by using *store-and-forward* technology.

Message Handling System

The CCITT *X.400* standard protocol for global *store-and-forward* messaging. The X.400 standard specifies everything from the type of data that a message can contain to rules for converting between different message types, such as from fax to text or vice versa.

See also **X.500**.

message switching

A routing method that uses *store-and-forward* techniques. Each message contains a *destination address* and is passed from source to destination through a series of intermediate nodes. At each intermediate node, the message is stored briefly, reviewed, and then forwarded to the next node. Message switching allows a network operating system to regulate traffic and to use the available communications links effectively.

Messaging API

Abbreviated MAPI. An application interface used to add messaging capabilities to any Microsoft Windows application. MAPI handles the details of message storage and forwarding and directory services.

See also **mail-aware application**.

metropolitan-area network

Abbreviated MAN. A public, high-speed network, operating at 100 megabits per second, or faster, capable of voice and data transmission over a distance of up to 80 kilometers (50 miles). A MAN is smaller than a *wide-area network* (WAN) but larger than a *local-area network* (LAN).

MFS

See **Macintosh File System**.

MHz

See **megahertz**.

MIB

Abbreviation for Management Information Base. A database of network configuration information used by *SNMP* and *CMIP* to monitor or change network settings. MIB provides a logical naming of all resources on the network related to the network's management.

See also **CMIS**.

m

Microchannel Architecture
See **MCA**.

microcode   Low-level instructions that define how a particular processor works by specifying what the processor does when it executes a *machine-language* instruction.

microcomputer   Any computer based on a single-chip processor. Many modern microcomputers are as powerful as mainframe models designed just a few years ago; they are also smaller and cheaper.

See also **workstation**.

microkernel   An alternative *kernel* design developed by researchers at Carnegie-Mellon University and implemented in the *Mach* operating system.

Traditionally, the kernel has been a monolithic piece of the operating system, resident in memory at all times. It takes care of operations as varied as virtual memory management, network support, file input/output, and task scheduling.

The microkernel is a stripped-down kernel that is only concerned with loading, running, and scheduling tasks. All other operating system functions (virtual memory management, disk input/output, and so on) are implemented and managed as tasks running on top of the microkernel.

micron   A unit of measurement. One millionth of a meter, corresponding to approximately $\frac{1}{25,000}$ of an inch. The core diameter of *fiber-optic cable* for networks is often specified in terms of microns; 62.5 microns is a common size.

microprocessor   A central processor unit (CPU) on a single chip, often referred to as the processor. The first microprocessor was developed by *Intel* in 1969. The microprocessors most often used in Apple Macintosh computers are the Motorola *680x0* series. In IBM and IBM-compatible computers, Intel *80x86* microprocessors are commonly used.

See also **DEC Alpha, 80286, 80386, 80486, Intel OverDrive, MIPS R4000, Pentium, PowerPC, P6.**

Microsoft BackOffice   A network *software suite* from Microsoft Corporation that consists of *Windows NT Server*, SQL Server, Microsoft SNA Server, Microsoft Mail, Microsoft Exchange, and

Microsoft System Management Server.

See also **Microsoft Office**.

Microsoft Bob   A new form of *graphical user interface*, known as a *social interface*, from Microsoft. Bob is aimed at new or occasional users, and is an innovative attempt to change the way that people interact with computers. Bob features easy-to-navigate screens that look like the rooms in a house, and you control Bob using choices presented by animated figures called guides. Several guides are available; you can choose a cuddly rabbit, Rover the dog, or a rather rude rat called Scuzz as your mentor. Bob includes a suite of eight applications, including a letter writer, e-mail, address book, checkbook program, and calendar, and you can run your existing DOS and Windows applications from within Bob.

Bob runs on top of DOS and Windows, and requires a computer with an Intel 80386 (or better) processor, VGA graphics, mouse, and 8 MB of memory.

Microsoft Corporation   The leading personal computer software company, founded in 1975 by Bill Gates and Paul Allen. Microsoft's greatest success was in supplying IBM with the *PC-DOS* operating system for the IBM PC, and then providing versions of *MS-DOS* to the clone manufacturers. It has been estimated that more than 100 million computers run DOS. Microsoft released Windows 3 in May 1990 and upgraded to version 3.1 in April 1992, selling many millions of copies. The release of *Windows NT* during 1993 consolidated Microsoft's position as a leading developer of operating systems, and Windows 95 will continue this trend.

In addition to MS-DOS and its extensive computer language products, Microsoft also markets a wide range of applications, including Microsoft Word, a word processor; Microsoft Excel, a spreadsheet; Microsoft Access and FoxPro databases; Microsoft Publisher, a desktop publishing program; and Microsoft Office, an integrated *software suite* that includes Access, Excel, Word, and PowerPoint.

The Microsoft consumer division now has over fifty different products, including popular multimedia titles such as Encarta and Cinemania, an interactive movie guide. Microsoft Press publishes and distributes computer-related books and CD-ROM products to bookstores.

m

Microsoft Corporation has seen phenomenal growth, from 1000 employees in 1985 with revenues of $140.4 million, to more than 15,000 employees in 1994 with revenues of $4.65 billion.

Microsoft Office   A very popular *software suite* from Microsoft Corporation that contains most of the core applications needed in a typical office. The Standard version of Microsoft Office includes Microsoft Word for Windows (word processor), Microsoft Excel (spreadsheet), Microsoft Mail (e-mail), and PowerPoint (presentation graphics); the Professional version also includes the Microsoft Access (database). Office requires 4 MB of memory (8 MB is recommended). A minimum installation takes 29 MB of hard disk space, while a complete installation occupies over 80 MB. More than six million copies of Microsoft Office have shipped, and the software is available on both the Macintosh and Windows *platforms.*

See also **SOHO.**

Microsoft Windows   A graphical operating environment from Microsoft that runs under DOS. Windows brings to DOS many of the graphical user interface features found in the Macintosh, including icons, dialog boxes, pull-down menus, and mouse support.

The three main components of Windows are Program Manager, which is the primary shell program that manages application execution and task switching; Print Manager, which organizes and coordinates Windows printing; and File Manager, which manages files, directories, and disks.

Windows also brings *multitasking* to the PC. In standard mode, several Windows applications can be run at the same time. In 386-enhanced mode, both Windows and non-Windows applications can be multitasked.

The Windows package supplied by Microsoft contains useful programs, including Write, a word processor; Paintbrush, a paint program; Terminal, a communications program; and several smaller utility programs and games.

Windows supports several *interprocess communication* channels, ranging from the Windows Clipboard, which lets you cut and paste information from one file to another, to more complex methods of communication, such as *Dynamic Data Exchange* (DDE) and *Object Linking and Embedding* (OLE).

Windows is preinstalled by over 400 hardware manufacturers, and the installed base is somewhere between 40 and 60 million systems worldwide. Not all PCs can run Windows; an 80286 (or higher) with at least 1 megabyte (MB) of memory is required to run Windows 3.1 in standard mode. An 80386 (or better) with at least 2 MB of memory is required to run in 386 enhanced mode. You also need a floppy disk drive and at least 10 MB of free hard-disk space. If you plan on using large applications or creating large data files, you will need much more hard-disk space.

Microsoft Windows 95
See **Windows 95.**

Microsoft Windows NT
See **Windows NT Server.**

micro-to-mainframe   Any form of connection that attaches a PC to a mainframe-based network. Often used to describe software (called *terminal-emulation* software) that allows the microcomputer to access data and applications on the mainframe system.

microwave   A method of radio transmission that uses high-frequency waves (in the range of 1 to 30 gigahertz) for *line-of-sight* broadband communications. It requires a repeater station every 20 miles or so because of the curvature of the earth. Microwaves can also be used for satellite communications.

midsplit   A special type of broadband cable system that splits the available frequencies into two groups: one for transmission and the other for reception.

See also **broadband network.**

MIGRATE   A Novell NetWare utility used to upgrade a NetWare 3.*x* server to NetWare 4.*x*. MIGRATE upgrades the server operating system and transfers existing *bindery objects*, *rights*, and *trustee assignments*.

If you want to upgrade from NetWare 2 to NetWare 4.*x*, you must use the *in-place migration* method to go from NetWare 2 to 3.12, and then upgrade to NetWare 4.*x*.

See also **across-the wire migration, BMIGRATE, INSTALL.**

m

milli- Abbreviated m. A prefix meaning one thousandth in the metric system, often expressed as 10^{-3}.

millisecond Abbreviated ms or msec. A unit of measurement equal to one thousandth of a second. In computing, hard disk and CD-ROM drive access times are often described in terms of milliseconds; the higher the number, the slower the disk system.

millivolt Abbreviated mv. A unit of measurement equal to one thousandth of a volt.

MIME Abbreviation for Multipurpose Internet Mail Extensions. An *Internet* specification that allows users to send multiple-part and multimedia messages, rather than simple ASCII text messages. A MIME-enabled e-mail application can send PostScript images, binary files, audio messages, and digital video over the Internet.
See also **uudecode, uuencode.**

minicomputer A medium-sized computer running a *multitasking* operating system capable of managing more than one hundred users simultaneously, suitable for use in a small company or a single

corporate or government department.
See also **mainframe computer, workstation.**

mini-hard disk A hard disk mounted on a Type III *PC Card*.
See also **PCMCIA.**

MIPS Acronym for millions of instructions per second. A measure of the processing speed of a computer's central processing unit (CPU).
See also **benchmark program.**

MIPS R4000 and R4400

A family of 64-bit microprocessors from MIPS Computer Systems.

The R4000 has a 1.3 million transistor design, with an 8 kilobyte (KB) data cache, an 8 KB instruction cache, and a *floating-point processor*. Internally, the R4000 runs at 100 MHz, double its external 50 MHz clock output.

The R4400, with 2.2 million transistors, is based on the R4000, but has larger cache units (16 KB data cache and 16 KB instruction cache) and runs internally at 150 MHz, externally at 75 MHz. Silicon Graphics acquired MIPS in June 1992.

MIRROR STATUS   A Novell NetWare server utility that lists the mirrored status of each partition on a server. There are five mirrored states:

- Not mirrored
- Fully synchronized—data is identical
- Out of synchronization—some data is not identical
- Orphaned—the integrity of the data is not guaranteed
- In the process of being re-mirrored

See also **disk duplexing, disk mirroring, RAID, SLED.**

MIS   See **Management Information System.**

mission-critical application
A computer application whose function is vital to the operation of the corporation using it; also called line-of-business application.

MJ   Abbreviation for modular jack. The jack used to connect telephone cables to a wall-mounted face plate.
See also **MMJ, RJ-11.**

MLID   See **multiple-link interface driver.**

MMJ   Abbreviation for modified modular jack. A six-pin connector developed by Digital Equipment Corporation used to connect serial lines to terminal devices. MMJ jacks have a side-locking tab and so can be distinguished from RJ-11 jacks, which have a center-mounted tab.
See also **MJ.**

MMU   See **memory management unit.**

mnemonic   Pronounced "ne-monic." A name or abbreviation used to help you remember a long or complex instruction. Programming languages use many different mnemonics to represent complex instructions.

MNP   Abbreviation for Microcom Networking Protocol. A set of communications protocols from Microcom that has become the standard for data compression and error detection and correction. The levels are as follows:

- **MNP 1 to 4:** Define hardware error control.
- **MNP 5:** Describes a method of data compression that achieves a 2-to-1 compression ratio.
- **MNP 6:** Describes a communication protocol that begins with

213

V.22 bis modulation, and then switches to *V.29* when possible.

- **MNP 7:** Describes a method of data compression that achieves a 3-to-1 compression ratio.
- **MNP 8:** Based on MNP 7, and adds a V.29 technique that lets half-duplex devices operate as full-duplex.
- **MNP 9:** Contains a proprietary technique that provides good performance over a wide variety of link types.
- **MNP 10:** Describes an extremely rigorous error control protocol, well suited for use on extremely noisy links. MNP 10 has been adopted for use in cellular modems.

mobile computing

1. The everyday use of a portable or laptop computer as a normal part of the workday.

2. Techniques used to establish links to a network by employees who move from one remote location to another, such as members of a sales staff; once the connection is made, users can access network resources as easily as if they were working from a computer in their office.

See also **laptop computer, PCMCIA, portable computer, wireless communications.**

modem   Contraction of MODulator/DEModulator, a device that allows a computer to transmit information over a telephone line.

The modem translates between the digital signals that the computer uses and analog signals suitable for transmission over telephone lines. When transmitting, the modem modulates the digital data onto a carrier signal on the telephone line. When receiving, the modem performs the reverse process to demodulate the data from the carrier signal.

Modems usually operate at speeds ranging from 2400 to 28800 bits per second over standard telephone lines, and at higher rates over leased lines.

See also **baud rate, external modem, internal modem, PCMCIA.**

modem eliminator   A device that allows two computers to be linked without using modems. In an asynchronous system, in which the serial ports of two PCs are connected, the modem eliminator is a *null-modem* cable. In synchronous systems, a modem eliminator must also provide timing functions to synchronize communications.

modem server See **asynchronous communications server**.

modulation In communications, the process used by a modem to add the digital signal onto the carrier signal, so that the signal can be transmitted over a telephone line. The frequency, amplitude, or phase of a signal may be modulated to represent a digital or analog signal.

See also **carrier signal, demo-dulation**.

module In programming, a self-contained portion of a larger program written, tested, and compiled separately. Normally, a module only performs one specific operation.

See also **NetWare Loadable Module, Virtual Loadable Module**.

MODULES A Novell NetWare server utility that displays information about the *NetWare Loadable Modules* (NLMs) installed on the server, including their long and short names and version number.

MONITOR A Novell NetWare server utility that displays information about the server, including the time elapsed since the server was booted, percent utilization of the server's processor, number of disk blocks available, the number of blocks waiting to be written to disk, the number of connections to the server, and the number of files being accessed. It also provides information about server disks, LAN drivers, and other attached mass-storage devices.

Monitrix for NetWare A package of network management utilities from Cheyenne Software, Inc. that includes hardware and software inventory, server monitoring, traffic monitoring, and virus protection. The package also includes automatic task scheduling, reporting functions, and replacements for certain NetWare utilities.

Mosaic A *World Wide Web* client program, originally written by the National Center for Supercomputing Applications (NCSA) at the University of Illinois. Mosaic uses a *graphical user interface* to give access to *Internet* resources, and allows users to navigate through *hypertext* documents quickly and easily using a mouse.

Mosaic is available in versions for Windows, Unix, and the Macintosh operating systems and requires that *TCP/IP* is installed

215

on the client computer and that a direct connection to the Internet is available.

See also Web browser.

motherboard   The main printed circuit board in a computer, containing the *central processing unit* (CPU), appropriate *coprocessor* and support chips, device controllers, and *memory*. It also includes *expansion slots* to give access to the computer's internal bus.

Motorola Inc.   A major manufacturer of microprocessors, including those used in Macintosh computers, founded in 1928 in Chicago. Motorola is also extensively involved in radio and data communications, automotive and industrial products, and the development of the *PowerPC*.

MOUNT   A Novell NetWare server utility used to load a volume onto the server, making the files on the volume available to users and applications. Using MOUNT, you can mount a single volume by name or mount all available volumes simultaneously with the MOUNT ALL command.

mount

1. The method by which nodes access network resources in the *NFS* (Network File System) and other networks.

2. To load a disk volume so that files and other resources can be accessed by users.

mouse   A small input device with one or more buttons used with *graphical user interfaces*. As the mouse moves, an on-screen mouse cursor follows; all movements are relative. Once the mouse pointer is in the correct position on the screen, you can press one of the mouse buttons to initiate an action or operation. Different user interfaces and file programs interpret mouse clicks in different ways.

A mouse has been standard equipment on the Macintosh family of computers for a long time. With the rising popularity of graphical user interfaces, such as Microsoft Windows, mouse use with DOS systems is becoming common.

You can connect a mouse to the computer in one of several ways:

● A bus mouse requires a separate expansion board in the computer.

• A serial mouse plugs into an unused serial port.

• A regular mouse plugs into the mouse port, as with Macintosh and IBM PS/2 computers. A wireless mouse is also available.

See also **trackball**.

ms   See **millisecond**.

MS-DOS   Acronym for Microsoft Disk Operating System. MS-DOS, like other operating systems, allocates system resources, such as hard and floppy disks, the monitor, and the printer, to applications that need them.

MS-DOS is a single-user, single-tasking operating system, with either a *command-line* or *shell* interface. It is the most ubiquitous operating system ever written, running more than 20,000 different applications on an estimated 100 million computers. Over the years, Microsoft has released several major upgrades:

• **MS-DOS 1.0:** First released in August 1981 along with the original IBM PC. It was based on the earlier CP/M operating system, used in 8-bit computers during the late 1970s. This similarity allowed software developers to port applications programs from CP/M to DOS.

• **MS-DOS 2.0:** Released in March 1983, with three times the number of commands as version 1.0. It added several important features borrowed from the *Unix* operating system, including hierarchical directories, pipes, filters, redirection, and the ability to work with a 10 megabyte (MB) hard disk.

• **MS-DOS 3.0:** Released in August 1984 along with the *80286*-based IBM PC/AT. It supported 1.2 MB floppy disks, a RAM disk, and larger hard disks. 3.1, released in November 1984, added some level of network support. 3.2, released in December 1985, added support for 3.5-inch floppy disks, the XCOPY command, and partitions of up to 32 MB on a hard disk. 3.3, released in April 1987 along with the IBM PS/2, supported a 3.5-inch 1.44 MB floppy disk, as well as multiple partitions of up to 32 MB for larger hard disks.

• **MS-DOS 4.0:** Released in November 1988 (written by IBM, not Microsoft). It added a shell menu program and support for hard disk partitions of up to 2 gigabytes. 4.01 was a bug-fix release.

• **MS-DOS 5.0:** Released in June 1991. It included an improved shell and menu interface

m

program, a full-screen editor, UNFORMAT and UNDELETE utilities, a task swapper, and support for 2.88 MB, 3.5-inch floppy disks. This version added the capability to take advantage of a computer's extended or expanded memory. DOS itself, along with selected device drivers, could be loaded into the *high memory area* to save more *conventional memory* for use by applications.

 • **MS-DOS 6.0:** Released in the spring of 1993. It added the DoubleSpace *file-compression program*, an enhanced backup and restore program, an *anti-virus program*, a hard *disk optimizer* and file *defragmenter*, and a more automatic memory configuration program. Several of these new utilities were licensed from Central Point Software or from Peter Norton Computing, rather than developed by Microsoft from scratch. 6.2 was a maintenance version, released late in 1993.

   MS-DOS is similar in operation to *PC-DOS*, the DOS version supplied with personal computers manufactured by IBM. However, some of the file sizes and names of device drivers are different. IBM's PC-DOS 6.1 supports tape backup systems and *PCMCIA* cards, has an enhanced text editor, and provides a program scheduler. PC-DOS 7 was released

by IBM in early 1995, and includes several major improvements, such as the Stacker data-compression application.

msec   See **millisecond**.

MTBF   See **mean time between failures**.

MTTR   See **mean time to repair**.

multicast   A special form of *broadcast* in which copies of the message are delivered to multiple stations but not to all possible stations.

multidrop line   A circuit connecting several stations or nodes on a single logical link (see the accompanying illustration); also called a multipoint line. A multidrop line

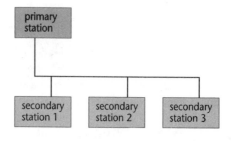

MULTIDROP LINE

is often used in IBM's *SNA* (Systems Network Architecture). It is controlled by a primary station, and the other nodes are considered to be secondary.

multilink   A printed circuit board that contains several different layers of circuitry. The layers are laminated together to make a single board, onto which the other discrete components are added.

multimedia   A computer technology that displays information using a combination of full-motion video, animation, sound, graphics, and text, with a high degree of user interaction.

multimedia extension   A software extension to an operating system that extends an application interface to include time-based media, such as music, sound, full-motion video, and animation. Multimedia extensions also include commands for synchronization and device control..

QuickTime is a multimedia extension to Apple's System 7 operating system. MMPM/2 brings multimedia support to IBM's OS/2. Microsoft includes several multimedia extension device drivers and utilities with Windows 3.1.

See also **Media Control Interface.**

multimode fiber   A *fiber-optic cable* with a wide core that provides multiple routes for light waves to travel. Its wider diameter prevents multimode fiber from carrying signals as far as *single-mode fiber.*

multiple DOS configurations
A DOS 6 feature that allows users to define different system configurations and choose the one they want to use on startup. This capability is useful when several people share the same computer system or when users want to be able to choose from several configurations.

multiple-link interface driver
Abbreviated MLID. A Novell *Open Datalink Interface* (ODI) device driver that manages the sending and receiving of packets to and from the physical local-area network (LAN) medium.

See also **link-support layer, ODINSUP.**

multiplexer   Often abbreviated mux. In communications, a device that merges several lower-speed transmission channels into one

m

high-speed channel at one end of the link. Another multiplexer reverses this process at the other end of the link to reproduce the low-speed channels; see the accompanying illustration.

See also **frequency-division multiplexing, statistical multiplexing, time-division multiplexing.**

multiplexing   In communications, a technique that transmits several signals over a single communications channel. *Frequency-division multiplexing* separates the signals by modulating the data into different carrier frequencies. *Time-division multiplexing* divides the available time among the various signals. *Statistical multiplexing* uses statistical techniques to dynamically allocate transmission space depending on the traffic pattern.

multipoint line   See **multidrop line.**

multiprocessing   The ability of an operating system to use more than one *central processing unit* (CPU) in a single computer. Symmetrical multiprocessing refers to the operating system's ability to assign tasks dynamically to the next available processor. Asymmetrical multiprocessing requires that the original program designer choose the processor to use for a given task when writing the program.

Multipurpose Internet Mail Extension   See **MIME.**

multiserver network   A single network that uses two or more file servers.

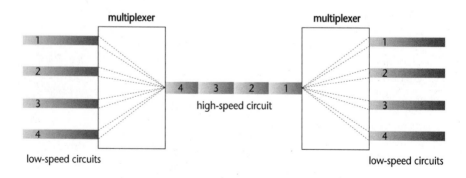

MULTIPLEXER

Multistation Access Unit
See **MAU**.

multitasking   The simultaneous execution of two or more programs in one computer.

multithreading   The concurrent processing of several *threads* inside the same program. Because several threads can be processed in parallel, one thread does not need to wait for another to finish before it can start.

multiuser   Describes an operating system that supports more than one simultaneous user. DOS and OS/2 are single-user operating systems. Unix and its derivatives and networking operating systems are multiuser systems.

mux   See **multiplexer**.

mv   See **millivolt**.

MVS   Acronym for Multiple Virtual Storage. IBM's standard operating system for large mainframe computers.
See also **VM**.

m

9-track tape A tape storage format that uses nine parallel tracks on $\frac{1}{2}$-inch, reel-to-reel magnetic tape. Eight tracks are used for data and one track is used for parity information. These tapes are often used as backup systems on minicomputer and mainframe systems; *digital audio tapes* (DATs) are more common on networks.

See also **quarter-inch cartridge.**

n See **nano-.**

NAEC Abbreviation for Novell Authorized Education Center. A private organization that provides Novell-approved training courses. See also **NEAP.**

NAK Abbreviation for negative acknowledgment. In communications, a *control code*, *ASCII* 21, sent by the receiving computer to indicate that the data was not properly received and should be sent again.

See also **ACK.**

NAME A Novell NetWare server utility that displays the name assigned to the server during NetWare installation.

named pipe A communications *Application Program Interface* (API) used by applications running on a network. Named pipes provide a software connection between a client and a server using routines similar to those used in normal operations for opening, reading, and writing to files.

See also **pipe, semaphore, shared memory.**

name-space NLM A specific type of *NetWare Loadable Module* (NLM) that allows non-DOS file-naming conventions, such as those used in OS/2, Unix, or the Macintosh system, to be stored in NetWare's directory and file-naming systems.

See also **ADD NAME SPACE.**

NAMPS Acronym for Narrowband Analog Mobile Phone Service. A proposed standard from Motorola that combines the *AMPS* (Advanced Mobile Phone Service) cellular standard with digital signaling information. NAMPS is designed to provide a higher level of performance and greatly increase communications capabilities.

nano- Abbreviated n. A prefix meaning one-billionth in the American numbering scheme, and one thousand millionth in the British system.

nanosecond Abbreviated ns. One-billionth of a second. The speed of computer memory and logic chips is measured in nanoseconds. Processors operating at clock speeds of 25 MHz or more need *dynamic RAM* (DRAM) with access times faster than 80 nanoseconds. *Static RAM* (SRAM) chips can be read in as little as 10 to 25 nanoseconds.

narrowband In communications, a voice-grade transmission channel of 2400 bits per second or less.

National Computer Security Center See NCSC.

NBACKUP In Novell NetWare 3.*x*, a workstation-based backup program for backing up files from directories in which users have the appropriate rights.

See also **SBACKUP**.

NCB Abbreviation for Network Control Block. The packet structure used by the *NetBIOS* transport protocol.

NCOPY A Novell NetWare workstation utility used to copy files and directories from one location on the network to another. NCOPY also specifies copying parameters, including whether subdirectories should be copied and whether extended attributes and name-space information should be retained.

NCP See **NetWare Core Protocol**.

NCSC Abbreviation for National Computer Security Center. A branch of the United States National Security Agency that defines security for computer products. The Department of Defense Standard 5200.28, also known as the Orange Book, specifies the following levels:

• **D:** A system that is not secure.

- **C1:** Requires an individual login, but allows group identification.
- **C2:** Requires an individual level of login by password, with an audit mechanism. This level of security is found in Novell NetWare 4.*x*, Windows NT 3.5 Server, and Banyan VINES network operating systems.
- **B1:** Requires Department of Defense security clearance levels.
- **B2:** Guarantees a path between the user and the security system and provides assurances that clearances cannot be changed.
- **B3:** Security based on a mathematical model that must be viable and repeatable.
- **A1:** The highest level of security, based on a mathematical model that can be proven.

An operating system that lets anyone have complete access, such as DOS, falls into the D category. C1 and C2 levels can be implemented in a commercial environment. At the B1 level, the computing environment changes radically, and many of the mandatory access-control mechanisms are impractical for normal commercial operations.

NCUPDATE   A Novell NetWare 4.*x* utility used to update a *NET.CFG* file with a new name

context after a container object has been renamed or moved.

NDIR   A Novell NetWare workstation utility used to find and sort information about files and directories. It includes the following options:

- Format options allow users to view, create, update, archive, and copy information about files and directories.
- Sort options allow users to specify display criteria, such as owner name, creation date, and file size.
- *Attribute* options allow users to sort file and directory information by attribute assignments.
- Restriction options allow users to restrict searches by owner, date, or size.

NDIS   Abbreviation for Network Driver Interface Specification. A device driver specification, originally developed by Microsoft and 3Com in 1990, that is independent of both the underlying network interface card hardware and the protocol being used. NDIS also provides protocol *multiplexing* so that multiple *protocol stacks* can be used at the same time in the same computer.

Windows NT includes the latest version, NDIS 3, which is

225

backward-compatible with the original NDIS and NDIS 2.

See also **ODINSUP, Open Data-link Interface.**

NEAP   Abbreviation for Novell Educational Academic Partner. A college or university that provides Novell-approved training courses as a part of its standard curriculum.

See also **Novell Authorized Education Center.**

near-end crosstalk   See **NEXT.**

negative acknowledge
See **NAK.**

NETADMIN   A Novell NetWare 4.*x* workstation utility used to manage *NetWare Directory Services* (NDS) objects. This utility has many of the same features and controls many of the same functions as the Windows-based program *NWADMIN.*

NETADMIN replaces the functions found in several NetWare 3.*x* utilities, including *DSPACE, SECURITY, SYSCON,* and *USERDEF.*

NetBEUI   Abbreviation for NetBIOS Extended User Interface, pronounced "net-boo-ee". A network device driver for the *transport layer* supplied with Microsoft's *LAN Manager, Windows for Workgroups,* and *Windows NT.* NetBEUI communicates with the network interface card via the *NDIS* (Network Driver Interface Specification).

See also **NetBIOS.**

NETBIOS   A Novell NetWare 3.*x* workstation utility used to determine if *NETBIOS.EXE* is loaded, and if so, which interrupts it is using.

NetBIOS   Acronym for network basic input/output system, pronounced "net-bye-os." A *session-layer* network protocol, originally developed in 1984 by IBM and Sytek, to manage data exchange and network access.

NetBIOS provides an *Application Program Interface* (API) with a consistent set of commands for requesting lower-level network services to transmit information from node to node, thus separating applications from the underlying network operating system. Many vendors provide either their own version of NetBIOS or an emulation of its communications services in their own products.

NETBIOS.EXE Novell NetWare's *NetBIOS* emulator.

NET.CFG A Novell NetWare workstation configuration file, similar to *CONFIG.SYS*, that contains information used to configure the workstation.

For normal network use, the default values established in this file usually work. In some cases, the NET.CFG values must be adjusted to work with particular applications or in certain configurations.

netiquette A contraction of NETwork etIQUETTE. The set of unwritten rules governing the use of *e-mail* and other computer and network services.

Netscape A popular *World Wide Web* browser that runs under Windows, *X Window*, and on the Macintosh. Netscape is manufactured by Netscape Communications Corporation.

NetSync A Novell NetWare utility used to synchronize NetWare binderies in mixed NetWare 3.*x* and 4.*x* networks.

See also **NETSYNC3, NETSYNC4, NWADMIN.**

NETSYNC3 A Novell NetWare *NetWare Loadable Module* that is loaded onto a NetWare 3.*x* server so that it can become part of a *NetSync* managed network.

NETSYNC4 A Novell NetWare *NetWare Loadable Module* that, when loaded onto a NetWare 4.*x* server, can manage up to twelve NetWare 3.*x* servers as part of the *NetSync* environment.

NETUSER A Novell NetWare 4.*x* workstation utility that offers a menu system used for performing simple user tasks, including the following:

- Managing print jobs
- Sending messages to other users
- Turning messaging on or off
- Mapping network drives
- Capturing ports to printers or print queues
- Changing the login script and password
- Attaching to servers

n

NETUSER replaces the NetWare 3.*x* utility *SESSION,* and can be invoked from either the workstation or the server.

This utility has many of the same features and controls many of the same functions as the Windows-based program *NWUSER.*

NetVIEW IBM *SNA* (Systems Network Architecture) management software that provides monitoring and control functions for SNA and non-SNA devices. This system relies heavily on mainframe data-collection programs, but it also incorporates Token Ring networks, Rolm CBXs, non-IBM modems, and PC-level products running under DOS or OS/2.

NetWare A series of popular *network operating systems* and related products from Novell, Inc. that run on Intel computers and support DOS, Microsoft Windows, Macintosh, OS/2, and Unix clients.

Almost 80 percent of PC-based local-area networks (LANs) use Novell NetWare products; approximately 66 percent of LAN sales went to NetWare 3.*x* during 1994, approximately 10 percent went to NetWare 4.*x*, and 2 percent went to *Personal NetWare.* Systems range from the peer-to-peer

Personal NetWare for a small number of users to the much larger NetWare 3.*x*, which can serve up to 250 users with 100,000 open files. Beginning in version 3.*x*, *NetWare Loadable Modules* (NLMs) allow network administrators to configure the network operating system running on the file server by adding individual modules as required for network security, workgroup productivity, or e-mail. The illustration on the following page shows the NetWare architecture.

Several different NetWare operating systems are available, including the following:

• **NetWare 2.*x*:** A 16-bit operating system that is often run on *80286* servers and is most suitable for smaller, self-contained networks that do not connect to external computing resources. It can access 12 megabytes (MB) of memory and manage a maximum volume size of 255 MB, although volumes cannot span multiple hard disks. NetWare 2.*x* supports DOS, Macintosh, and OS/2 clients.

• **NetWare 3.*x*:** A 32-bit operating system that is run on *80386* (and later) processors and is suitable for larger, multisegment networks, with up to 250 nodes per server. NetWare 3.*x* can access up to 4 gigabytes (GB) of RAM (random-access memory) and up to 32 terabytes (TB) of storage. A maximum of 100,000 files can be open concurrently on the file server, and the maximum file size is 4 GB. *Disk mirroring, disk duplexing,* support for optical disks, and *UPS-*monitoring functions are all available.

- **NetWare 4.x:** Adds support for *optical disks, CD-ROMs, data*

compression, and improved login *security* mechanisms, as well as the *Network Directory Services* (NDS), which is based on the CCITT *X.500* directory standard and replaces the bindery database of versions 2.*x* and 3.*x*. NetWare 4.1 is the first version of NetWare to integrate *Message Handling*

Layer 7: application layer	Service Advertising Protocol (SAP)	NetWare Loadable Modules (NLM)
Layer 6: presentation layer		
Layer 5: session layer		
Layer 4: transport layer		
Layer 3: network layer	Net BIOS extended user interface (Net BEUI)	Transmission Control Protocol Internet Protocol TCP/IP
Layer 2: data-link layer	Network Driver Interface Specification (NDIS)	
Layer 1: physical layer	network interface card and cabling	

NETWARE

Service with the directory, and it also adds *System Fault Tolerance.* NetWare 4.*x* is suitable for larger, multisegment *internetworks,* supporting up to one thousand nodes per server. It includes a set of user and administrator utilities featuring a graphical user interface, and it is available in several languages.

Unlike with other software products, NetWare users do not always change to the next highest level of software release as a matter of course—from NetWare 3.*x* to NetWare 4.*x*, for example. Novell expends much time and effort in maintaining several parallel levels of network operating systems.

See also **SuperNOS, UnixWare.**

NetWare command files   Text
files created by the network administrator containing a series of NetWare commands and the appropriate modifying parameters.

Similar to DOS batch files, NetWare command files execute NetWare commands just as though you had typed them at the NetWare console. NetWare command files have the file-name extension .NCF; *AUTOEXEC.NCF* for server configuration at startup

and BSTART.NCF for Btrieve initialization are common examples.

NetWare Core Protocol
Abbreviated NCP. A Novell NetWare upper-layer procedure used by a server when responding to workstation requests. It includes routines for manipulating directories and files, opening semaphores, printing, and creating and destroying connections.

NetWare Directory Database
Abbreviated NDD. A Novell NetWare 4.*x* database, often referred to as the Directory, that organizes *NetWare Directory Services* (NDS) objects in a hierarchical tree structure, known as the Directory tree.

NetWare Directory Services
Abbreviated NDS. A Novell NetWare 4.*x* global naming service that maintains information on, and provides access to, every resource on the network, including users, groups, printers, volumes, and servers.

NDS manages all network resources as objects in the *NetWare Directory Database* (NDD), independent of their actual physical location. NDS is global to the network, and information is replicated so that a local failure cannot bring down the whole system.

NDD replaces the *bindery*, the system database for earlier releases of NetWare. The bindery managed the operation of a single NetWare server; NDS supports the whole network, including multiserver networks. *Bindery emulation* provides compatibility with previous versions of NetWare.

NDS is based on the 1988 CCITT *X.500* standard.

See also **container object, leaf object.**

NetWare DOS Requester   The *DOS client* portion of the Novell NetWare 4.*x* network operating system. The Requester replaces the *NetWare shell* used by earlier Novell network operating systems.

See also **NetWare Requester for OS/2, NET*x*.COM.**

NetWare Express   Novell's private electronic information service that gives access to Novell support information via the GE Information Services system, GEnie. NetWare Express includes the NetWare Buyer's Guide, product information, press releases, trade show dates, advanced technical support, the *Network Support Encyclopedia*, and a large

Novell library. There is a fee for this service.

NetWare for SNA   A Novell NetWare *NLM* that connects Novell workstations to an *SNA* (Systems Network Architecture) host computer.

NetWare Hub Services   PC-based software from Novell that supports the management of any *hub* card that complies with the NetWare Hub Management Interface (HMI) standard.

NetWare/IP   A set of *NetWare Loadable Modules* (NLMs) that enables existing NetWare 3.*x* and 4.*x* servers to use *IP* as a transport protocol option, so that users can run NetWare network services and applications in a TCP/IP environment. NetWare/IP can also function as a *gateway*, connecting NetWare and NetWare/IP networks.

NetWare Link Services Protocol   Abbreviated NLSP. The NetWare *IPX* link-state protocol used by IPX *routers* to share information about their routes with other devices on the network. NLSP allows large or small *internetworks* to be connected without causing routing inefficiencies.

n

NLSP runs with NetWare versions 3.*x* and 4.*x*, as well as with Novell's Multiprotocol Router (MPR) Version 3.0.

See also **RIP, SAP.**

NetWare Lite A *peer-to-peer network* operating system from Novell for DOS workstations, which makes drives, files, and printers available to all the users on the network. NetWare Lite is limited to a maximum of 25 simultaneous users, but supports up to 255 nodes on the same network. NetWare Lite has been replaced by *Personal NetWare.*

NetWare Loadable Module

Abbreviated NLM. Server management programs and LAN drivers that run on a server under Novell NetWare's network operating system. NLMs can be loaded and unloaded dynamically, without the server being down, and provide better service than applications that run outside the core operating system. Several kinds of NLM are available:

• **Utilities and application modules** that allow you to look at or change various configuration options. These NLMs have the .NLM file-name extension.

• **Name-space modules** allow non-DOS file naming conventions

to be used when storing files. These NLMs have the .NAM file-name extension.

• **Disk drivers** give access to hard disks; they have the .DSK file-name extension.

• **LAN drivers** control communications between the network operating system and the network interface cards; they have a .LAN file-name extension.

See also **value-added process, Virtual Loadable Module.**

NetWare Management System

Abbreviated NMS. A system responsible for managing the network. NMS communicates using a network-management protocol and builds a map of network resources, which in turn can send messages to the server indicating unusual or error conditions on the network.

See also **NMAGENT.**

NetWare Multiprotocol Router

Novell's PC-based software that allows network administrators to connect local-area networks (LANs) using *IPX, IP, OSI,* or *AppleTalk Filing Protocol* (AFP) over a wide range of LANs and wide-area networks (WANs).

See also **PC-based router.**

NetWare Multiprotocol Router Plus
Novell's PC-based software that provides wide-area connectivity for dispersed *heterogeneous networks* over *T1, fractional T1, X.25,* and low-speed synchronous *leased lines.* NetWare Multiprotocol Router Plus replaces three earlier products: NetWare Link/64, NetWare Link/T1, and NetWare Link/X.25.

See also **PC-based router.**

NetWare NFS
A Novell *NetWare Loadable Module* (NLM) that adds *NFS* (Network File System) server capability to an existing NetWare 3.*x* or 4.*x* file server. Once loaded, Unix NFS clients see the NetWare server as another NFS server.

NetWare NFS Gateway
A Novell *NetWare Loadable Module* (NLM) that lets a NetWare server mount a *Unix* file system as a NetWare *volume.* Complete NetWare security is maintained, and access to the Unix system is based on the NetWare client's privileges.

NetWare Requester for OS/2
Part of the NetWare client software for *OS/2* that directs network requests from the workstation to the network.

The Requester replaces the *NetWare shell* used by earlier Novell network operating systems. It allows application servers and their workstations to communicate on the network without using a NetWare server, so that users can run advanced distributed applications on their OS/2 workstations.

See also **NetWare DOS Requester.**

NetWare Runtime
A single-user version of the Novell NetWare 4.*x* or 3.*x* network operating system that provides NetWare services to clients of *NetWare Loadable Modules* (NLMs).

NetWare shell
The Novell NetWare program loaded into each workstation's memory that allows the workstation to access the network. The shell captures the workstation's network requests and forwards them to a NetWare server. In earlier versions of NetWare, the shell program was specific to the version of DOS in use. The term shell is not used in NetWare 4.*x*.

See also **NetWare DOS Requester, NetWare Requester for OS/2, NETx.COM.**

n

NetWare System Fault Tolerance

Abbreviated NetWare SFT. Previously an add-on product from Novell, now integrated into NetWare 4.1, SFT provides *fault tolerance*, so that critical operations are always accessible to users.

See also **SFT**.

NetWare Tools

Novell NetWare 4.*x* utilities that allow users to perform a variety of network tasks, such as accessing network resources, mapping drives, managing printing, and sending messages to other network users. NetWare Tools programs are installed separately from the server installation program, and they are available for DOS and OS/2 workstations.

NetWare Users International

Abbreviated NUI. An organization created to support distributed NetWare user groups, first formed in the mid-1980s. NUI now has 150 regional chapters and more than 140,000 members worldwide. Users can present a united voice to Novell, giving feedback on new products and how to support and improve existing products.

NetWare Video

A Novell NetWare *NetWare Loadable Module* for NetWare 3.*x* and 4.*x* that allows up to twenty-five users at a time to access Audio-Video Interleaved (AVI) video files located on the file server. AVI files can often be very large, and can bog down a busy network very quickly. In an attempt to alleviate this problem, NetWare Video separates the audio and video components at the server and sends them to the workstation, where they are recombined by a special NetWare Video driver.

NetWire

Novell's online information service accessed through the commercial service CompuServe, provides product information, press releases, technical support, downloadable patches, upgrades, and utilities.

To access NetWire, log in to CompuServe and type GO NET-WIRE, or use Services ➤ Go and enter NETWIRE into the Go dialog box in CIM (CompuServe Information Manager).

network

A group of computers and associated peripheral devices connected by a communications channel capable of sharing files and other resources between several users. A network can range from a *peer-to-peer network* connecting a small number of users in an office or department, to a *local-area network* (LAN) connecting many users over permanently installed cables and dial-up lines, to a *metropolitan-area network* (MAN) or *wide-area network* (WAN) connecting users on several different networks spread over a wide geographic area.

network adapter   See **network interface card.**

network administrator   The person responsible for the day-to-day operation and management of a network; also known as a system administrator. Duties of the network administrator can include the following:

- Planning for future expansion
- Installing new workstations and network peripheral devices
- Adding and removing authorized users
- Backing up the system and archiving important files
- Assigning and changing passwords
- Troubleshooting network problems
- Monitoring system performance
- Evaluating new products

- Installing hardware and software updates
- Training users

See also **configuration management.**

network analyzer   Any device that decodes and analyzes data transmitted over the network. A network analyzer may be hardware, software, or a combination of the two. Some analyzers troubleshoot network problems by decoding *packets*; others create and transmit their own packets.

network architecture   The design of a network, including the hardware, software, access methods, and the protocols in use. Several well-accepted network architectures have been defined by standards committees and major vendors. For example, the International Standards Organization (ISO) developed the seven-layer *ISO/OSI model* for computer-to-computer communications, and IBM designed *SNA* (Systems Network Architecture). Both of these architectures organize network functions into layers of hardware and software, with each layer building on the functions provided by the previous layer.

n

The ultimate goal is to allow different computers to exchange information freely in as transparent a fashion as possible.

network backbone
See **backbone.**

network board   See network interface card.

network control program
Abbreviated NCP. In an *SNA* (Systems Network Architecture) environment, performs the routing, error control, testing, and addressing of SNA devices.

network device driver   Software that controls the physical function of a *network interface card*, coordinating between the card and the other workstation hardware and software.

network directory   A directory located on a computer other than the one currently being used. Depending on access privileges, the rest of the disk may or may not be available to the user. On the Macintosh, a network directory is often referred to as a shared folder.
See also **network drive.**

network drive   A drive located on a computer other than the one currently being used that is available to users on the network.
See also **local drive, network directory.**

Network Driver Interface Specification   See **NDIS.**

Network File System   Abbreviated NFS. A distributed file-sharing system developed almost a decade ago by Sun Microsystems, Inc. NFS allows a computer on a network to use the files and peripheral devices of another networked computer as if they were local. NFS is platform-independent and runs on mainframes, minicomputers, RISC-based workstations, *diskless workstations*, and personal computers. NFS has been licensed and implemented by more than three hundred vendors.
See also **NetWare NFS, NetWare NFS Gateway.**

Network Information Services
Abbreviated NIS. A recent name for the security and file-access databases on Unix systems, previously known as the Yellow Pages. The NIS for most Unix systems

comprises the Unix host files /etc/hosts, /etc/passwd, and /etc/group.

network interface card

Abbreviated NIC. In networking, the PC *expansion board* that plugs into a personal computer or server and works with the network operating system to control the flow of information over the network. The network interface card is connected to the network media (*twisted pair*, *coaxial*, or *fiber-optic cable*), which in turn connects all the network interface cards in the network. Novell NetWare documentation uses the term network board rather than the more common term network interface card.

See also **PCMCIA**.

network layer

The third of seven layers of the *ISO/OSI* model for computer-to-computer communications. The network layer defines protocols for data routing to ensure that the information arrives at the correct destination node and manages communications errors.

Network Management Protocol

See **NMP**.

network operating system

Abbreviated NOS. In typical *client/server architecture* local-area networks (LANs), the NOS consists of two parts. The largest and most complex part is the system software running on the file server. This system software coordinates many functions, including user accounts and network access information, security, resource sharing, administrative functions, UPS and power monitoring, data protection, and error detection and control. A much smaller component of the NOS runs on each of the networked PCs or workstations attached to the network. Examples of client/server NOSs include Novell *NetWare*, *Banyan VINES*, and Microsoft *LAN Manager*.

In *peer-to-peer networks*, a part of the NOS is installed on each PC or workstation attached to the network and runs on top of the PC operating system. In some cases, the NOS may be installed on one PC designated as a file server, but this PC is not dedicated to the file server function; it is also available to run applications. Examples of peer-to-peer network operating systems include *LANtastic*, *Personal NetWare*, *PowerLAN*, and *Windows for Workgroups*.

n

network printer   See **print server.**

Network Support Encyclopedia
Abbreviated NSE. Novell's electronic database available in two volumes:

• **Standard Volume:** Includes Technotes, Novell lab bulletins, and product information.

• **Professional Volume:** Adds troubleshooting decision trees, NetWare application notes, and additional product manuals.

The NSE is accessible via *NetWare Express* or as a CD-ROM subscription, updated several times a year.

network topology   See **topology.**

NETx.COM   The workstation shell software used in Novell NetWare 2.*x* and 3.*x* networks. This program is loaded into memory on the workstation and begins transmission when the workstation requests network resources. In earlier versions of NetWare, NETx.COM was specific to the version of DOS running on the workstation. The only way to unload NETx.COM from memory is to reboot the workstation. NETx.COM has been replaced by NET.EXE, which runs with all versions of DOS.

In NetWare 4.*x*, a *Virtual Loadable Module* (VLM) provides backward compatibility with NETx.COM and older versions of the *NetWare shell.*

New Technology File System
See **NTFS.**

NexGen   Manufacturer of microprocessors, specializing in clones of *Intel's* popular Pentium chip.

The Nx586 is a clone of Intel's Pentium chip, available in 70, 75, 84, and 93 MHz versions, with a 32-bit address bus, 64-bit data bus, and 32K cache (16K code, 16K data). The Nx586 is not *pin-compatible* with the Pentium, and is therefore not a direct replacement; the chipset is only available from NexGen, and requires a unique motherboard design.

See also **AMD, Cyrix, P6.**

NEXT   Acronym for near-end crosstalk. Any interference that occurs close to a connector at either end of a cable. NEXT is usually measured near the source of the test signal.

See also **crosstalk.**

NFS   See **Network File System.**

NIC   See **network interface card.**

NII   Abbreviation for the National Information Infrastructure. A planned high-speed, public-access information service, designed to reach millions of schools, homes, and businesses throughout the United States.

NLICLEAR   A Novell NetWare 3.*x* server *NetWare Loadable Module* (NLM) that clears incomplete and unauthenticated logins so that the connection can be reused.

NLIST   A Novell NetWare 4.*x* workstation utility that provides a search function for objects in the *NetWare Directory Services* (NDS) database; you can view information on users, groups, volumes, servers, and queues. NLIST contains the functions previously found in *SLIST*, and *USERLIST* under NetWare 3.*x*.

NLM   See **NetWare Loadable Module.**

NLSP   See **NetWare Link Services Protocol.**

NMAGENT   A Novell NetWare server utility used with network hub and management programs.
   See also **NetWare Management System.**

NMENU   A Novell NetWare workstation utility that executes menus created for workstation users.

NMP   Abbreviation for Network Management Protocol. A set of protocols developed by AT&T designed to control certain network devices, such as modems and *T1 multiplexers.*

node   Any device attached to the network capable of communicating with other network devices. In Novell NetWare, a workstation is often called a node.

node number   The number that uniquely identifies a network interface card and distinguishes it from all others. Node numbers can be assigned in different ways. *Ethernet* node numbers are factory-set, so that no two Ethernet boards have the same number. *ARCnet* node numbers are set by jumpers or switches on each individual network interface card.

n

239

noise   In communications, extraneous signals on a transmission channel that degrade the quality or performance of the channel. Noise is often caused by interference from nearby power lines, electrical equipment, or spikes in the AC line voltage.

See also **crosstalk, NEXT.**

nominal velocity of propagation
   The speed at which a signal moves through a cable, expressed as a percentage or fraction of the speed of light in a vacuum. Some cable testers use this speed, along with the time it takes for a signal to return to the testing device, to calculate cable lengths.

nondedicated server   A server
upon which applications are available, while network management software runs in the background. Nondedicated servers are common in *peer-to-peer networks*.

non-preemptive multitasking
   Any form of *multitasking* in which the operating system cannot preempt a running task and move to the next task in the queue. The cooperative multitasking scheme used in Microsoft Windows is non-preemptive.

Programs are easy to write for this environment; however, a single badly written program can take over the whole system. By refusing to relinquish the processor, such a program can cause serious problems for other programs running at the same time. Poorly written non-preemptive multitasking can produce a kind of stuttering effect on running applications, depending on how the programs behave.

See also **preemptive multitasking, time-slice multitasking.**

nonvolatile memory   Any form of memory that holds its contents when power is removed. *ROM* (read-only memory), EPROM (erasable programmable read-only memory), and EEPROM (electrically erasable programmable read-only memory) are all nonvolatile memory.

no parity   See **parity.**

Norton Administrator for Networks   A package of network
management utilities from Symantec Corporation that includes hardware and software inventory, client monitoring, application metering, software distribution, and

virus detection. Several report formats are also available.

notebook computer A small, portable computer, about the size of a computer book, with a flat screen and a keyboard that fold together. A notebook computer is lighter and smaller than a laptop computer. Recent advances in battery technology allow them to run for as long as nine hours between charges. Some models use *flash memory* rather than conventional hard disks for program and data storage; other models offer a range of business applications in ROM (read-only memory). Many offer *PCMCIA* expansion connections for additional peripheral devices, such as modems, fax modems, and network connections.

See also **laptop computer, palmtop computer.**

Novell AppWare A suite of software development tools from Novell, used to create custom and commercial cross-network applications. AppWare contains two major components:

• **Visual AppBuilder:** A development system for creating

applications with prewritten, reusable software *modules.*

• **AppWare Bus:** An architecture that allows the development tools to take advantage of these reusable software modules.

Novell, Inc. A leading *network operating system* software company. Independent surveys show that Novell can claim up to 70 percent of the network operating system market with products such as Novell *NetWare* 2.*x*, 3.*x*, and 4.*x* and *Personal NetWare.* Novell has grown by a carefully planned series of acquisitions over the years, including Digital Research, Inc., developers of DR-DOS, bought in 1991; UNIX Systems Laboratories (USL), acquired from AT&T in 1993; and WordPerfect Corporation in 1994.

Novell Authorized Education Center See **NAEC.**

Novell DOS A version of DOS, originally developed by Digital Research and called DR-DOS, now owned by Novell, Inc., and called Novell DOS. Novell DOS 7 includes built-in *peer-to-peer networking*, network management

n

utilities, *file compression*, and *preemptive multitasking*. It is compatible with MS-DOS, PC-DOS, and Microsoft Windows applications.

Novell Education Academic Partner   See NEAP.

Novell NetWare   See NetWare.

Novell NetWare Lite   See NetWare Lite.

NPATH   A Novell NetWare 4.*x* utility used to determine the location of files as well as other related information.

.

NPRINT   A Novell NetWare workstation utility used to print a file that has been formatted for a printer.

NPRINTER   A Novell NetWare *Netware Loadable Module* that allows any printer attached to a server to be a network printer, without the need for a separate print server.

ns   See nanosecond.

NSFNET   Abbreviation for National Science Foundation Network. The NSFNET is not the Internet, but it is certainly a part of the Internet.

NTFS   Abbreviation for NT File System. The native file system used by *Windows NT*, which supports the following:

• Up to 256 characters for file names

• A wide range of *permissions* for sharing files

• A transaction log, which allows Windows NT to complete any incomplete file-related tasks before continuing if the operating system is interrupted

• The *file allocation table* (FAT) file system and the *High-Performance File System* (HPFS) used by OS/2

NUC   Novell NetWare software for a *UnixWare* client connecting to a Novell file server; NUC starts the NetWare Unix Client for connecting to the server.

NUI   See **NetWare Users International**.

null   A character that has all the binary digits set to zero (ASCII 0), and therefore has no value. In programming, a null character is used for several special purposes, including padding fields or serving as delimiter characters. In the C programming language, for example, a null character indicates the end of a character string.

null modem   A short *RS-232-C* cable that connects two personal computers so that they can communicate without the use of modems. The cable connects the two computers' serial ports, and certain lines in the cable are crossed over so that the wires used for sending by one computer are used for receiving data by the other computer; see the accompanying illustration.

See also **modem eliminator.**

NUT   A Novell NetWare server utility that is the *NetWare Loadable Module* (NLM) utility user interface for NetWare 3.*x*

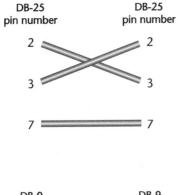
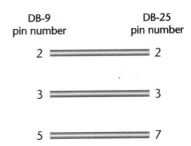
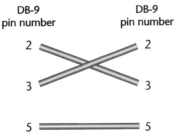

NULL MODEM

modules. It must be loaded on NetWare 3.*x* servers in order for most utilities to function. In NetWare 4.x, NUT allows you to use NetWare 3.x NLMs that use NUT's library of functions and routines.

See also **NWSNUT.**

NVER   A Novell NetWare workstation utility that displays network, server, and *OS/2 Requester* version information.

NWADMIN   A Novell NetWare 4.*x* workstation utility that combines most of the functions of the *NETADMIN, PCONSOLE, FILER, PARTMGR,* and *RCONSOLE* utilities under a single *graphical user interface.*

NWEXTRACT   A Novell NetWare 4.*x* workstation utility that allows a network administrator to reinstall a NetWare system file after it has been accidentally deleted from the server. NWEXTRACT locates and uncompresses the specified file from CD-ROM, and then stores the file in the default location on the server.

NWSNUT   A Novell NetWare server utility that is the *NetWare Loadable Module* (NLM) utility user interface for NetWare 4.*x* modules. It must be loaded on 4.*x* servers in order for most utilities to function.

See also **NUT.**

NWUSER   A Novell NetWare 4.*x* workstation utility that lets users display or modify their workstation's drive mappings, server attachments, and print queues using a simple graphical user interface.

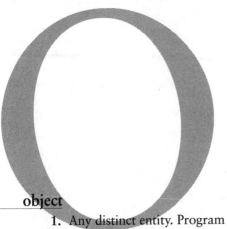

object

1. Any distinct entity. Program objects can represent applications such as word processors, spreadsheets, and so on. Folder objects can represent a directory and contain a group of files, a group of programs, or a group of other folders. Data-file objects can include information such as text, memos, letters, spreadsheets, video, and sound. Device objects can be printers, fax modems, plotters, servers, and CD-ROMS.

2. In *Object Linking and Embedding* (OLE), an object can be any user-selected group of data, such as a block of text, a set of spreadsheet cells, a chart, sound, or a graphical image. This data can be embedded in or linked to another document created by a different OLE application.

3. In *object-oriented programming*, a program consists of a set of related but self-contained objects that can contain both code and data.

See also **container object, leaf object, NetWare Directory Services.**

Object Linking and Embedding
Abbreviated OLE, pronounced "oh-lay." A Microsoft protocol for application-to-application exchange and communications using data objects. OLE works at a much higher level, with greater user involvement and more convenience, than *Dynamic Data Exchange* (DDE), the other interprocess method.

Data objects can be either embedded or linked. If the source data in its original form is actually stored inside the other application program's data file, the data is embedded. In this case, there are two separate copies of the data: the original data and the embedded copy. Any changes made to the original document will not be made in the compound document unless the embedded object is updated.

If the data still exists in a separate file and a set of pointers to this data is stored in the other application program's data file, the data is linked. In this case, only one copy of the data exists; any changes made in the original document will be made automatically in the compound document.

To discover if an application supports OLE, check the Edit menu for commands such as Paste Link, Paste Special, and Insert Object. If these commands are present, the application supports OLE.

See also **OpenDoc**.

object-oriented

A term that can be applied to any computer system, operating system, programming language, application, or graphical user interface that supports the use of *objects*.

object-oriented graphics

Graphics that are constructed from individual components, such as lines, arcs, circles, and squares. The image is defined mathematically rather than as a set of dots, as in a bitmapped graphic. Object-oriented graphics are used in illustration, drawing, and CAD programs, and are also known as vector graphics or structured graphics.

Object-oriented graphics allow the user to manipulate a part of an image without redrawing. Unlike bitmapped graphics, all or parts of object-oriented graphics can be resized or rotated without introducing any distortion.

object-oriented programming

Abbreviated OOP. A programming model that views a program as a set of self-contained *objects*. These objects interact with other objects by passing messages between them. Object-oriented programming also lets you create procedures that work with objects whose exact type may not be known until the program actually runs.

In object-oriented programming, each object contains both data and code and is completely self contained. The program incorporates an object by making it part of a layered hierarchy. Object-oriented programming is the result of many years of theoretical development, and it is seen by many to be the current extension of the theory behind modular programming, in which code is combined into reusable modules.

OCR   See **optical character recognition**.

octet   See **byte**.

ODBC   Abbreviation for Open Database Connectivity. An *Application Program Interface* (API) from Microsoft that allows a single application to access many different types of database and file formats.

odd parity   See **parity**.

ODI   See **Open Data-link Interface.**

ODINSUP   Abbreviation for Open Data-link Interface/Network Driver Interface Specification Support, also written as ODI/NDIS Support.

A Novell interface that allows the coexistence of two network driver interfaces: Microsoft's *NDIS* (Network Driver Interface Specification) and Novell's *ODI* (Open Data-link Interface). ODINSUP allows a DOS or Microsoft Windows workstation to connect to dissimilar networks through a single network interface card, and to use them as if they were a single network.

ODINSUP also allows NDIS protocol stacks to communicate through the ODI's *link-support layer* (LSL) and *multiple-link interface driver* (MLID), so that ODI and NDIS protocol stacks can coexist in the same system, using a single ODI MLID.

OEM   Abbreviation for original equipment manufacturer. The

original manufacturer of a hardware subsystem or component. For example, Canon makes the print engine used in many laser printers, including those from Hewlett-Packard (HP); in this case, Canon is the OEM and HP is a *value-added reseller* (VAR).

OFF   A Novell NetWare server utility that clears messages from the server screen. This command performs the same function as does the *CLS* command.

offline   Describes a printer or other peripheral device that is not in ready mode, and is therefore unavailable for use.
See also **online.**

offline reader   An application that lets you read postings to *USENET newsgroups* without having to stay connected to the *Internet.*

The program downloads all the newsgroup postings you have not read and disconnects from your service provider. You can then read the postings at your convenience without incurring online charges or tying up your telephone line. If you reply to any of these postings, the program will automatically upload them to the

O

247

right newsgroup the next time you connect to your service provider.

OLE   See **Object Linking and Embedding.**

online

1. Most broadly, any work done on a computer instead of by more traditional manual means.

2. Any function available directly on a computer, such as an application's help system.

3. Describes a peripheral device, such as a printer or modem, when it is directly connected to a computer and ready to operate.

4. In communications, describes a computer connected to a remote computer over a network or a modem link.

See also **offline.**

online service   A service that provides an online connection via modem for access to various services. Online services fall into four main groups:

- **Commercial services:** Services such as America Online, CompuServe, and Prodigy charge a monthly membership fee for access to online *forums, e-mail*

services, software libraries, and online conferences. Some of the larger services, such as America Online and CompuServe, provide you with free software you run on your computer to access their services; GEnie and Delphi users must provide their own *communications software.*

- **Internet:** The Internet is a worldwide network of computer systems located at government and educational institutions. The Internet is not always easy to access nor is it always easy to use, but the wealth of information available is staggering. The main problem for casual users is that there is no central listing of everything that is available.

- **Specialist databases:** Specific databases aimed at researchers can be accessed through online services such as Dow Jones News/Retrieval for business news and Lexis and Nexis for the legal information and news archives.

- **Local Bulletin boards:** A small network of two or three computers, giving access to special-interest information, software libraries, e-mail, online conferences, and games. There are thousands of small, local bulletin board systems (BBSs), often run from private homes, by local PC Users Groups or by local schools.

open architecture   A vendor-independent computer design that is publicly available and well understood within the industry. An open architecture allows the user to configure the computer easily by adding expansion cards.

See also **closed architecture.**

Open Data-link Interface   Abbreviated ODI. A Novell specification, released in 1989, that allows multiple *network interface card device drivers* and *protocols* to share a single network interface card without conflict. (See the accompanying illustration.)

ODI defines an interface that separates device drivers from *protocol stacks* and lets multiple protocol stacks share the same network hardware. Here are the main components:

- The *multiple-link interface driver* (MLID) manages the sending and receiving of packets to and from the network.

- The *link-support layer* (LSL) is the interface layer between the device driver and the protocol stacks. Any ODI LAN driver can communicate with any ODI protocol stack via the LSL.

O

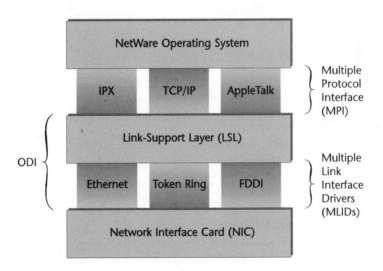

OPEN DATA-LINK INTERFACE

The MLI (Multiple-Link Interface) communicates with the network interface cards through an MLID and consists of three main components:

- The media-support module (MSM) manages the details of interfacing ODI MLIDs to the LSL and to the operating system.
- The topology-specific module (TSM) manages operations that are specific to a particular media type, such as Ethernet or Token Ring.
- The hardware-specific module (HSM) is specific to a particular network interface card. It handles adapter initialization, reset, shutdown, packet reception, timeout detection, and multicast addressing.

See also **NDIS, ODINSUP.**

OpenDoc A specification for creating compound documents from Apple, IBM, Borland, and Novell. OpenDoc manages text, spreadsheets, graphics, sound, and video as objects that can be created in one application and then inserted into another.

OpenDoc is similar in many respects to Microsoft's *Object Linking and Embedding* (OLE) specification, but OpenDoc provides for greater network support, and also has a certification process

to ensure that applications work together (something that Microsoft does not currently have with OLE).

Open Shortest Path First
See **OSPF.**

Open Systems Interconnection
See **ISO/OSI model.**

OpenView A popular network management package from Hewlett-Packard that includes a server platform, Network Node Manager, OperationsCenter, and other support services. OpenView is based on HP-UX, a Unix variant.

operating system Abbreviated OS. That software responsible for allocating system resources, including memory, processor time, disk space, and peripheral devices such as printers, modems, and monitors. All applications use the operating system to gain access to these resources as necessary. The operating system is the first program loaded into the computer as it boots, and it remains in memory throughout the session.

See also **kernel, microkernel, network operating system.**

optical character recognition

Abbreviated OCR. The computer recognition of printed or typed characters. OCR is usually performed using a standard optical scanner and special software, although some systems use special readers. The text is reproduced just as though it had been typed. Certain advanced systems can even resolve neatly handwritten characters.

See also **document management**.

optical drive
A high-capacity disk-storage device that uses a laser to read and write information. Because optical drives are relatively slow, they are used for archiving information and for other applications for which high access speed is not critical.

See also **high-capacity storage system, jukebox**.

Orange Book
The US Department of Defense Standard 5200.28, which specifies security levels.

See also **security**.

organization object
In Novell NetWare 4.*x*, a *container object* that helps to organize other objects in the tree. You must have at least one organization object; usually the name of your company or department, and each organization object must appear one level below the *root object*.

See also **leaf object, NetWare Directory Services**.

original equipment manufacturer
See OEM.

OS/2
A 32-bit *multitasking* operating system for Intel 80386 (or later) processors. OS/2 supports the *file allocation table* (FAT) file system, the *High-Performance File System* (HPFS), and installable file systems, such as a CD-ROM file system.

OS/2 was developed jointly by Microsoft and IBM as the successor to DOS, and Windows was developed as a stop-gap measure until OS/2 was ready. When Microsoft chose to back Windows, placing considerable resources behind the breakthrough release of Windows 3.0, IBM took control of OS/2 development. In spring 1992, IBM released OS/2 version 2.0, which won many industry awards for its technical achievements. The following OS/2 versions have been released by IBM:

- **OS/2 2.0:** Allowed multitasking of up to 240 separate

DOS sessions, along with Windows, OS/2 1.*x* and 2.*x* programs, and use of up to 4 gigabytes (GB) of memory. OS/2 2.0 was released with an *object-oriented* graphical user interface; a set of built-in desktop applications, including personal productivity programs, graphics, and games; and a structured programming language called REXX.

- **OS/2 2.1:** Released in 1993, adds support for Windows 3.1 programs, including those requiring Windows Enhanced mode. Other features include support for more 256-color SuperVGA chipsets, better CD-ROM and *SCSI* interface support, and support for *PC Cards*, Advanced Power Management for portable computers, enhanced support for pen-based systems, and the MultiMedia Presentation Manager (MMPM/2).
- **OS/2 for Windows:** Released at the end of 1993 for users who already have Windows 3.1 installed on their system.
- **OS/2 Warp:** Also known as OS/2 Version 3.0. Released in late 1994 as a significant upgrade to OS/2, and included a BonusPak of major applications programs encompassing multimedia, desktop fax capabilities, and one of the best and most complete sets of Internet access tools available anywhere.

- **OS/2 Warp Connect:** Released in 1995 with strong network support, including Peer for OS/2, which added peer-to-peer networking between OS/2 systems, as well as requesters for NetWare, *LAN Server, Windows NT Server*, and IBM's *LAN Distance*. Warp Connect also included additional TCP/IP support, and a version of *Lotus Notes* called Lotus Notes Express.

OS/2 client   Any computer running *OS/2* that connects to a network. OS/2 client workstations support *IPX/SPX, NetBIOS*, and *named pipes*.

OSI   Abbreviation for Open Systems Interconnection. See **ISO/OSI model.**

OSPF   Abbreviation for Open Shortest Path First. A routing protocol used on *TCP/IP* networks that takes into account network loading and *bandwidth* when routing information over the network. *Routers* maintain a map of the network and swap information on the current status of each network link. OSPF incorporates least-cost routing, equal-cost routing, and *load balancing*.

See also **RIP.**

output   Computer-generated information that is displayed on the
screen, printed, written to disk or
tape, or sent over a communications link to another computer.
See also **input/output.**

outsourcing   To subcontract
a company's data processing
operations to outside contractors
rather than maintain corporate
hardware, software, and staff.
Outsourcing is often used as a
cost-cutting mechanism, although
the cost savings can be very difficult to quantify.
See also **downsizing.**

O

P6 The latest microprocessor in the 80x86 family from Intel. The 32-bit P6 has a 64-bit data path between the processor and cache, and runs at 133 MHz, although a version of the chip capable of running at 166 MHz is expected shortly. The P6 contains the equivalent of 5.5 million transistors, and is aimed at the server and very high-end desktop markets.

P See **peta-.**

PABX See **private automatic branch exchange.**

packet Any block of data sent over a network. Each packet contains sender, receiver, and error-control information, in addition to the actual message. Packets may be fixed- or variable-length, and they will be reassembled if necessary when they reach their destination. The actual format of a packet depends on the protocol that creates the packet; some protocols use special packets to control communications functions in addition to data packets.

See also **Ethernet packet, packet switching.**

packet assembler/disassembler
See **PAD.**

Packet Burst Protocol
Abbreviated PBP. A Novell NetWare protocol built on top of *IPX* that speeds up the transfer of multi-packet *NetWare Core Protocol* (NCP) data transfers between a workstation and a server by removing the need to sequence and acknowledge every packet. Using PBP, a workstation or server can transmit a burst of up to 128 packets before requiring an acknowledgment, thus reducing network traffic.

packet filter A process used by *bridges* to limit protocol-specific traffic to one segment of the network, to isolate e-mail domains, and to perform other traffic-control functions. The network administrator sets the packet filtering specifications for each bridge. If a packet matches the specifications, the bridge can either accept or reject it.

255

Packet-level Procedure   See **PAP.**

packet-switched network   A network that consists of a series of interconnected circuits that route individual *packets* of data over one of several routes, offering flexibility and high reliability.

A packet-switched network may also be called a "cloud" because it contains many different possible connections and routes that a packet might take to reach its destination.

The term often refers to networks using the international standard *X.25*.

See also **packet switching.**

packet switching   A data-transmission method that simultaneously routes and transmits data *packets* from many different customers over a communications channel or telephone line, thus optimizing use of the line.

An addressed packet is routed from node to node until it reaches its destination, although related packets may not all follow the same route to that destination. Because long messages may be divided into several packets, packet sequence numbers are used

to reassemble the original message at the destination node.

See also **packet-switched network.**

PAD   Abbreviation for packet assembler/disassembler. A device that is connected to a *packet-switched network* and that converts a serial data stream from a character-oriented device, such as a *bridge* or *router*, into packets suitable for transmission. It also disassembles packets back into characters for transmission to the character device. PADs are often used to connect a terminal or computer to an *X.25* packet-switched network.

paged memory management unit   Abbreviated PMMU. A specialized chip designed to manage *virtual memory*. High-end processors, such as the Motorola 68030 and 68040 and the Intel 80486 and Pentium, have all the functions of a PMMU built into the chip itself.

page-mode RAM   A memory-management technique used to speed up the performance of *dynamic RAM* (DRAM).

In a page-mode memory system, the memory is divided into pages

by specialized DRAM chips. Consecutive accesses to *memory addresses* in the same page result in a
page-mode cycle that takes about
half the time of a regular DRAM
cycle. For example, a normal
DRAM cycle can take from 130 to
180 nanoseconds, while a typical
page-mode cycle can be completed
in 30 to 40 nanoseconds.

palmtop computer   A small,
battery-powered *portable computer*, often weighing about a
pound, that you can hold in one
hand and operate with the other.

Many palmtop computers have
small screens of eight lines by
forty characters and tiny keyboards. Some models have Lotus
1-2-3 or similar software already
built into ROM (read-only memory). Most run a customized version of DOS; others use
proprietary operating systems
that require custom-written software. The main difference between palmtop computers and
laptop computers is that palmtops
are usually powered by off-the-
shelf batteries. Because of this
power limit, palmtops do not
have floppy or hard disk drives.

See also **notebook computer,
PDA.**

PAP

   1. Abbreviation for Packet-
level Procedure, an *X.25 full-
duplex* protocol for the transfer
of *packets* between a computer
and a modem.

   2. Abbreviation for Printer Access Protocol, a part of the *Apple-
Talk Filing Protocol* used to
manage network printing.

parallel communications   The
transmission of information from
computer to computer, or from
computer to peripheral device, in
which all the *bits* that make up
the character are transmitted at
the same time over a multiline
cable.

See also **serial communications.**

parallel port   An *input/output
(I/O) port* that manages information 8 *bits* at a time, often used to
connect a parallel printer.

See also **parallel communications, RS-232-C, serial communications, serial port.**

parallel processing   A computing method that can be performed
by systems containing two or
more processors operating simultaneously. Parallel processing uses
several processors, all working on

p

257

different aspects of the same program at the same time, in order to share the computational load.

Parallel processing computers can achieve incredible speeds; the Cray X-MP48 peaks at 1000 million floating-point operations per second (1000 MFLOP) using four extremely powerful processors, while parallel-hypercube systems, first marketed by Intel, can exceed 65,536 processors with speeds of up to 262 billion floating-point operations per second (262 GFLOP).

What is all this speed used for? Applications such as weather forecasting, where the predictive programs can take as long to run as the weather actually takes to arrive, 3-D seismic modeling, groundwater and toxic flow studies, and modeling full-motion dinosaur images used in movies.

parent directory   In a hierarchical directory system, such as that used by DOS, OS/2, and Unix, the directory immediately above the *current directory*. The special symbol .. is shorthand for the name of the parent directory.

See also **period and double-period directories.**

parity   In communications, a simple form of error checking that uses an extra or redundant bit after the data bits but before the stop bit or bits. Parity may be set as follows:

- **Odd parity:** Indicates that the sum of all the 1 bits in the byte plus the parity bit must be odd. If the total is already odd, the parity bit is set to 0; if it is even, the parity bit is set to 1.

- **Even parity:** If the sum of all the 1 bits is even, the parity bit must be set to 0; if it is odd, the parity bit must be set to 1.

- **Mark parity:,** The parity bit is always set to 1 and is used as the eighth bit.

- **Space parity:** The parity bit is set to 0 and is used as the eighth bit.

- **None:** If parity is set to none, there is no parity bit, and no parity checking is performed.

The parity settings used by both communicating computers must match. Most online services, such as CompuServe, use no parity and an eight-bit data word.

See also **asynchronous transmission, parity checking, parity error.**

parity bit   An extra or redundant bit used to detect transmission errors. See also **parity.**

parity checking   A check mechanism applied to a character or series of characters that uses the addition of extra or redundant *parity bits*. Parity checking is useful for a variety of purposes, including asynchronous communications and computer memory coordination.
See also **parity**.

parity error   A mismatch in *parity bits* that indicates an error in transmitted data.
See also **parity**.

partition

1. A portion of a hard disk that the operating system treats as if it were a separate drive. In DOS, a hard disk can be divided into several partitions. A primary DOS partition, generally assigned the drive letter C, might contain files that start the computer running. You could also set up an extended DOS partition and a non-DOS partition used for a different operating system. In Novell NetWare, a server must have a NetWare partition defined in order to function as a part of the NetWare file system. Other partitions can manage file systems used by other operating systems.

2. In Novell NetWare 4.*x*, a grouping or collection of objects in the *NetWare Directory Services* (NDS) global database. Each partition consists of a *container object*, all the objects contained in it, and data about all those objects. Partitions do not include any information about the file system or the directories or files contained there.
See also **disk mirroring, leaf object, PARTMGR, root object, volume**.

partition table   In Novell NetWare Directory Services (NDS), a list on each server containing the NDS *replicas*. For each replica on the server, the partition table contains the partition name, type, time stamp, and partition state.

PARTMGR   A Novell NetWare 4.*x* workstation utility used to manage *partitions* (collections of objects) or *replicas* (copies of partitions) in the *NetWare Directory Database* (NDD). The Windows-based utility, *NWADMIN*, is also used to manage partitions.

passive hub   A device used in some networks to split a transmission signal, allowing additional *hubs* to be added to the network, sometimes at the expense of distance.

See also **active hub.**

password A security method that identifies a specific, authorized user of a computer system or network by a unique string of characters. The user must type these characters to gain access to the computer or network.

In general, passwords should be a mixture of letters and numbers, and longer than six characters. Here are some general guidelines:

- Passwords should be kept secret and changed frequently. The worst passwords are the obvious ones: people's names or initials, place names, phone numbers, birth dates, or complete English words. There are a limited number of words in the English language, and it is easy for a computer to try them all relatively quickly.

- Change all passwords every 90 days, and change those associated with high security privileges every month.

- Some systems provide default passwords, such as MANAGER, SERVICE, or GUEST, as part of the installation process.

These default passwords should be changed immediately.

- Limit concurrent sessions to one per system.

- Do not allow more than two or three invalid password attempts before disconnecting.

- Do not allow generic accounts.

- Promptly remove the accounts of transferred or terminated people, as well as all unused accounts.

- Review the security log files periodically.

See also **NCSC, security.**

password protection The use of one or more passwords to prevent unauthorized access to computer systems.

See also **password, NCSC, security.**

patch panel A panel, usually located in a wiring closet, that contains rows of telephone-type modular jacks. A patch panel allows the network administrator to connect, disconnect, move, and test network devices by changing these connections.

path The complete location of a directory or file in the file system.

See also **filespec.**

PAUDIT   A Novell NetWare 3.*x* workstation utility that displays the contents of the audit file NET$ACCT.DAT, created when server *accounting* is enabled. In NetWare 4.*x*, this function is performed by the *ATOTAL* workstation utility.

PB   See **petabyte**.

PBP   See **Packet Burst Protocol**.

PBX   See **private branch exchange**.

PC-based router   A router that operates on a standard Intel-based personal computer, such as the *NetWare Multiprotocol Router* or *Multiprotocol Router Plus*.

PC Card   A term that describes add-in cards that conform to the *PCMCIA* (Personal Computer Memory Card International Association) standard. A PC Card uses a 68-pin connector with longer power and ground pins that will always engage before the signal pins do.

PC Card slot   An opening in the case of a *portable computer*,

intended to receive a *PC Card*; also known as a *PCMCIA* slot.

PC-DOS   The version of the DOS operating system supplied with PCs made by IBM. PC-DOS and *MS-DOS* began as virtually identical operating systems, with only a few minor differences in device driver names and file sizes, but after the release of DOS 6 (MS-DOS 6.2 and PC-DOS 6.1), the two grew much further apart.

   PC-DOS 7 was released by IBM in 1995, and includes the REXX programming language, enhanced PCMCIA support, the popular Stacker file-compression program from Stac Electronics, and FILEUP, an application used to synchronize files between portable and desktop PCs.

PCI local bus   Abbreviation for Peripheral Component Interconnect local bus. A specification introduced by Intel in 1992 for a local bus that allows up to ten PCI-compliant *expansion cards* to be plugged into the computer. One of these expansion cards must be the PCI controller card, but the others can include a video card, network interface card, SCSI interface, or any other basic function.

261

The PCI controller exchanges information with the computer's processor, either 32 or 64 bits at a time, and allows intelligent PCI adapters to perform certain tasks concurrently with the main processor by using *bus-mastering* techniques.

PCI is compatible with *ISA, EISA,* and *MCA* expansion buses for backward compatibility with older technologies. PCI can operate at a bus speed of 32 MHz, and can manage a maximum throughput of 132 megabytes per second with a 32-bit data path, or a rate of 264 megabytes per second with a 64-bit data path.

See also **local bus, Plug-and-Play.**

PCMCIA Abbreviation for Personal Computer Memory Card International Association. A nonprofit association, formed in 1989, with more than 320 members in the computer and electronics industries, that developed a standard for credit-card-sized, plug-in adapters designed for portable computers.

Several versions of the standard have been approved by PCMCIA:

- **Type I:** The thinnest PC Card, only 3.3 millimeters (0.13 inch) thick, used for memory enhancements, including *dynamic RAM, static RAM,* and *flash memory.*
- **Type II:** A card used for modems or network interface cards, 5 millimeters (0.2 inch) thick; may also hold a Type I card.
- **Type III:** A 10.5 millimeter (0.4 inch) card, used for *mini-hard disks* and other devices that need more space, including wireless network interface cards; may also hold two Type I or Type II cards.

Version 1 of the hardware standard was released in September 1990. Version 2, issued in September 1991, added software for input/output PC Cards for modems and disk drives. Version 2.01 contained minor corrections to the earlier standards, but no new specifications.

Software known as *socket services* provides a standard interface to the hardware; software known as *card services* coordinates access to the PC Cards themselves.

In theory, each PCMCIA adapter can support 16 PC Card sockets (if there is enough space), and up to 255 adapters can be installed in a PC that follows the PCMCIA standard; in other words, PCMCIA allows up to 4080 PC Cards on one computer.

The majority of PCMCIA devices are modems, *Ethernet* and

Token Ring network adapters, dynamic RAM, and flash memory cards, although mini-hard disks, *wireless LAN* adapters, and *SCSI* adapters are also available.

PCMCIA slot   See PC Card slot.

PC Memory Card International Association
See PCMCIA.

PCONSOLE   A Novell NetWare workstation utility used to set up and manage *print queues* and *print servers* on the network.

PDA   Abbreviation for personal digital assistant. A tiny, pen-based, battery-powered *palmtop computer* that combines personal organization software with fax and e-mail facilities into a unit that fits into your pocket. PDAs are available from several manufacturers, including Apple's Newton, and others from Casio, Tandy, Toshiba, Motorola, Sharp, Sony, GRiD, and AT&T.

PDN   See public data network.

peer-to-peer   A network *architecture* in which two or more nodes can communicate with each other

directly, without the need for any intermediary devices. In a peer-to-peer system, a node can be both a client and a server.

See also peer-to-peer network.

peer-to-peer network   A local area network in which drives, files, and printers on each PC can be available to every other PC on the network, eliminating the need for a dedicated file server. Each PC can still run local applications.

Peer-to-peer networks introduce their own system management problems, including administration and responsibility for system backup, reliability, and security. Peer-to-peer systems are often used in relatively small networks, with two to ten users, and can be based on DOS, OS/2, or Unix.

Popular peer-to-peer network operating systems include Novell's *Personal NetWare*, Artisoft's *LANtastic*, and *PowerLAN* from Performance Technology.

pen computer   A computer that accepts handwriting as input. Using a pen-like stylus, users print neatly on a screen. The computer translates this input using pattern-recognition techniques. Users can also choose selections from on-screen menus using the stylus.

P

Pen extensions to PC-DOS, Microsoft Windows, and OS/2 are available. In the future, pen computing may be used for filling in forms, such as job applications, insurance reports, and medical records.

See also **PDA.**

Pentium   A 64-bit microprocessor introduced by Intel in 1993. After losing a courtroom battle to maintain control of the *x*86 designation, Intel has named this member of its family the Pentium rather than the 80586 or the 586. The Pentium represents the continuing evolution of the *80486* family of microprocessors and adds several notable features, including 8 K instruction code and data *caches*, and a built-in *floating-point processor* and *memory management unit*. It also has a *superscalar* design and dual *pipelining*, which allow the Pentium to execute more than one instruction per clock cycle.

Available in a whole range of clock speeds, from 60 MHz all the way up to 180 MHz versions, the Pentium is equivalent to 3.1 million transistors, more than twice that of the 80486.

See also **P6.**

PerfectOffice   A popular *software suite* from Novell. The Standard version of PerfectOffice bundles WordPerfect (word processor), Quattro Pro (spreadsheet), WordPerfect Presentations (presentation graphics), InfoCentral (personal information manager), Envoy (portable document creator and viewer), and GroupWise client (previously available as WordPerfect Office). The Professional version adds the Paradox database and the VisualAppBuilder development tool.

period and double-period directories   In a hierarchical directory system, such as that used by DOS, OS/2, and Unix, a shorthand way of referring to directories. The period (.) represents the *current directory*, and the double period (..) represents the directory immediately above the current directory.

See also **parent directory, root directory.**

Peripheral Component Interconnect   See **PCI local bus.**

permanent swap file   A swap file that, once created, is used over and over again. This file is used in *virtual memory* operations, where hard-disk space is used in place of *RAM* (random-access memory).

See also **swap file, temporary swap file.**

permission   In a network or *multiuser* environment, the ability of a user to access certain system resources. Permissions are based on the rights given to *user accounts* by the network administrator.

See also **rights.**

personal communications services   Abbreviated PCS. A class of applications that includes wireless communications for *portable computer* users.

personal digital assistant   See **PDA.**

Personal Information Manager   Abbreviated PIM. A multipurpose software package that combines a word processor, database, and other accessory modules to allow the user to manipulate data in a less structured way than required by conventional programs. A PIM can store notes, memos, names and addresses, appointments, and to-do lists, and it may be part of the software used in a *PDA* (personal digital assistant).

Personal NetWare   Novell's *peer-to-peer network* replacement for *NetWare Lite*, released in 1994, that provides DOS and Microsoft Windows users with the ability to share files, printers, CD-ROMs, and other resources, as well as run standard network applications. Other features include simplified network administration, increased security, and a single login so that users can view or access all network resources at once.

Personal NetWare can manage up to fifty workstations per server and up to fifty servers on each network, giving a maximum of 2500 nodes per network.

peta-   Abbreviated P. A metric system prefix for one quadrillion, or 10^{15}. In computing, based on the *binary* system, peta has the value of 1,125,899,906,842,624, or the power of 2 (2^{50}) closest to 1 quadrillion.

petabyte Abbreviated PB. Usually 1,125,899,906,842,624 bytes
(2^{50}), but may also refer to 1 quadrillion bytes (10^{15}).

PGP Abbreviation for Pretty
Good Privacy. A popular shareware public-key *encryption*
program, written by Phil
Zimmermann, available at no
charge from certain Internet sites.

physical address See **hardware
address.**

physical drive A real device in
the computer that you can see or
touch, as opposed to a conceptual
or *logical drive*. One physical
drive may be divided into several
logical drives, which are parts of
the hard disk that function as if
they were separate disk drives.
See also **partition, volume.**

physical layer The first and lowest of the seven layers in the
ISO/OSI model for computer-to-
computer communications. The
physical layer defines the physical, electrical, mechanical, and
functional procedures used to connect the equipment.

physical unit See **PU.**

PIM See **Personal Information
Manager.**

pin-compatible A description of
a chip or other electronic component with connecting pins exactly
equivalent to the connecting pins
used by a different device. With a
pin-compatible chip, you can easily
upgrade a system by replacing the
older chip with the newer version.
See also **plug-compatible.**

PING A Novell NetWare 4.*x*
menu utility used to determine if
a network node is reachable.
PING sends out a special diagnostic packet, an *ICMP* echo request
packet, which forces the node to
acknowledge that the packet
reached its destination.
See also **ping.**

ping A method of testing for network connectivity by transmitting
a special diagnostic packet (an
ICMP echo request) to a specific
node on the network, thus forcing
the node to acknowledge that the
packet reached its destination.
When ping is used with
TCP/IP systems, it is said to be an
acronym for Packet Internet
Groper. It is often used as a verb,
as in "ping that workstation to
see if it is awake."

pinouts   The configuration and purpose of each pin in a multi-pin connector.

pipe   A section of memory that can be used by a command to pass information to a second command for processing. In DOS and OS/2, a pipe is symbolized by the vertical bar (|) character.

A special form of pipe, known as a *named pipe*, originated in the Unix operating system. A named pipe allows two processes to exchange information. This concept has been extended in several network operating systems as a method of interprocess communication, allowing data to be exchanged between applications running on networked computers.

pipelining

1. In processor architecture, a method of fetching and decoding instructions that ensures that the processor never needs to wait; as soon as one instruction is executed, the next one is ready.

2. In *parallel processing*, the method used to pass instructions from one processing unit to another.

platform

1. An operating system environment, such as a NetWare platform or a Unix platform.

2. A computer system based on a specific microprocessor, such as an Intel-based platform or a PowerPC-based platform.

platform-specific routers
Routers based on a specific and proprietary hardware architecture, which is usually vendor-specific.

plenum cable   Cable with a special Teflon coating designed for use in suspended ceilings, inside walls, or between floors. This Teflon coating provides low flame-spread and low, nontoxic smoke in the case of an accident. Plenum cables should meet the CMR (Communications Riser Cable) or CMP (Communications Plenum Cable) specifications of the National Electric Code, and are often used for cable runs in air return areas.

Plug-and-Play   Abbreviated PnP. A standard from Compaq, Microsoft, Intel, and Phoenix that

p

defines automatic techniques designed to make PC configuration simple and straightforward. Currently, ISA expansion boards are covered by the specification, but the standard may soon cover *SCSI* and *PCMCIA* buses also.

PnP adapters contain configuration information stored in non-volatile memory, which includes vendor information, serial number, and checksum information. The PnP chipset allows each adapter to be isolated, one at a time, until all cards have been properly identified by the operating system.

The PnP-compatible BIOS isolates and identifies PnP cards at boot time, and when you insert a new card, the BIOS performs an auto-configuration sequence enabling the new card with appropriate settings.

New PCs with flash BIOS will be easy to upgrade so that they can take advantage of PnP; older systems with ROM-based BIOS will need a hardware change before they can take full advantage of PnP.

See also **PCI local bus, Plug-and-Pray.**

Plug-and-Pray   What most of us will do when our *Plug-and-Play* systems do not work automatically.

plug-compatible   Any hardware device designed to work in exactly the same way as a device manufactured by a different company. For example, all external serial devices are plug-compatible, because you can replace one with another without changing the cabling or connector.

See also **pin-compatible.**

PMMU   See **paged memory management unit.**

PnP   See **Plug-and-Play.**

POH   Abbreviation for power-on hours.

See also **mean time between failures.**

point of presence   Abbreviated POP. A connection to the telephone company or to long-distance carrier services.

point-to-point link   A direct connection between two, and only two, locations or nodes.

Point-to-Point Protocol   Abbreviated PPP. A *TCP/IP* protocol used to transmit *IP* packets over serial lines and telephone connections. PPP allows a PC to establish a temporary direct connection to the Internet via modem, and appear to the host system as if it were an Ethernet port on the host's network.

PPP provides router-to-router, host-to-router, and host-to-host connections, and also provides an automatic method of assigning an *IP* address so that mobile users can connect to the network at any point.

See also **SLIP.**

polling   A method of controlling the transmission sequence of devices on a shared circuit or *multidrop line* by sending an inquiry to each device asking if it wants to transmit. If a device has data to send, it sends back an acknowledgment, and the transmission begins. Three methods are in common use:

- **Roll-call polling:** A master station uses a polling list to locate the next node to poll.

- **Hub polling:** A node polls the next node in sequence.

- **Token-passing polling:** A token is passed to the next node in sequence. This node can transmit or pass the token to the next device.

port

1. To move a program or operating system from one hardware platform to another. For example, *Windows NT* portability refers to the fact that the same operating system can run on both *Intel* and *reduced instruction set computing* (RISC) architectures.

2. The point at which a communications circuit terminates at a network, serial, or parallel interface card.

portable   Describes the degree to which a program can be moved easily to various different computing environments with a minimum number of changes. Applications written for the Unix operating system are often described as portable applications.

portable computer   Any computer light and small enough to be carried easily. The first portable DOS-based computers were known as *luggable computers* because they were definitely not

p

easy to carry. Later models fall into three general categories:

- **Laptop computers:** Small enough to be used in an airplane seat and powerful enough to run major operating systems, including DOS, Microsoft Windows, OS/2, and popular business applications. Extended battery life is making the laptop a serious alternative to the desktop system.

- **Notebook computers:** Smaller than a laptop and about the size of a textbook or student notebook, but still capable of running DOS, Microsoft Windows, and major applications. A notebook computer will easily fit into a briefcase.

- **Palmtop computers:** Very small computers with a tiny display and nonstandard keyboard, often designed for a specific purpose, such as reading utility company meters or tracking UPS parcel deliveries. Some can run DOS, but must use a proprietary operating system that requires custom software.

Major advances in battery life and the use of *flash memory* are part of the continuing development of portable computers.

See also **docking station, PCMCIA, PDA.**

port multiplier   A concentrator that provides multiple connections to the network.

POSIX   Acronym for Portable Operating System Interface for Computer Environments. A collection of *IEEE standards* that defines a complete set of *portable* operating system services. POSIX is based on Unix operating system services, but it can be implemented by many other operating systems.

POST   See **power-on self test.**

Postal Telephone and Telegraph   See **PTT.**

power conditioning   The use of protective and conditioning devices to filter out power surges and spikes and ensure clean power. There are three main types of power conditioning:

- **Suppression device:** Protects against sudden destructive transient voltages.

- **Regulation device:** Modifies the power waveform back to a clean sine wave. A *UPS* (uninterruptible power supply) is a common form of voltage regulator. It may be online, actively modifying the power, or offline and available only after the line voltage drops below a certain level.

- **Isolation device:** Protects against noise. These types of devices are often expensive.

Because power conditioning is expensive, usually just the servers or hosts in a network are protected. *Surge suppressors* may be used with workstations or other important network nodes, such as *bridges* or *routers*.

See also **blackout, brownout, power surge, spike, surge.**

PowerLAN A popular *peer-to-peer* networking operating system from Performance Technology. PowerLAN offers a complete Windows interface, flexible network printing, connections to NetWare-based and Windows-based networks, and powerful user and group management tools.

Power Mac A series of computers from Apple Computer, Inc. based on the *PowerPC* 601 chip. Several systems are available, including the 7100/66, based on the 66 MHz PowerPC chip, and the 8100/80, based on the 80 MHz chip.

Although the Power Macs run on the PowerPC chip rather than the traditional Motorola chips, they run a version of the Macintosh operating system, and look and feel just like 68000-based computers. They can also run DOS software under emulation with SoftWindows.

The most interesting computer in the range is the Power Macintosh 6100/66 DOS Compatible, which has both a PowerPC chip and an 80486 DX2/66 chip; users flip between the Macintosh System 7 and DOS/Windows with the touch of one key.

p

power-on hours Abbreviated POH. See **mean time between failures.**

power-on self test Abbreviated POST. A set of diagnostic programs loaded from ROM (read-only memory) before any attempt is made to load the operating system, designed to ensure that the major system components are present and operating. If a problem is found, the POST *firmware* writes an error message in the screen, sometimes with a diagnostic code number indicating the type of fault located.

PowerPC   A family of microprocessors jointly developed by Apple, Motorola, and IBM.

The *32-bit* 601 houses 2.8 million transistors, runs at 110 MHz,
and is designed for use in high-
performance, low-cost PCs. The
66 MHz 602 is targeted at the
consumer electronics and entry-
level computer markets. The low-
wattage 603e is aimed at
battery-powered computers, the
604 is for high-end PCs and workstations, and the top-of-the-line
620 is designed for servers and
very high performance applications. The 620 is a 64-bit chip.

PCs based on the PowerPC
chip usually include a minimum
of 16 MB of memory; a 540 MB
hard disk; *PCI local bus* architecture, including a local-bus based
graphics adapter; and a CD-ROM.

power supply   A part of the computer that converts the power
from a wall outlet into the lower
voltages, typically 5 to 12 volts
DC (direct current), required internally in the computer. PC power
supplies are usually rated in
watts, ranging from 90 to 300
watts. If the power supply in a
computer fails, nothing works—
not even the fan.

power surge   A sudden, brief,
and often destructive increase in
line voltage. A power surge may
be caused by an electrical appli-
ance, such as a photocopier or elevator, or by power being reapplied
after an outage.

See also **power conditioning,
surge, surge suppressor.**

PPP   See **Point-to-Point Protocol.**

preemptive multitasking   A
form of *multitasking* in which the
operating system executes an application for a specific period of
time, according to its assigned priority. At that time, it is preemp-
ted, and another task is given
access to the central processing
unit (CPU) for its allocated time.
Although an application can give
up control before its time is up,
such as during input/output waits,
no task is ever allowed to execute
for longer than its allotted time
period.

See also **cooperative multitasking, time-slice multitasking.**

presentation layer   The sixth of
seven layers of the *ISO/OSI model*
for computer-to-computer communications. The presentation layer

defines the way in which data is formatted, presented, converted, and encoded.

Primary Rate ISDN   Abbreviated PRI. An *ISDN* (Integrated Services Digital Network) service that provides 23 B (bearer channels), capable of speeds of 64 kilobits per second (Kbps), and a D (data channel), also capable of 64 Kbps. The combined capacity of 1.544 megabits per second is equivalent to one *T1* channel.
See also **Basic Rate ISDN.**

PRINTCON   A Novell NetWare workstation utility used to create, view, or modify print-job configurations on the network. Configuration options include the printer to be used, the *print queue* to process the job through, the print-device mode, the printer form number, and the number of copies.
See also **CAPTURE, NPRINT, PCONSOLE.**

PRINTDEF   A Novell NetWare workstation utility used to create, view, and modify printer definitions on the network.
See also **CAPTURE, NPRINT, PCONSOLE.**

printer emulation   The ability of a printer to change modes so that it behaves like a printer from another manufacturer. For example, many dot-matrix printers offer an Epson printer emulation in addition to their own native mode. Most laser printers offer a Hewlett-Packard LaserJet emulation.
See also **emulator, terminal emulation.**

print queue   A list of documents waiting to be printed on a particular network printer. In Novell NetWare, print queues are created through *NETADMIN* or *PCONSOLE*. A corresponding directory is created for each print queue. In NetWare 2.*x* and 3.*x*, the print queue directory is placed in the SYS:SYSTEM directory of the current server. In NetWare 4.*x*, it is placed in the QUEUES directory on the specified volume.

print server   A server that handles printing for all users on the network. A print server collects print jobs sent by applications running on other networked PCs, places them in a *print queue* on the hard disk, and routes them to one or more printers attached to the print server.

273

Novell NetWare print servers run as *NetWare Loadable Modules* (NLMs) on a NetWare server and can manage up to 256 printers and any number of print queues.

See also **local printer.**

print spooler   In an operating system or network operating system, the software that coordinates print jobs sent to a shared printer when that printer is busy. Each print job is stored in a separate file and is printed in turn when the printer becomes free.

private automatic branch exchange   Abbreviated PABX. An automatic telephone system that serves a particular location, such as an office, providing connections from one extension to another, as well as a set of connections to the external telephone network. Many PABXs handle computer data and may include *X.25* connections to a *packet-switched network.*

See also **private branch exchange.**

private branch exchange   Abbreviated PBX. A telephone system, usually owned by the customer, that serves a particular location, such as an office, providing connections from one extension to another, as well as a set of connections to the external telephone network.

See also **private automatic branch exchange.**

private leased circuit   A leased communications circuit, available 24 hours a day, seven days a week, that connects a company's premises with a remote site.

privileged mode   An operating mode supported in protected mode in Intel processors that allows the operating system and certain classes of device driver to manipulate parts of the system, including memory and input/output ports.

privilege level

1. Those *rights* granted to a user or a group of users by the network administrator that determine the functions the user can execute. Rights form an important component of network *security*, and can include supervisor rights, read, write, erase, and modify rights, and several others.

2. A form of protection built into Intel microprocessors. The Intel microprocessor architecture provides two broad classes of

protection. One is the ability to separate *tasks* by giving each task a separate address space. The other mechanism operates within a task to protect the operating system and special processor registers from access by applications.

Within a task, four privilege levels are defined. The innermost ring is assigned privilege level 0 (the highest, or most trusted level) and the outermost ring is privilege level 3 (the lowest, or least privileged level). Rings 1 and 2 are reserved for the operating system and operating system extensions; level 3 is available to applications. This protection is maintained by complex circuitry in the processor's *memory management unit*.

See also **DOMAIN.**

PRN In DOS and OS/2, the logical device name for a printer, usually the first *parallel port*, which is also known as LPT1.

process In a *multitasking* operating system, a program or a part of a program. All EXE and COM files execute as processes, and one process can run one or more other processes.

See also **session, thread.**

programming language A language used to write a program that the computer can execute. Almost two hundred different programming languages exist. An example is the popular C language, which is well-suited to a variety of computing tasks. With C, programmers can write anything from a device driver, to an application, to an operating system.

Certain kinds of tasks, particularly those involving artificial intelligence (LISP or Prolog), process control (Forth), or highly mathematical applications (FORTRAN and APL), can benefit from a more specific language.

Programming languages are also divided into low-level languages, such as assembly language, and high-level languages, such as Pascal, C, and C++.

See also **machine language.**

propagation delay In communications, any delay between the time a signal enters the transmission channel and the time it is received. This delay is relatively small across a local-area network (LAN), but can become considerable in satellite communications,

p

where the signal must travel from one earth station to the satellite and back to earth again. Unusually long delays may require specialized hardware to ensure that the link is not broken prematurely.

property   In Novell NetWare 4.*x*, a characteristic of an object in *NetWare Directory Services*; also known as an attribute. User object properties include name, telephone number, and e-mail address.

proprietary software   Software developed in-house by a particular business or government agency, and never made available commercially to the outside world. The operating systems used in certain *palmtop* computers and *PDAs* (personal digital assistants) may also be considered to be proprietary, because they are specific to one system and are not generally available anywhere else.

protected mode   In Intel processors, an operating state that supports advanced features. Protected mode in these processors provides hardware support for *multitasking* and *virtual memory* management, and it prevents programs from accessing blocks of memory that belong to other executing programs.

In 16-bit protected mode, supported on 80286 and higher processors, the central processing unit (CPU) can address a total of 16 megabytes of memory directly; in 32-bit protected mode, supported on *80386* and higher processors, the CPU can address up to 4 gigabytes of memory. OS/2 and most versions of Unix that run on these processors execute in protected mode.

See also **real mode, virtual 8086 mode.**

PROTOCOL   A Novell NetWare server utility that displays a list of the protocols and frame types registered on the server.

protocol   In networking and communications, the formal specification that defines the procedures to follow when transmitting and receiving data. Protocols define the format, timing, sequence, and error checking used on the network.

See also **communications protocol, ISO/OSI model, protocol stack.**

protocol analyzer   A hardware or combined hardware and software product used to analyze the performance data of the network, and to find and troubleshoot network problems. Protocol analyzers can translate network information because they are programmed to understand many different network protocols. For example, on a Novell NetWare system, an analyzer can capture and decode *NetWare Core Protocol* (NCP), *SPX*, and *IPX* infor-mation.

Protocol analyzers vary greatly in complexity. Network General Corporation's high-end Sniffer can decode approximately 140 different protocols. *LANalyzer for Windows* converts a networked PC into a NetWare-specific analyzer.

protocol converter   A combined hardware and software product that converts from one protocol to another, used when two dissimilar networks are connected.

See also **gateway**.

protocol stack   The several layers of software that define the computer-to-computer or computer-to-network protocol. The protocol stack on a Novell NetWare system will be different from that used on a

Banyan VINES network or on a Microsoft LAN Manager system.

See also **ISO/OSI model, SNA**.

protocol suite   See **protocol stack**.

PSC   A Novell NetWare workstation utility used to control print servers and printers and to display network printer information.

PSERVER   A Novell NetWare server utility that links a print server to the server operating system. Use *PCONSOLE* to set and configure the print server before using PSERVER.

PTT   Abbreviation for Postal Telephone and Telegraph. The official government body that administers and manages the telecommunications systems in many European countries.

PU   Abbreviation for physical unit. The name used in IBM's *SNA* (Systems Network Architecture) to indicate a physical device and its associated resources within the network.

See also **LU**.

p

public data network   Abbreviated PDN. Any government-owned or -controlled commercial *packet-switched network*, offering wide-area services to data-processing users.

PUBLIC directory   In Novell NetWare, the SYS:PUBLIC directory, created during installation. This directory allows general access to the network and contains utilities and programs for network users.

NetWare users on a DOS-based workstation have a search drive mapped to SYS:PUBLIC through the system login prompt. They also have read and file-scan rights to the directory. NetWare users on an OS/2-based workstation access NetWare utilities through the SYS:PUBLIC/OS2 directory.

See also **public files.**

public files   Files and utilities that can be accessed by all NetWare users. Public files are located in the SYS:PUBLIC directory for DOS users, and in the SYS:PUBLIC/OS2 directory for users of OS/2-based workstations.

See also **PUBLIC directory.**

public key encryption   An *encryption* scheme that uses two keys. The public key encrypts the data, and a corresponding private key decrypts the data.

public network   Normal voice telephone systems, also called the direct distance dial (DDD) network.

punch-down block   A connecting device used for telephone lines; also known as a quick-connect block. The wires are pushed into metal teeth that strip the insulation away and make a good connection.

PUPGRADE   A Novell NetWare utility that upgrades NetWare 3.*x* printer definitions, print objects, and print job configurations to NetWare 4.*x*.

See also **INSTALL.**

PURGE   A Novell NetWare workstation utility used to remove information about deleted files from the server. When a file is deleted from NetWare, the network operating system retains all information about the file, thus allowing the SALVAGE utility to recover any files deleted by accident. However, the space that a deleted file occupies is made available to the system and may be reused if disk space is at a premium. In this case the file is overwritten and cannot be recovered by SALVAGE; the file must be reloaded from a backup.

See also **DELETED.SAV directory.**

PVC   Abbreviation for permanent virtual circuit. A fixed communications circuit, created and maintained even when no data is being transmitted. A PVC has no setup overhead, and gives improved performance for periodic transmissions that require an immediate connection.

See also **SVC.**

p

¼-inch cartridge   See **quarter-inch cartridge.**

QIC   See **quarter-inch cartridge.**

quadrature amplitude modulation   In communications, a data-encoding technique used by modems that operate at 2400 bits per second or more. Quadrature amplitude modulation is a combination of phase and amplitude change that can encode multiple bits on a single carrier signal. For example, the CCITT *V.42bis* standard uses four phase changes and two amplitudes to create sixteen different signal changes.
See also **trellis-coded modulation.**

quarter-inch cartridge   Abbreviated QIC. A set of tape standards defined by the Quarter-Inch

Cartridge Drive Standards, a trade association established in 1987. Several standards are in use today. Table Q.1 on the following page lists the most common capacities and densities of the DC-2000 series of minicartridges.
Other QIC data cartridge formats allow for higher capacities; QIC 1350 allows for up to 1.35 gigabytes (GB) of tape storage, QIC-2100 allows for up to 2.6 GB, and QIC-5010 allows for up to 13 GB.

query language   In a database management system, a programming language that allows a user to extract and display specific information from a database. *Structured Query Language* (SQL) is an international database query language that allows the user to issue high-level commands or statements, such as SELECT or INSERT, to create or modify data or the database structure.

question mark   A wildcard character used in many operating systems to represent a single character in a file name or file-name extension.
See also **asterisk.**

queue   A temporary list of items
waiting for a particular service,
stored on disk in a special directory. For example, a print queue
is a list of documents waiting to
be printed on a network printer.
See also **print queue**.

quick-connect block   See
punch-down block.

TABLE Q.1: *QIC Minicartridge Standards*

DECIMAL	CHARACTER	CONTROL COMBINATION
Standard	Capacity (Uncompressed)	Bits per Inch
QIC-40	60 MB	10,000
QIC-80	125 MB	14,700
QIC-100	40 MB	10,000
QIC-128	128 MB	16,000
QIC-3010	255 MB	22,125
QIC-3020	500 MB	44,250
QIC-3030	580 MB	40,600
QIC-3040	840 MB	40,600
QIC-3080	1.6 GB	60,000
QIC-3090	2 GB	93,333
QIC-3070	4 GB	67,773

RAD Abbreviation for Rapid Application Development. A set of client/server application-development tools designed to speed up the development of robust applications for *SQL* databases.

radio-frequency interference

Abbreviated RFI. Many electronic devices, including radios, televisions, computers, and peripherals, can interfere with other signals in the radio-frequency range by producing electromagnetic radiation. The use of radio frequencies is generally regulated by government agencies.

See also **Class A certification, Class B certification, extremely low-frequency emission, FCC.**

RAID Acronym for redundant array of inexpensive disks. In networking and *mission-critical applications*, a method of using several hard disk drives (often *SCSI* or *Integrated Drive Electronics*

(IDE) drives) in an array to provide *fault tolerance* in the event that one or more than one drive fail.

Each of the different levels of RAID is designed for a specific use:

- **RAID 0:** Data is striped over one or more drives, but there is no redundant drive. RAID 0 provides no fault tolerance because the loss of a hard disk means a complete loss of data. Some classification schemes omit RAID 0 for this reason.

- **RAID 1:** Two hard disks of equal capacity duplicate or mirror each other's contents. One disk continuously and automatically backs up the other disk. This method is also known as *disk mirroring* or *disk duplexing*, depending on whether one or two independent hard-disk controllers are used.

- **RAID 2:** Bit-interleaved data is written across several drives, and then parity and error-correction information is written to additional separate drives. The specific number of error-correction drives depends on the allocation algorithm in use.

- **RAID 3:** Bit-interleaved data is written across several drives, but only one parity drive is used. If an error is detected, the data is reread to resolve the problem.

The fact that data is reread in the event of an error may add a small performance penalty.

- **RAID 4:** Data is written across drives by sectors rather than at the bit level, and a separate drive is used as a parity drive for error detection. Reads and writes occur independently.
- **RAID 5:** Data is written across drives in sectors, and parity information is added as another sector, just as if it were ordinary data.

There is not much difference in speed or quality among these levels. The appropriate level of RAID for any particular installation depends on network usage. RAID levels 1, 3, and 5 are available commercially, and levels 3 and 5 are proving popular for networks.

See also **disk striping, disk striping with parity, SLED.**

RAM   Acronym for random-access memory. The main system memory in a computer, used for the operating system, applications, and data.

See also **dynamic RAM, static RAM.**

RAM chip   A semiconductor storage device, either *dynamic RAM* or *static RAM.*

RAM cram   A slang expression used to describe the increasing demands made upon limited memory space, especially the inability to run large applications in a PC with 1 megabyte of RAM (random-access memory) running DOS.

RAM disk   An area of memory managed by a special device driver and used as a simulated disk; also called virtual drive. Because the RAM disk operates in memory, it works much faster than a regular hard disk. However, anything stored on a RAM disk will be erased when the computer is turned off, so contents must be copied onto a real disk to be saved.

See also **disk cache.**

random access   Describes the ability of a storage device to go directly to the required *memory address* without needing to read from the beginning every time data is requested. In a random-access device, the information can be read directly by accessing the appropriate memory address. There is nothing random or haphazard about random access; a more precise term is direct access.

See also **sequential access.**

random-access memory
See **RAM**.

RCONSOLE   A Novell Net-
Ware workstation utility that allows network administrators to
manage routers and servers from
a remote PC using a modem or
from a workstation on the network. RCONSOLE establishes
the connection to the server and
converts the PC into a virtual server console.

In NetWare 3.*x*, use *ACON-
SOLE* to perform this function.

See also **REMOTE, RSPX**.

read-after-write verification
A method of checking that data is
written to a hard disk correctly.
Data is written to the disk, and
then read back and compared
with the original data still held in
memory. If the data read from the
disk matches, the data in memory
is released. If the data does not
match, that block on the disk is
marked as bad, and another attempt is made to write the data
elsewhere on the disk.

README file   A text file which
contains information about the software, placed on a set of distribution
disks by the manufacturer. The file
name may vary slightly; it might be
READ.ME, README.TXT, or
README.DOC, for example.
README files may contain last-
minute, important information
that is not in the program manuals or online help system.

You should always look for a
README file when installing a
new program on your system; it
may contain information perti-
nent to your specific configuration. You can open a README
file in any word processor or text
editor.

read-only   Describes a file or
other collection of information
that may only be read; it may not
be updated in any way or deleted.
Certain important operating system files are designated as read-
only files to prevent accidental
deletion. Also, certain types of
ROM (read-only memory) and
some devices, such as archive
backup tapes and CD-ROMs, can
be read but not changed.

read-only memory   See ROM.

real mode
1. An operating state supported by all processors in the Intel 80*x*86 family, and the only
operating mode supported by
DOS. In real mode, the processor

can directly address 1 megabyte of memory. Unlike protected mode, real mode does not offer any advanced hardware features for memory management or multitasking.

2. In Microsoft Windows, an operating mode that runs Windows using less than 1 megabyte of extended memory. Real mode is not available in Windows 3.1 or later.

See also **protected mode.**

reboot   To restart the computer and reload the operating system, usually after a *crash.*

See also **boot.**

Receive Data   See **RXD.**

record locking   See **file and record locking.**

recursion   In programming, the ability of a subroutine to call itself. Recursion is often used when solving problems that repeat the same processing steps. However, some limiting factor must be present; otherwise, the program will never stop running.

Red Horde   A nickname for *Novell, Inc.,* a leading network operating system software company.

redirector   A software module loaded onto all the workstations on a network that intercepts application requests for file- and printer-sharing services and diverts them to the file server for action. Redirectors are often DOS *terminate-and-stay-resident* (TSR) programs.

See also **NetWare shell, NETx.COM, requester.**

reduced instruction set computing   Abbreviated RISC, pronounced "risk." A processor that recognizes only a limited number of assembly-language instructions.

RISC chips are relatively cheap to produce and debug, because they usually contain fewer than 128 different instructions. RISC processors are commonly used in workstations, and they can be designed to run up to 70 percent faster than processors that use complex instruction set computing (CISC).

See also **complex instruction set computing, IBM RS/6000, instruction set.**

redundant array of inexpensive disks   See **RAID.**

<u>reentrant</u>   Describes a programming technique that allows one copy of a program to be loaded into memory and shared. When one program is executing reentrant code, a different program can interrupt and then start or continue execution of that same code.

Many operating system service routines use reentrant code so that only one copy of the code is needed. The technique is also used in *multithreaded* applications, in which different events are taking place concurrently in the computer.

REGISTER MEMORY   A
Novell NetWare server utility that informs the network operating system that the server contains more than the default amount of memory. All numbers must be entered as hexadecimal numbers.

See also **MEMORY**.

REINITIALIZE SYSTEM   A
Novell NetWare 4.*x* server utility that reexecutes the commands in the NETINFO.CFG configuration file; if the file contains any new commands, they are also executed.

relational database   A database model in which the data always appears from the point of view of the user to be a set of two-dimensional tables, with the data presented in rows and columns.

The rows in a table represent records, which are collections of information about a specific topic, such as the entries in a doctor's patient list. The columns represent fields, which are the items that make up a record, such as the name, address, city, state, and zip code in an address list database.

See also **database model.**

REMAPID   A Novell NetWare
4.*x* *NetWare Loadable Module* loaded onto a NetWare 3.*x* server so that passwords are correctly managed in a NetSync environment.

See also **NETSYNC3, NET-SYNC4.**

REMIRROR PARTITION
A Novell NetWare server utility used to restart *disk mirroring* of a logical disk partition.

See also **MIRROR STATUS.**

REMOTE   A Novell NetWare
server utility used to access the server console from a PC, a workstation, or by using a modem.

See also **RCONSOLE, RSPX.**

r

287

remote boot   A technique used to boot a workstation from an image file on the file server rather than from a local drive attached directly to the workstation.

remote connection   A workstation-to-network connection, made using a modem and telephone line, that allows data to be sent or received over greater distances than those allowed by conventional cabling. Also known as remote access.

See also **mobile computing, remote user, wireless communications.**

remote-control program   A program that allows the user to link two PCs together, so that one of the computers controls the operation of the other. The connection may be over a dedicated serial or *SCSI* line, a local-area network (LAN), or a modem-to-modem communications link. Each computer runs a copy of the remote-control program.

Remote-control programs are particularly useful for troubleshooting problems at computers located far from the technical support center, installing or removing demonstration software without needing to visit the customer site, training remote users, and *telecommuting.*

Popular remote control programs include Symantec's pcAnywhere, Microcom's Carbon Copy, Traveling Software's LapLink for Windows, and Farallon's Timbuktu.

See also **mobile computing, wireless communications.**

remote digital loopback test
A capability of certain modems that allows the whole circuit to be tested.

See also **loopback.**

Remote File Service   See **RFS.**

Remote Procedure Call   Abbreviated RPC. A set of procedures used to implement *client/server architecture* in distributed programming. RPC describes how an application initiates a process on another network node and how it retrieves the appropriate result.

remote resource   Any device not attached to the local node, but available through the network.

remote user   A user who logs in to the network using a modem and telephone line from a site located some distance away from the main network.

See also **mobile computing, remote connection, wireless communications.**

REMOVE   A Novell NetWare 3.*x* workstation utility that allows a network administrator to remove all of a user's or group's *trustee* assignments from a file or directory by removing the name from its trustee list. In NetWare 4.*x*, this function is provided by *RIGHTS*.

See also **REVOKE, SYSCON.**

REMOVE DOS   A Novell NetWare server utility that unloads DOS from the file server memory and makes that memory space available to the network operating system.

RENDIR   A Novell NetWare workstation utility that allows users to rename directories.

repeater   A simple hardware device that moves all *packets* from one local-area network (LAN)

segment to another by regenerating, retiming, and amplifying the electrical signals. The main purpose of a repeater is to extend the length of the network transmission medium beyond the normal maximum cable lengths.

See also **active hub, bridge, brouter, router.**

replica   In Novell *NetWare Directory Services* (NDS), a copy of a directory *partition*. Replicas are designed to eliminate a single point of failure and to provide faster access to users across a *wide-area network* (WAN).

NetWare 4.*x* contains three major types of replica:

• **Master replica:** The original, used to create new partitions in the *NetWare Directory Database* (NDD).

• **Read-Write replica:** Used to read or update NDD information.

• **Read-Only replica:** Used to display but not modify NDD information.

A fourth replica type is important to NDS communications:

• **Subordinate reference:** A link between a parent partition and a child partition, containing a list of the servers in which replicas of the child partition are

r

stored, their addresses, and replica types, as well as other NDS partition information.

See also **partition table.**

requester Special software loaded onto a networked workstation to manage communications between the network and the workstation. This software may also be referred to as a shell, *redirector*, or client, depending on the networking system in use.

See also **NetWare shell, NetWare DOS Requester, NETx.COM.**

Request To Send See **RTS.**

reserved memory In DOS, a term used to describe that area of memory between 640 kilobytes and 1 megabyte, also known as upper memory. Reserved memory is used by DOS to store system and video information.

See also **memory management.**

reserved word See **keyword.**

RESET ROUTER A Novell NetWare server utility used to reset or recreate the *routing table* in the file server. Router tables are automatically reset every two minutes, so this command is not used often.

resource Any part of a computer system that can be used by a program as it runs. Resources include memory, hard and floppy disks, networking components, the operating system, printers, and other output devices, as well as queues, security features, and other less well-defined data structures.

response time The time lag between sending a request and receiving the data. Response time can be applied to a complete computer system, as in the time taken to look up a certain customer record, or to a system component, as in the time taken to access a specific cluster on disk.

REVOKE A Novell NetWare 3.*x* workstation utility that allows a network administrator to remove a specific right from the *Inherited Rights Mask* without removing the user or the group from the file or directory's *trustee* list. In NetWare 4.*x*, this function is provided by *RIGHTS*.

See also **REMOVE, SYSCON.**

RFC   Abbreviation for Request for Comments. One of a large set of over 1,000 Internet documents that contain descriptions of protocols, standards, notes for new users, and other information.

RFI   See **radio frequency interference.**

RFS   Abbreviation for Remote File Service. A distributed file system network *protocol* that allows programs running on a computer to use network resources as though they were local. Originally developed by AT&T, RFS has been incorporated as a part of Unix *System V Interface Definition.*

RG-58   A 50-ohm *coaxial cable*, used in Ethernet networks, that conforms to the IEEE 802.3 10Base2 standard.

RG-59   A 75-ohm *coaxial cable* used in *ARCnet.*

RG-62   A 93-ohm *coaxial cable* used in *ARCnet* local-area networks (LANs) or in IBM 3270 applications.

RIGHTS   A Novell NetWare workstation utility that displays the user's current file, directory, or volume *rights.*
See also **GRANT.**

rights   The privileges granted to a user or a group of users by the network administrator. Rights determine the operations that users can perform on the system. For example, Novell NetWare 3.*x* directory system rights are supervisor, read, write, erase, create, modify, access control, and file scan. In NetWare 4.*x*, NDS rights are grouped as directory rights, file rights, object rights, and property rights.

rightsizing   The process of matching a corporation's goals to the computing and network solutions available to maximize business effectiveness in reaching that goal.
See also **downsizing, outsourcing, service bureau.**

ring network   A network *topology* in the form of a closed loop or circle, with each node in the network connected to the next; see the illustration on the following page. Messages move in one direction around the system.

r

291

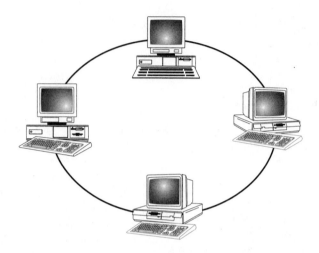

RING NETWORK

When a message arrives at a node, the node examines the address information in the message. If the address matches the node's address, the message is accepted; otherwise, the node regenerates the signal and places the message back on the network for the next node in the system. It is this regeneration that allows a ring network to cover greater distances than *star networks* or *bus* networks. Ring networks normally use some form of *token-passing* protocol to regulate network traffic.

See also **token-ring network.**

RIP   Abbreviation for Routing Information Protocol. A *routing* protocol used on *TCP/IP*

networks that maintains a list of reachable networks and calculates the degree of difficulty involved in reaching a specific network from a particular location by determining the lowest *hop count*.

RISC   See **reduced instruction set computing.**

riser cable   Any cable that runs vertically between floors in a building. Riser cable may be run through special conduits or inside the elevator shaft.

RJ-11   A commonly used modular telephone connector. RJ-11 is a four wire (two-pair) connector most often used for voice communications; see the accompanying illustration.

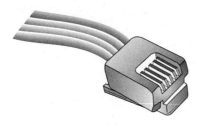

RJ-11

RJ-12   A commonly used modular telephone connector. RJ-11 is a six wire (three-pair) connector most often used for voice communications.

RJ-45   A commonly used modular telephone connector. RJ-45 is an eight wire (four-pair) connector used for data transmission over *unshielded twisted-pair cable* (UTP) and leased telephone line connections; see the accompanying illustration.

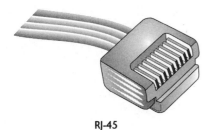

RJ-45

RLL encoding   See **run-length limited encoding.**

rlogin   A Unix utility that establishes a terminal to remote host connection on a TCP/IP network. Once the connection is established, any commands you enter will run on the remote system.

roll back   The ability of a database management system to abort a transaction against the database before the transaction is complete and return to a previous stable condition. See also **roll forward, Transaction Tracking System.**

roll forward   The ability of a database management system to recreate the data in the database by rerunning all the transactions listed in the transaction log. See also **roll back.**

ROM   Acronym for read-only memory. A semiconductor-based memory system that stores information permanently, retaining its contents when power is switched off. ROMs are used for *firmware*, such as the *BIOS* used in the PC. In some portable computers, applications and even the operating system are stored in ROM. See also **flash memory.**

r

293

ROM BIOS   See **BIOS**.

root directory   In a hierarchical directory structure, such as that used in DOS, OS/2, and Unix, the directory from which all other directories must branch. You cannot delete the root directory.

See also **backslash, parent directory, period and double-period directories**.

root object   In Novell NetWare 4.x *NetWare Directory Services*, the highest access point in the Directory tree.

See also **container object, leaf object**.

ROT-13   A simple *encryption* scheme often used to scramble *posts* to *USENET newsgroups*. ROT-13 makes the article unreadable until the text is decoded, and is often used when the subject matter might be considered offensive. Many newsreaders have a built-in command to unscramble ROT-13 text, and if you use it, don't be surprised by what you read; if you think you might be offended, don't decrypt the post.

ROUTE   A Novell NetWare server utility that configures and controls the routing of NetWare

packets across an IBM *bridge* to a *Token Ring* network.

router   An intelligent connecting device that can send *packets* to the correct local-area network (LAN) segment to take them to their destination; see the illustration on the opposite page. Routers link LAN segments at the *network layer* of the *ISO/OSI model* for computer-to-computer communications. The networks connected by routers can use similar or different networking *protocols*.

A router may be one or more of the following types:

• **Central router:** Acts as a network *backbone*, connecting many LANs together.

• **Peripheral router:** Connects individual LANs to either a central router or to another peripheral router.

• **Local router:** Operates within the limits of its LAN driver's cable-length limitations.

• **Remote router:** Connects beyond its device driver limitations, perhaps through a modem or remote connection.

• **Internal router:** Part of a network file server.

• **External router:** Located in a workstation on the network.

See also **bridge, brouter, gateway**.

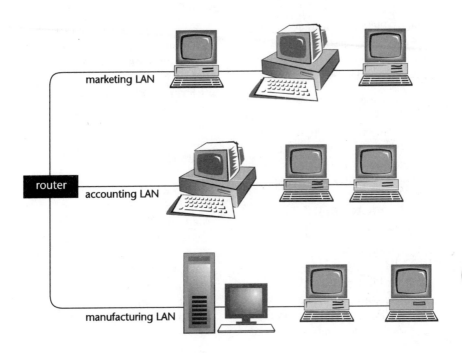

marketing LAN

router
accounting LAN

manufacturing LAN

ROUTER

routing The process of directing message *packets* from a source node to the destination node.

Routing Information Protocol See **RIP.**

routing protocol The protocol that enables *routing* by the use of a specific routing algorithm that determines the most appropriate path between the source and destination nodes.
See also **OSPF, RIP.**

routing table A table stored in a *router* used to keep track of routes to specific network destinations.

RPL A Novell NetWare server utility that allows users to boot *diskless workstations* from files on the server.
See also **remote boot.**

RPRINTER A Novell NetWare 3.*x* workstation utility that allows a local printer attached to a workstation to act as a network printer.

295

Once RPRINTER is loaded, a local printer can receive jobs from a *print server*. In NetWare 4.*x*, this function is provided by *NPRINTER*.

RS232   A Novell NetWare server utility that sets up an asynchronous communications port on the server, so that a workstation can establish a *remote connection* to the server via modem.

See also **ACONSOLE, REMOTE**.

RS-232-C   A recommended standard interface established by the Electronic Industries Association (*EIA*). The standard defines the specific electrical, functional, and mechanical characteristics used in *asynchronous transmissions* between a computer (*DTE*) and a peripheral device (*DCE*). RS is the abbreviation for recommended standard, and the C denotes the third revision of that standard. RS-232-C is compatible with the CCITT *V.24* and V.28 standards, as well as ISO IS2110.

RS-232-C uses a 25-pin or 9-pin *DB connector*. The accompanying illustration shows the *pinouts* used in a DB-25 male connector. It is used for serial communications between a computer and a peripheral device, such as a printer, modem, or mouse. The maximum cable limit of 15.25

Signal	Pin number		Pin number	Signal
secondary transmitted data	14		1	protective ground
DCE transmitter signal element timing	15		2	transmitted data
secondary received data	16		3	received data
receiver signal element timing	17		4	request to send
no defined signal designation	18		5	clear to send
secondary request to send	19		6	data set ready
data terminal ready	20		7	signal ground/common return
signal quality detector	21		8	received line signal detector
ring indicator	22		9	+ voltage
data signal rate selector	23		10	- voltage
DTE transmitter signal element timing	24		11	no defined signal designation
no defined signal designation	25		12	secondary received line signal detector
			13	secondary clear to send

RS-232-C INTERFACE

meters (50 feet) can be extended by using high-quality cable, line drivers to boost the signal, or *short-haul modems.*

RS-422   A recommended standard (RS) interface established by the Electronic Industries Association (*EIA*).

The standard defines the electrical and functional characteristics used in a balanced serial interface, but does not specify a connector. Manufacturers who use this standard use many different types of connectors with nonstandard pin configurations. Serial ports on the Macintosh are RS-422 ports.

RS-423   A recommended standard (RS) interface established by the Electronic Industries Association (*EIA*). The standard defines the electrical and functional characteristics used in an unbalanced serial interface, but does not specify a connector. Manufacturers who use this standard use many different types of connectors with non-standard pin configurations.

RS-449   A recommended standard (RS) interface established by the Electronic Industries Association (*EIA*). The standard defines the specific electrical, functional,

and mechanical characteristics used in serial binary data interchange, and it is often used with *synchronous transmissions.*

RS-449 may be implemented using a 37-pin or 9-pin *DB connector*; the illustration on the following page shows a DB-37 male connector.

RS-485   A recommended standard (RS) interface established by the Electronic Industries Association (*EIA*), which is similar to *RS-422*, except that the associated drivers are tri-state rather than dual-state. RS-485 can be used in multipoint applications, where one computer controls up to sixty-four different devices.

RS-530   A recommended standard (RS) interface established by the Electronic Industries Association (*EIA*).

The standard defines the specific electrical, functional, and mechanical characteristics used in transmitting serial binary data, either synchronously or asynchronously, using a 25-pin *DB connector.*

RS-530 works in conjunction with *RS-422* (balanced electrical circuits) or *RS-423* (unbalanced

r

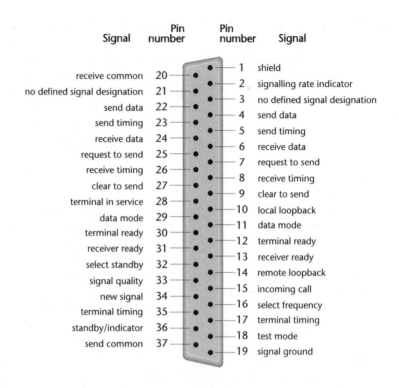

Signal	Pin number	Pin number	Signal
		1	shield
receive common	20	2	signalling rate indicator
no defined signal designation	21	3	no defined signal designation
send data	22	4	send data
send timing	23	5	send timing
receive data	24	6	receive data
request to send	25	7	request to send
receive timing	26	8	receive timing
clear to send	27	9	clear to send
terminal in service	28	10	local loopback
data mode	29	11	data mode
terminal ready	30	12	terminal ready
receiver ready	31	13	receiver ready
select standby	32	14	remote loopback
signal quality	33	15	incoming call
new signal	34	16	select frequency
terminal timing	35	17	terminal timing
standby/indicator	36	18	test mode
send common	37	19	signal ground

RS-449 INTERFACE

electrical circuits) and allows data rates from 20 kilobits per second to 2 megabits per second. The maximum distance depends on the electrical interface in use. RS-530 is compatible with CCITT V.10, V.11, X26; MIL-188/114, and *RS-449*. See the illustration on the opposite page.

RS/6000   See **IBM RS/6000.**

RSPX   A Novell NetWare server utility that loads the *SPX* driver on to the server so that work-stations can access the server console.   See also **RCONSOLE, REMOTE.**

RTDM   A Novell NetWare 4.*x* server utility that allows the server to migrate data to another file system, or to a device such as a

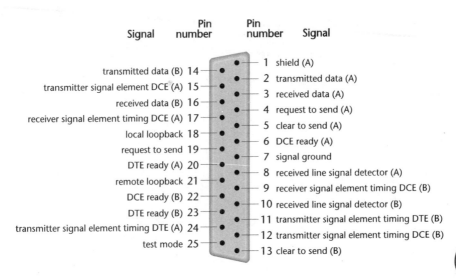

Signal	Pin number		Pin number	Signal

transmitted data (B) 14
transmitter signal element DCE (A) 15
received data (B) 16
receiver signal element timing DCE (A) 17
local loopback 18
request to send 19
DTE ready (A) 20
remote loopback 21
DCE ready (B) 22
DTE ready (B) 23
transmitter signal element timing DTE (A) 24
test mode 25

1 shield (A)
2 transmitted data (A)
3 received data (A)
4 request to send (A)
5 clear to send (A)
6 DCE ready (A)
7 signal ground
8 received line signal detector (A)
9 receiver signal element timing DCE (B)
10 received line signal detector (B)
11 transmitter signal element timing DTE (B)
12 transmitter signal element timing DCE (B)
13 clear to send (B)

RS-530 INTERFACE

tape drive or CD-ROM disc changer.

RTS   Abbreviation for Request To Send. A hardware signal defined by the *RS-232-C* standard to request permission to transmit.
See also **CTS**.

run-length limited encoding

Abbreviated RLL encoding. An efficient method of storing information on a hard disk. Compared with older, less efficient methods, such as modified frequency modulation encoding (MFM), RLL encoding effectively doubles the storage capacity of a disk.
See also **advanced run-length limited encoding**.

run-time version   A special, limited-capability release of software bundled with a single product that allows that product to run, but does not support any of the other applications capable of running in that same environment. The run-time version provides some but not all the features of the full product.

r

299

RXD   Abbreviation for Receive Data. A hardware signal defined by the *RS-232-C* standard to carry data from one device to another.

   See also **TXD**.

680x0　A family of 32-bit microprocessors from Motorola, used in Macintosh computers and many advanced workstations. The 680x0 is popular with programmers, because it uses a linear-addressing mode to access memory, rather than the segmented-addressing scheme used by Intel coprocessors.

Several models have been developed:

- **68000:** The first microprocessor in this family, which used a 32-bit data word with a 16-bit data bus, and could address 16 megabytes of memory.
- **68020:** A 32-bit microprocessor, which runs at 16 MHz, 20 MHz, 25 MHz, or 33 MHz and is capable of addressing up to 4 gigabytes of memory. The 68020 was used in the Macintosh II computer, but has been replaced by the 68030.
- **68030:** Has a *paged memory management unit* built-in, so it does not need external hardware to handle this function. The 68030 is used in the Macintosh II and SE computers.
- **68040:** Incorporates a built-in *floating-point processor* and *memory management unit*, along with independent 4 kilobyte data and instruction caches, and it can perform parallel execution by using multiple, independent instruction queues. The 68040 incorporates 1.2 million transistors and is capable of executing 20 million instructions per second; it is used in the Macintosh Quadra line of computers.

See also **PowerPC**.

S3 86C9xx　A family of fixed-function graphics accelerator chips from S3 Corporation. These chips, the 86C801, 86C805, 86C924, and 86C928, are used in many of the accelerated graphics adapters that speed up Microsoft Windows' video response.

SAA　See **Systems Application Architecture**.

Saber LAN Workstation　A network management package from Saber Software Corporation that includes hardware and software inventory, server monitoring, client monitoring and control, traffic statistics, application metering, and software distribution. The package also includes several smaller but very useful features, including reporting functions, an automatic task scheduler, and print-queue management.

sag   A short-term drop in line voltage to between 70 and 90 percent of the nominal voltage.

See also **power conditioning, spike, surge.**

SALVAGE   A Novell NetWare 3.*x* workstation utility that helps users recover deleted files.

When files are first deleted, they remain in their original directory, and when complete directories are deleted, they are copied into a directory called *DE-LETED.SAV*, located in the volume's root directory. Deleted files and directories are actually saved until the hard-disk space they occupy is required by the operating system for a new file, when they are purged from the system.

As long as deleted files have not been overwritten, SALVAGE can recover both deleted files and files from deleted directories. SAL-VAGE cannot recover an entirely deleted directory structure. In Net-Ware 4.*x*, this function is provided by *FILER*.

salvageable files   In Novell Net-Ware, files and directories that may be recovered using the SAL-VAGE or FILER commands.

SAP   Abbreviation for Service Advertising Protocol. A protocol that provides a method for servers, printers, and other devices to *advertise* their services on a Novell NetWare network and allows routers to create and maintain a database of current internetwork server information. SAP packets are normally broadcast every 60 seconds.

SAS   Abbreviation for single-attached station. In the Fiber Distributed Data Interface (*FDDI*), a device attached to only one of the dual, counter-rotating rings. Noncritical devices, such as workstations, are often connected using SASs, because they are less expensive than *DASs* (dual-attached stations).

SATAN   Abbreviation for Security Administrator Tool for Analyzing Networks. A software package, available free over the Internet, that allows network administrators to identify gaps in their security systems. Critics of the program argue that SATAN lets hackers exploit the information contained in the program on how to infiltrate these security systems, but so far, the program seems to have acted as a wake-up call for network administrators.

See also **intruder, security.**

SBACKUP   A Novell NetWare server utility that allows a network administrator to back up to and restore data from a mass-storage device attached to the server. Data can be backed up from both the server and from DOS, Microsoft Windows, or OS/2 workstations on the network, and can be backed up in OS/2 *HPFS, NFS,* or *FTAM* formats.

See also **NBACKUP, Storage Management Services.**

Scalar Processor Architecture
See **SPARC.**

SCAN FOR NEW DEVICES
A Novell NetWare server utility that searches for devices added to the server since the server was last booted.

SCHDELAY   A Novell NetWare 4.*x* server utility that allows the network administrator to give a priority level to *processes* running

on the server by assigning a number to each process. This number specifies the number of central processor unit (CPU) cycles to be skipped before the process is allowed to run again. This ability to assign priority levels effectively lets the network administrator slow down a process when the server is very busy. The default setting of 0 means that the process will run every time it is scheduled; a setting of 3 allows the process to run only every third time it is scheduled.

script   A small program or *macro* invoked at a particular time. For example, a *login script* may execute the same specific set of instructions every time a user logs in to a network or computer system. A communications script may send the user-identification information to an online information service each time a subscriber dials up the service.

SCSI   Acronym for Small Computer System Interface, pronounced "scuzzy." A high-speed parallel interface defined by the ANSI X3T9.2 committee. SCSI is used to connect a computer to peripheral devices using just one port. Devices connected in this way are said to be "daisy-chained" together, and

S

303

each device must have a unique identifier or priority number.

SCSI has been standard on the Macintosh since the Mac Plus was introduced, and it is available on the IBM RS/6000, IBM PS/2 Model 65, and higher computers. It can also be installed in an IBM-compatible computer as a single expansion board, with a special 50-pin connector extending through the back of the computer case.

Today, SCSI is often used to connect hard disks, tape drives, CD-ROM drives, and other mass storage media, as well as scanners and printers.

There are several SCSI interface definitions:

- **SCSI-1:** A 1986 definition of an *8-bit* parallel interface with a maximum data transfer rate of 5 megabytes per second.
- **SCSI-2:** This 1994 definition broadened the 8-bit data bus to *16-* or *32-bits* (also known as Wide SCSI), doubling the data transfer rate to 10 or 20 megabytes per second (also known as Fast SCSI). Wide SCSI and Fast SCSI can be combined to give Fast-Wide SCSI, with a 16-bit data bus and a maximum data-transfer rate of 20 megabytes per second. SCSI-2 is backward compatible with SCSI-1, but for maximum benefit, you should use

SCSI-2 devices with a SCSI-2 controller.

- **SCSI-3:** This definition increased the number of connected peripherals from seven to sixteen, increased cable lengths, added support for a *serial interface* and for a *fiber optic* interface. Data transfer rates depend on the hardware implementation, but data rates in excess of 100 megabytes per second are possible.

See also **Enhanced Small Device Interface, Integrated Drive Electronics, ST506 Interface.**

SCSI bus   Another name for the *SCSI* interface and communications protocol.

SCSI terminator   The *SCSI* interface must be correctly terminated at both ends to prevent signals echoing on the bus. Many SCSI devices have built-in terminators that engage when they are needed. With some older SCSI devices, you must add an external SCSI terminator that plugs into the device's SCSI connector.

scuzzy   See **SCSI.**

SDLC   Abbreviation for Synchronous Data Link Control. The data-link protocol most widely used in networks that conform to IBM's *SNA* (Systems Network Architecture).

SDLC is a *bit-oriented* synchronous protocol that organizes information into well-defined units known as frames; see the accompanying illustration. SDLC is similar to the *HDLC* (High-level Data Link Control) protocol defined by the *International Standards Organization* (ISO).

See also **data-link layer.**

SEARCH A Novell NetWare server utility that sets search paths for startup files and *NetWare Loadable Modules.* SEARCH corresponds in scope to the *MAP* command used to map disks.

search drive A drive that the operating system searches when the requested file is not located in the current directory.

See also **current drive.**

second source In computer hardware, an alternative supplier of an identical product. Second sources are a safety net for the buyer, because there are at least two suppliers for one product.

SECURE CONSOLE A Novell NetWare server utility that allows authorized users to access the console, but preserves network security by allowing only *NetWare Loadable Modules* (NLMs) to be loaded from the SYS volume, not from another hard disk or a floppy disk.

SECURITY A Novell NetWare 3.*x* workstation utility that checks system security by searching user accounts for missing passwords, passwords that match user names, passwords that are less than five characters long, and passwords that have not been changed for a long time. It also searches for other users with supervisor security clearances and for accounts without *login scripts*. There is no equivalent command in NetWare 4.*x*.

data start field	address field	control field	information field	cyclic redundancy check	data redundancy check	end flag

SDLC

security   Operating system controls used by the network administrator to limit users' access to approved areas. Security is usually implemented in the operating system at several levels: login and *password* security, account security, directory security, and file attributes security. Many personal computer operating systems do not provide much security.

If the computer system allows many users to dial in from remote locations over normal telephone lines, security should also extend to preventing unauthorized access via these lines. Data may also be encrypted by any of several methods, including the *Data Encryption Standard* (DES). When top-secret data is processed on a network, *diskless workstations* are often used to minimize the opportunity for copying the data.

The United States Department of Defense Standard 5200.28, also known as the Orange Book, specifies the following security levels:

- **Class D:** A system that is not secure; most PC operating systems fall into this category.
- **Class C1:** Requires an individual login, but allows group identification.
- **Class C2:** Requires an individual level of login by password, with an audit mechanism. This

level of security is found in Novell NetWare 4.*x*, Windows NT Server, and Banyan VINES network operating systems.

- **Class B1:** Requires Department of Defense security clearance levels.
- **Class B2:** Guarantees a path between the user and the security system and ensures that clearances cannot be changed.
- **Class B3:** Security based on a mathematical model that must be viable and repeatable; the system must be managed by a network administrator in charge of security, and must remain secure when shut down.
- **Class A1:** The highest level of security, based on a mathematical model that can be proven.

An operating system that lets anyone have complete access, such as DOS or the Macintosh System 7, falls into the D category. C1 and C2 levels can be implemented in a commercial environment. After the B1 level, the computing environment changes radically, and many of the mandatory access-control mechanisms become impractical for normal commercial operations. See also **intruder.**

semaphore   An *interprocess communication* signal that indicates the status of a shared system re-source, such as *shared memory,* in a multitasking operating system.

There are several types of semaphore:

- **Event semaphore:** Allows a *thread* to tell other threads that an event has occurred and it is safe for them to resume execution.
- **Mutual exclusion (mutex) semaphore:** Protects system re-sources, such as files, data, and peripheral devices, from simulta-neous access by several *processes.*
- **Multiple wait (muxwait) semaphore:** Allows threads to wait for multiple events to take place, or for multiple resources to become free.

SEND   A Novell NetWare server utility used to send a message from the server console to work-stations logged in to the network. Messages can be sent to specific users or to a particular *connec-tion number.*

See also **BROADCAST.**

sequel   See **Structured Query Language.**

Sequenced Packet Exchange
See **SPX.**

sequential access   An access method used by some storage de-vices, such as tapes, that requires them to start at the beginning to find a specific storage location. If the in-formation is toward the end of the tape, access can take a long time.

See also **random access.**

serial communications   The transmission of information from computer to computer, or from com-puter to peripheral device, one bit at a time. Serial communications can be synchronous and control-led by a clock, or asynchronous and coordinated by start and stop bits embedded in the data stream. The sending and receiving devices must both use the same baud rate, parity setting, and other communi-cation parameters.

See also **asynchronous transmis-sion, duplex, synchronous trans-mission, RS-232-C, RS-442, RS-443, RS-449, RS-485, RS-530.**

Serial Line Internet Protocol
See **SLIP.**

serial port   A computer input/out-put port that supports *serial com-munications,* in which information is processed on bit at a time. *RS-232-C* is a common protocol used

S

on serial ports when communicating with modems, printers, mice, and other peripherals.

See also **parallel port.**

SERVER A DOS program that boots the server and starts the NetWare operating system. After you bring down a server, use this command to start it up again.

See also **DOWN.**

server Any computer that makes access to files, printing, communications, and other services available to users of the network. In large networks, a dedicated server may run a special *network operating system*; in smaller installations, a nondedicated server may run a personal computer operating system with *peer-to-peer networking* software running on top.

A server typically has a more advanced processor, more memory, a larger cache, and more disk storage than a single-user workstation; a server may also have several processors rather than just one. Many servers also have large power supplies, *UPS* (uninterruptible power supply) support, and *fault-tolerance* features, such as *RAID* (redundant array of inexpensive disks) technology.

See also **access server, communications/modem server, file server, print server.**

server application In *Object Linking and Embedding* (OLE), an application that creates OLE objects.

See also **client application.**

Server Message Block See **SMB.**

Service Advertising Protocol See **SAP.**

service bureau A company that provides data processing or business software development services to its customers. By using a service bureau, a company can avoid the high hardware and personnel costs associated with running its own in-house services.

See also **downsizing, outsourcing, rightsizing.**

service provider A general term used to describe those companies providing a connection to the *Internet* or to other communications services. Access methods vary from high-speed dedicated access to dialup methods using *SLIP* or *PPP.*

SERVMAN   A Novell NetWare 4.*x* utility used to manage the server and view network information, including operating system performance parameters and *IPX/SPX* settings. It also provides information about the number of running processes, *NetWare Loadable Modules* (NLMs) installed, volumes mounted, users logged in, and name spaces loaded.

SESSION   A Novell NetWare 3.*x* workstation utility used to perform common tasks, including attaching to other file servers, logging out of a particular server, managing drive mappings, listing the groups on a server, sending messages, and changing to another server.

In NetWare 4.*x*, these functions are performed by *NETUSER*.

session

1. The time during which a program is running on either a local or a remote computer.

2. A DOS or Microsoft Windows program run as a separate protected task under certain *multitasking* operating systems, such as OS/2 and Windows NT.

3. In communications, the name for the active connection between a mainframe terminal (or a personal computer emulating a terminal) and the computer itself. Many different transactions or message exchanges may take place during a single session.

See also **process, thread.**

session layer   The fifth of seven layers of the *ISO/OSI model* for computer-to-computer communications. The session layer coordinates communications and maintains the *session* for as long as it is needed, performing security, logging, and administrative functions.

SET   A Novell NetWare server command used to establish operating system parameters from the command line, including parameters for communications, the memory pool, file and directory caching, the disk and file system, locking, transaction tracking, the *NetWare Core Protocol* (NCP), and error handling.

Most operating system parameters are originally set to default values that allow for efficient operation. However, under certain circumstances, some parameters may need to be adjusted.

The SET command is also used by other operating systems, including DOS, OS/2, and Unix, to establish environment values.

SETPASS A Novell NetWare workstation utility used to change a user's password.

SET TIME A Novell NetWare server utility used to establish the server's internal time and date. It does not affect the time synchronization settings used to validate network time across all servers.
See also **SERVMAN, SET.**

SET TIME ZONE A Novell NetWare server utility used to set a time reference in *CLIB* (the C language library). Parameters include time zone, hours from Greenwich Mean Time (GMT), and daylight saving time.

SETTTS A Novell NetWare workstation utility used to display and set the logical and physical record locks for the *Transaction Tracking System.*

setup string See **control code.**

SFT See **System Fault Tolerance.**

SGML Abbreviation for Standard Generalized Markup Language. A standard (ISO 8879) for defining the structure and managing the contents of any digital document. *HTML*, used in many *World Wide Web* documents on the Internet, is a part of SGML.

shadow memory In PCs based on the *80386* (or later) processor, the technique of copying the contents of the *BIOS ROM* (read-only memory) into faster *RAM* (random-access memory) when the computer first boots up; also known as shadow RAM or shadow ROM. RAM is usually two to three times faster than ROM, and the speedier access reduces the time required to execute a BIOS routine, so the processor spends more time working and less time waiting.

shadow RAM See **shadow memory.**

shadow ROM See **shadow memory.**

shared folder In a networked Macintosh, a folder that is available to other users, either without restriction or through a password. A shared folder in the Macintosh is comparable to a *network directory* on a PC.

shared memory   An *interprocess communications* technique in which the same memory is accessed by more than one program running in a *multitasking* operating system. *Semaphores* or other management elements prevent the applications from colliding, or trying to update the same information at the same time.

shell   Software used for the interface between the user and the operating system. The DOS command interpreter is a form of shell, but DOS also offers the DOSSHELL program. Microsoft Windows uses the Program Manager. The Macintosh shell is the Finder. The two most common shells in the Unix operating system are the C shell and the Bourne shell.
　　See also **kernel, NetWare shell.**

shielded cable   Cable protected against electromagnetic and *radio-frequency interference* (RFI) by metal-backed mylar foil and plastic or PVC.
　　See also **unshielded cable.**

shielded twisted-pair cable
　　Abbreviated STP. Cable with a foil shield and copper braid

surrounding the pairs of wires; see the accompanying illustration.
　　The wires have a minimum number of twists per foot of cable length; the greater the number of twists, the lower the *crosstalk.* STP offers high-speed transmission for useful distances, and it is often associated with *Token Ring* networks, but its bulk quickly fills up wiring conduits.
　　See also **shielded cable, unshielded twisted-pair cable.**

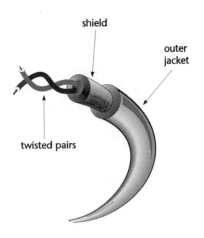

SHIELDED TWISTED-PAIR CABLE

short circuit   Often abbreviated to short. A circuit that is accidentally completed at a point too close to its origin to allow normal or complete operation. In cabling, a short circuit often occurs when two stripped wires touch.

shortcut keystroke   See **key combination**.

shortest-path routing   A routing algorithm in which paths to all network destinations are calculated. The shortest path is then determined by a cost assigned to each link.

short-haul modem   A simple, low-cost modem that can transmit information only over short distances, such as from one side of a building to the other side.
   See also **long-haul modem**.

SIG   See **special interest group**.

signal-to-noise ratio   Abbreviated SNR. The ratio between the desired signal and the unwanted noise at a specific point in a cable; a measure of signal quality. SNR is particularly important in networks using *unshielded twisted-pair cable* (UTP). SNR specifications for *Token Ring* networks are much more stringent than those for *10BaseT* or *ARCnet*.

Simple Mail Transfer Protocol   See **SMTP**.

Simple Network Management Protocol   See **SNMP**.

single large expensive disk   See **SLED**.

single login   An authentication process that allows users to log in to a complex network only once rather than requiring them to log in to each separate network element. Additional connections and drive mappings are managed in the background as a part of the authentication process. Also known as single sign-on.

single-mode fiber   Narrow diameter *fiber-optic cable* in which lasers rather than LEDs are used to transmit signals through the cable.
   Single-mode fiber allows only one route for a light wave to pass through, and it can transmit signals over considerable distances. For this reason, it is often used in telephone networks rather than in local-area networks.
   See also **multimode fiber**.

single-user system   A computer system designed for use by one person at a time, often on a personal computer. DOS, the Macintosh System 7, OS/2, and Windows NT are examples of single-user operating systems. Unix and most network operating systems are multiuser systems.

site license   A software license that covers all the installed copies of a software package at a specific location or locations. Some large corporations and government institutions prefer to negotiate a site license rather than try to pay for and keep track of all the individual copies they use. A site license may allow unlimited copies for internal use, or it may limit the number of copies of a program the corporation can use concurrently.

   See also **application metering**.

slash

   1. With many operating systems, used to separate *command-line switches* that alter the default settings for an operating system command.

   2. In Microsoft Windows File Manager, used in combination with the Ctrl key (Ctrl-/) to select all the currently unselected files.

See also **backslash**.

SLED   Abbreviation for single large expensive disk. The traditional alternative to *RAID* (redundant array of inexpensive disks), used by most networks.

SLIP   Abbreviation for Serial Line Internet Protocol. A protocol used to run *IP* over serial lines or telephone connections using modems. SLIP allows a PC to establish a temporary direct connection to the Internet via modem, and appear to the host system as if it were a port on the host's network. SLIP is slowly being replaced by *PPP* (Point-to-Point Protocol).

SLIST   A Novell NetWare 3.*x* workstation utility that displays a list of all the available file servers on the network, along with each server's network number, node address, and current status. In NetWare 4.*x*, this function is provided by *NLIST.*

Small Computer System Interface   See SCSI.

small office/home office
   See SOHO.

S

smart hub   A *concentrator*, used in Ethernet or ARCnet networks, with certain network-management facilities built into firmware that allow the network administrator to control and plan network configurations; also known as an intelligent hub.

In Token Ring networks, a smart hub is known as a Controlled Access Unit (CAU). A CAU can determine if nodes are operating, connect and disconnect nodes, and monitor node activity.

smart terminal   See **intelligent terminal**.

SMB   Abbreviation for Server Message Block. A distributed file-system network protocol, developed by Microsoft and adopted by many other vendors, that allows a computer to use the files and other resources of another computer as though they were local. For network transfers, SMBs are *encapsulated* within the *NetBIOS* network control block packet.

SMDS   Abbreviation for Switched Multimegabit Data Service. A high-speed *metropolitan-area*

network (MAN) service based on the *802.6* standard for use over *T1* and *T3* circuits.

See also **ATM**.

SMODE   A Novell NetWare 3.*x* workstation utility that lets users display or specify search mode settings for executable files. In NetWare 4.*x*, this function is provided by *FLAG*.

SMS   See **Storage Management Services**.

SMTP   Abbreviation for Simple Mail Transfer Protocol. The *TCP/IP* protocol for exchanging e-mail. Many third-party vendors sell host software for Unix capable of exchanging SMTP e-mail with proprietary e-mail systems, such as IBM's PROFS.

SNA   Abbreviation for Systems Network Architecture. IBM's proprietary terminal-to-mainframe protocol, introduced in 1974. SNA describes a seven-layer system, with each layer building on the services provided by the previous layer; see the illustration on the opposite page. Devices on an SNA system are usually connected using the *SDLC* protocol, running over serial lines. SNA is not compatible with the seven-layer *ISO/OSI model*.

SNA gateway   A hardware and software device that connects an *SNA* (Systems Network Architecture) mainframe to a local-area network.

sneakernet   An informal method of file sharing in which a user copies files on to a floppy disk and then carries them to a co-worker in the next office.

SNMP   Abbreviation for Simple Network Management Protocol. A standard protocol, part of the *TCP/IP* suite, used to manage and monitor nodes on a network. The illustration on the following page shows how the SNMP manager and agent are organized.

Two versions of SNMP currently exist:

• **SNMP 1:** Provides a method for setting and monitoring configuration information.

• **SNMP 2:** Adds increased security, the ability to communicate between management stations, and the ability to transfer a large amount of data at the same time.

S

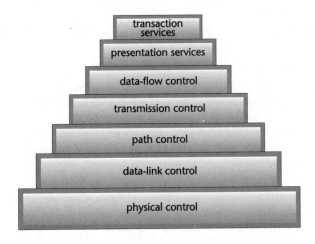

SNA

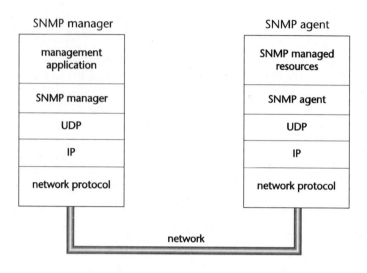

SNMP manager   SNMP agent

SNMP

SNR   See **signal-to-noise ratio.**

social interface   A form of *graphical user interface* that replaces icons with images representing real objects. Microsoft's Bob uses a social interface with a representation of a house containing several rooms, including a family room, study, garage, and attic. Scattered around the rooms are the objects used to start Bob's programs; when you click on the calendar on the wall, your appointment book opens, and so on.

Apple Computer's online service eWorld also uses a social interface.

socket

1. A general-purpose *interprocess communication* mechanism, originally developed in the Unix world.

2. That part of an *IPX internetwork* node address that represents the destination of an IPX packet. Certain sockets are reserved by NetWare for particular applications. For example, IPX delivers all *NetWare Core Protocol* (NCP) request packets to socket 451h.

socket services   Part of the software support needed for *PCMCIA* hardware devices in a *portable computer*, controlling the interface to the hardware.

Socket services is the lowest layer in the software that manages PCMCIA cards. It provides a BIOS-level software interface to the hardware, effectively hiding the specific details from higher levels of software. Socket services also detect when you insert or remove a PCMCIA card and identify the type of card it is.

See also **card services, device driver.**

software   An *application program* or *operating system* that a computer can execute. Software is a broad term that can imply one or many programs, and it can also refer to applications that may consist of more than one program.

software interrupt   An *interrupt* generated by an instruction in a program, often called a trap.

See also **hardware interrupt.**

software license   A license to use a software package subject to certain conditions. These conditions usually define the rights of the purchaser and limit the liability of the program's publisher.

See also **application metering, site license.**

software piracy   The illegal copying and distribution of copyrighted software. Copying software, like duplicating any copyrighted material, is illegal. In an attempt to discourage software piracy, the *Software Publishers Association* (SPA) has run several advertising campaigns, including a billboard showing a pair of handcuffs and the message "Copy software illegally and you could get this hardware absolutely free." The SPA has been successful in persuading companies to inventory their software, so that corporations know which software copies they have purchased legally.

Software Publishers Association   Abbreviated SPA. An association of software developers and distributors most notable for their tactics in fighting *software piracy*, including extremely blunt advertising campaigns and unannounced visits to companies suspected of acts of piracy.

software suite   A selection of business applications sold as a single integrated package. The Standard version of a software suite usually includes a word processor, spreadsheet, presentation graphics, and an e-mail program, and

S

317

the Professional version will often add a database program. The cost of the suite is significantly less than the cost of purchasing each application separately. Additional benefits include inter-application communications, easy installation of the whole package, and re-duced training time.

Microsoft Office, *PerfectOffice* from Novell, and *Lotus SmartSuite* are all examples of popular suites.

SOHO Abbreviation for small of-fice/home office. That portion of the market for computer services occupied by small offices and home-based businesses rather than the large corporate buyers. SOHO is a small but growing market sector characterized by very well-informed buyers.

Over thirteen million Ameri-cans run a small business from home, and more than forty mil-lion work at home either full time or part time. This large number of home offices is the result of many factors in the economy, including corporate downsizing and cheaper, more capable computers and office equipment, and is a trend that is likely to continue.

See also **telecommuting.**

Solaris A Unix-based operating system from SunSoft that runs on

Intel processors and supports a *graphical user interface*, *e-mail*, the *Network File System* (NFS), and *Network Information Ser-vices* (NIS). Solaris brings a com-mon look-and-feel to both *SPARC* and Intel platforms.

See also **System V Interface Definition.**

source address The *address* por-tion of a *packet* or *datagram* that identifies the sender.

See also **destination address.**

source routing IBM's *Token Ring* method of routing data frames through a network consist-ing of multiple local-area net-works (LANs) by specifying the route to be traveled in each frame. The route is actually deter-mined by the end stations through a discovery process supported by source-*bridge routers*.

IBM bridges can be of two types:
- **Single-route broadcasting:** Allows certain bridges to pass the packet, so that only a single copy arrives on each ring in the network.
- **All-routes broadcasting:** Sends the packet across all the possible routes in the network, so as many copies of the packet ar-rive at the destination as there are bridges in the network.

SPA See **Software Publishers Association.**

space parity See **parity.**

spanning tree A network segment that is free of logical loops; a network structure that has a root node and one path, usually the shortest distance, that connects all the other nodes. This tree structure is used in bridged networks to make routing decisions, especially if multiple paths connect nodes, because these loops could lead to packets looping on their way to their destination.

spanning tree algorithm A technique based on the IEEE *802.1* standard that finds the most desirable path between segments of a multilooped, bridged network. If multiple paths exist in the network, the spanning tree algorithm finds the most efficient path and limits the link between the two networks to this single active path. If this path fails because of a cable failure or other problem, the algorithm reconfigures the network to activate another path, thus keeping the network running.

SPARC Acronym for Scalable Processor ARChitecture. A 32-bit *reduced instruction set computing* (RISC) processor from Sun Microsystems. See also **SPARCstation.**

SPARCstation A Sun Microsystems family of Unix workstations based on the *SPARC* processor. SPARCstations range from small, diskless desktop systems to high-performance, tower servers in multiprocessor configurations.

special interest group Abbreviated SIG. A group that meets to share information about a specific topic, such as particular hardware, software, programming languages, or operating systems. A SIG is often part of a user group or other organization.

SPEED A Novell NetWare server utility that displays the server's central processing unit (CPU) relative speed setting.

spike A short, transient electrical signal, often of very high amplitude. See also **power conditioning, power surge, surge suppressor.**

SPOOL A Novell NetWare 3.*x* server utility used to set up default print queues for print jobs created with either *NPRINT* or *CAPTURE.*

spooler See **print spooler.**

SPX Abbreviation for Sequenced Packet Exchange. A set of Novell NetWare protocols implemented on top of *IPX* to form a *transport-layer* interface. SPX provides additional capabilities over IPX. For example, it guarantees packet delivery by having the destination node verify that the data was received correctly. If no response is received within a specified time, SPX retransmits the packet. If several retransmissions fail to return an acknowledgment, SPX assumes that the connection has failed and informs the operator. All packets in the transmission are sent in sequence, and they all take the same path to their destination node.

SPXCONFIG A Novell NetWare server utility used to set configuration parameters for *SPX,* including watchdog timeouts, retry counts, maximum concurrent SPX settings, and *IPX socket* table size.

SPXS A Novell NetWare server utility used with a *STREAMS-*based *SPX* protocol.

SQE See heartbeat.

SQL See **Structured Query Language.**

SRAM See **static RAM.**

ST506 Interface A popular hard-disk interface standard developed by Seagate Technologies, first used in IBM's PC/XT computer. The interface is still used in systems with disk capacities smaller than about 40 megabytes. ST506 has a relatively slow data-transfer rate of 5 megabits per second.

A later variation of ST506, called ST412, adds several improvements. Because these two interfaces are so closely related, they are often referred to as ST506/412.

See also **Enhanced Small Device Interface, Integrated Drive Electronics, SCSI.**

star-dot-star A commonly available file specification (*.*), which uses the asterisk *wildcard* character. It is equivalent to specifying any combination of file name and file-name extension.

StarLAN A *network operating system* from AT&T that implements *CSMA/CD* protocols on *twisted-pair cable* (TP) transmitting at 1 megabit per second (Mbps); a subset of *802.3*. In 1988, StarLAN was renamed StarLAN 1, and StarLAN 10 was launched. StarLAN 10 is a 10 Mbps *Ethernet* version that uses TP or *fiber-optic cable*.

star network A network topology in the form of a star. At the center of the star is a wiring *hub* or concentrator, and the nodes or workstations are arranged around the central point representing the points of the star; see the accompanying illustration. Wiring costs tend to be higher for star networks than for other configurations, because each node requires its own individual cable. Star networks do not follow any of the IEEE standards.

See also **bus network, ring network, topology.**

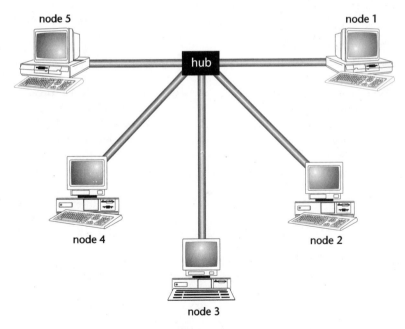

STAR NETWORK

start bit   In *asynchronous transmissions*, a start bit is transmitted to indicate the beginning of a new data word.

See also **data bits, parity, stop bit(s)**.

STARTUP.NCF   A Novell NetWare server configuration boot file that loads the NetWare server's disk driver, along with *name spaces* and certain *SET* parameters.

static RAM   Abbreviated SRAM, pronounced "ess-ram." A type of computer memory that retains its contents as long as power is applied; it does not need constant refreshment, as required by *dynamic RAM* (DRAM) chips.

An SRAM chip can store only about one-fourth of the information that a DRAM chip of the same complexity can hold. However, SRAM, with access times of 10 to 25 nanoseconds, is much faster than DRAM, at 80 nanoseconds or more, and is often used in *caches*. SRAM is four to five times as expensive as DRAM.

statistical multiplexing   Abbreviated stat mux. In communications, a method of sharing a transmission channel by using statistical techniques to allocate resources. A statistical multiplexer can analyze traffic density and dynamically switch to a different channel pattern to speed up the transmission. At the receiving end, the different signals are merged back into individual streams.

See also **frequency-division multiplexing, time-division multiplexing**.

stop bit(s)   In *asynchronous transmissions*, stop bits are transmitted to indicate the end of the current data word. Depending on the convention in use, one or two stop bits are used.

See also **data bits, parity, start bit**.

Storage Management Services   Abbreviated SMS. A set of Novell *NetWare Loadable Modules* and other software that allows data to be backed up and retrieved from the server and from workstations attached to the network. SMS is independent of both the hardware used to create the backup and also the file systems (DOS, OS/2, Macintosh, or Unix) actually being backed up or restored.

See also **SBACKUP**.

store-and-forward   A method that temporarily stores messages at intermediate nodes before forwarding them to the next destination. This technique allows routing over networks that are not available at all times and lets users take advantage of off-peak rates when traffic and costs might be lower.

See also **message switching**.

STP   See **shielded twisted-pair cable**.

straight-tip connector   Abbreviated ST. A *fiber-optic cable* connector that maintains the perfect alignment of the ends of the connected fibers, required for efficient light transmission; see the accompanying illustration.

STRAIGHT-TIP CONNECTOR

streaming tape   A high-speed tape backup system designed to optimize throughput; the tape is not stopped during a backup. To use streaming tape, the computer and backup software must be fast enough to keep up with the tape drive.

See also **DC-2000, tape cartridge**.

STREAMS   A Novell *NetWare Loadable Module* (NLM) that provides a common interface between NetWare and transport protocols such as *IPX/SPX*, *TCP/IP*, *SNA*, and *OSI*. STREAMS allows services to be provided across the network regardless of the transport protocol in use, because the protocol is transparent to the operating system.

streams   A function of Unix that provides flexible communications paths between *processes* and *device drivers*.

StreetTalk   The distributed global naming and directory service for *Banyan VINES* network operating system. The StreetTalk database contains all the necessary information about all nodes and devices on the network, and

S

323

this database is updated every 90 seconds.

Under StreetTalk, all users, printers, and servers have a three-part StreetTalk address in the form of device or user name, domain name, and organization name; StreetTalk also allows nicknames for nodes and devices.

See also **domain directory services, Enterprise Network Services, global directory services, NetWare Directory Services, X.500.**

string   See **character string.**

structured graphics   See **object-oriented graphics.**

Structured Query Language
Abbreviated SQL, pronounced "sequel." In *relational database* management systems, a query language developed by IBM for use in mainframe applications. SQL has been adopted by Oracle Corporation for use in its database management systems, running on all platforms, not just mainframes. SQL contains about sixty commands and is used to create, modify, query, and access data organized in tables. It can be used either as an interactive interface or as embedded commands in an application.

Many databases implement SQL queries behind the scenes, enabling communication with database servers in systems with *client/server architecture.*

SQL is an *ANSI* standard in the United States, as well as a worldwide *International Standards Organization* (ISO) standard. The most recent version of the standard was published in 1992.

structured wiring   A planned cabling system for *enterprise-wide network* communications, including both voice and data. AT&T's Premises Distribution Systems and IBM's Cabling System are both structured wiring designs.

subdirectory   A directory within another directory. The *root directory* is the top-level directory, from which all other directories must branch. In common use, subdirectory is synonymous with directory or folder.

See also **current directory, parent directory, period and double-period directories.**

SuperFAT   See **file allocation table.**

SuperNOS   A planned future integration of Novell NetWare and UnixWare into a single unified network operating system that takes advantage of the best features available in both systems. Time will tell.

superpipelining   A preprocessing technique used by some microprocessors in which two or more execution stages (such as fetch, decode, execute, or write back) are divided into two or more pipelined stages, giving considerably higher performance.

superscalar   A microprocessor architecture that contains more than one execution unit, or pipeline, allowing the processor to execute more than one instruction per clock cycle. For example, the *Pentium* processor is superscalar, with two side-by-side pipelines for integer instructions. The processor determines whether an instruction can be executed in parallel with the next instruction in line. If it does not detect any dependencies, the two instructions are executed.

See also **complex instruction set computing, reduced instruction set computing.**

superserver   A computer specifically designed for use as a network server. A superserver is a very high-performance system, often characterized by scalable input/output channels, complex *multiprocessing* features, and a large price tag. It may have several central processing units (CPUs), large amounts of error-correcting memory, *cache memory*, and hard-disk space, as well as *fault-tolerant* features, such as redundant power supplies.

superuser   A special Unix *privilege level*, with unlimited access to all files, directories, and commands, that allows system managers to perform certain functions.

surface test   A test contained in the Novell NetWare installation program that finds and marks bad blocks on the server hard disk. The test can be run as either a destructive test or a nondestructive test. A destructive test destroys any existing data on the disk as it reads and writes test patterns. A nondestructive test does not destroy existing data, but reads and saves the data, performs the tests, and then rewrites the original data back again. On a large hard disk, a surface test can take more than 24 hours to complete.

S

325

surge   A short, sudden, and often destructive increase in line voltage. A voltage-regulating device, known as a *surge suppressor*, can protect computer equipment against surges.

See also **power conditioning, spike.**

surge protector   See **surge suppressor.**

surge suppressor   A voltage-regulating device placed between the computer and the AC line connection that protects the computer system from *power surges*; also known as a surge protector.

See also **power conditioning.**

SVC   Abbreviation for Switched Virtual Circuits. A connection that exists for only as long as it is in use; the connection is broken when the transmission is complete.

See also **PVC.**

SVID   See **System V Interface Definition.**

swap file   On a hard disk, a file used to store parts of running programs that have been swapped out of memory temporarily to make room for other running programs. A swap file may be permanent, always occupying the same amount of hard-disk space even though the application that created it may not be running, or temporary, created as and when needed.

See also **permanent swap file, temporary swap file, virtual memory.**

swapping   The process of exchanging one item for another. In a *virtual memory* system, swapping occurs when a program requests a virtual memory location that is not currently in memory. Swapping may also refer to changing floppy disks as needed when using a single floppy disk drive.

Switched Multimegabit Data Services   See **SMDS.**

symmetrical multiprocessing   A *multiprocessing* design that assigns a task to a processor in response to system load as the application starts running. This design makes for a much more flexible system than *asymmetrical multiprocessing*, in which the programmer matches a specific task to a certain processor while writing the program.

In symmetrical multiprocessing, the overall workload is

shared by all processors in the system; system performance increases as more processors are added into the system. The drawback is that symmetrical multiprocessing operating systems are much harder to design than asymmetrical multiprocessing operating systems.

synchronization   The timing of separate elements or events to occur simultaneously. In computer-to-computer communications, the hardware and software must be synchronized so that file transfers can take place.

See also **asynchronous transmission, synchronous transmission.**

synchronous transmission   A transmission method that uses a clock signal to regulate data flow. In synchronous transmissions, *frames* are separated by equal-sized time intervals. Timing must be controlled precisely on the sending and the receiving computers. Special characters are embedded in the data stream to begin synchronization and to maintain synchronization during the transmission, allowing both computers to check for and correct any variations in timing.

See also **asynchronous transmission.**

Synchronous Data Link Control   See SDLC.

syntax   The formal rules of grammar as they apply to a specific programming language or operating system command; in particular, the exact sequence and spelling of command elements required for the command to be interpreted correctly.

syntax error   An error in the use of a programming language or operating system command *syntax*, such as misspelling a keyword or omitting a required space.

SYSCON   A Novell NetWare 3.*x* workstation utility used to manage the file servers on the network; most of the supervisory tasks associated with the file server can be performed with SYSCON, including setting up accounts and account restrictions, assigning file-system rights, and managing users. In NetWare 4.*x*, these functions are performed through NETADMIN or NWADMIN.

System 7   A version of the Macintosh system software, released in 1991. System 7 adds many improvements, including *non-preemptive multitasking*, context-sensitive balloon help, a *virtual memory* implementation, *peer-to-peer* file sharing on networked Macintoshes, *inter-application communications*, and outline fonts for the screen and printer.

system administrator　See network administrator.

SYSTEM directory　In Novell NetWare, the SYS:SYSTEM directory created during installation. This directory contains NetWare operating system files and directories, as well as *NetWare Loadable Modules* (NLMs) and network administrator utilities.

System Fault Tolerance　Abbreviated SFT. A method of duplicating data on several hard disks so that if one disk fails, the data is still available from another disk. Several levels of hardware and software SFT are available in Novell NetWare, with each level of redundancy decreasing the possibility of catastrophic data loss. For example, SFT I includes *Hot-Fix* redirection, and SFT II adds *disk duplexing* and *disk mirroring*. SFT III uses duplicate servers, so that all transactions are recorded on both; if one fails, the other can take over.

See also **disk striping, RAID, Transaction Tracking System.**

Systems Application Architecture　Abbreviated SAA. A set of IBM standards, first introduced in 1987, that defines a consistent set of interfaces for future IBM software. Three standards are defined:

- **Common User Access (CUA):** A graphical user interface definition for products designed for use in an *object-oriented* operating environment. The OS/2 desktop follows CUA guidelines in its design, and Microsoft Windows implements certain CUA features.

- **Common Programming Interface (CPI):** A set of *Application Programming Interfaces* (APIs) designed to encourage independence from the underlying operating system. The standard database query language is *Structured Query Language* (SQL).

- **Common Communications Support (CCS):** A common set of communications protocols that interconnect SAA systems and devices.

Systems Network Architecture
See **SNA.**

System V See **System V Interface Definition.**

System V Interface Definition
Abbreviated SVID. A standard for the Unix operating system, based on Unix System V release 4, designed to ease application migration between the different derivatives of Unix.
See also **POSIX.**

SYSTIME A Novell NetWare workstation utility used to synchronize a workstation's time and date with the server's time and date.

SYS volume In Novell NetWare, the name of the first file server volume. The SYS volume contains the following default directories:

- **SYSTEM directory:** Contains files and directories for the NetWare operating system.
- **PUBLIC directory:** Contains files and directories for end users.
- **LOGIN directory:** Contains login utilities and operating system boot image files for use by diskless workstations.
- **MAIL directory:** Contains directories for each user.
- **DELETED.SAV directory:** Contains recently deleted directories and their associated files.

In NetWare 4.*x*, several additional default directories may also be installed, including those associated with NetWare language services in non-English environments.

S

10/100   A term used to indicate that a device can support both *Ethernet* (at a data transfer rate of 10 megabits per second) and *Fast Ethernet* or *100VG-AnyLAN*.(at a data transfer rate of 100 megabits per second).

3+   A network operating system, originally developed by 3Com, that implemented *Xerox Network System* (XNS) transport protocols and Microsoft MS-Net file sharing.

10Base2   An implementation of the *802.3* Ethernet standard on *thin Ethernet* (*RG-58*) coaxial cable; sometimes called thinnet or cheapernet wire. 10Base2 has a data-transfer rate of 10 megabits per second and a maximum cable-segment length of 185 meters (610.5 feet). A *T-connector* attaches the thin coaxial cable to the *BNC* connector on the Ethernet adapter.

10Base5   An implementation of the *802.3* Ethernet standard on *thick Ethernet* coaxial cable; sometimes called thicknet. 10Base5 has a data-transfer rate of 10 megabits per second and a maximum cable-segment length of 500 meters (1650 feet), over a *bus* topology. The cable attaches to the Ethernet adapter with a vampire, or piercing, connector and a *transceiver*.

10BaseF   Emerging *802.3* standards that define the use of Ethernet over *fiber-optic cable*. Several standards are included:
- **10BaseFP (fiber passive):** For desktops.
- **10BaseFL (fiber link):** For intermediate *hubs* and workgroups.
- **10BaseFB (fiber backbone):** For central facility lines between buildings.

10BaseT   An implementation of the *802.3* Ethernet standard over *unshielded twisted-pair* (UTP) wiring: the same wiring and *RJ-45* connectors used with modern telephone systems. The standard is based on a star topology, with each node connected to a central wiring center, and a maximum cable-segment length of 100 meters (330 feet).

286 See 80286.

386DX See 80386DX.

386SX See 80386SX.

387 See 80387.

387SX See 80387SX.

3720 A general description for the family of products from IBM that includes terminals, printers, and terminal cluster controllers. 3270 products all communicate with a mainframe computer using the *SNA* (Systems Network Architecture) protocol.

T See **tera-**.

T1 A long-distance, point-to-point circuit, providing twenty-four channels of 64 kilobits per second (Kbps), giving a total bandwidth of 1.544 megabits per second (Mbps). The standard T1 frame is 193 bits long, made up of twenty-four 8-bit voice samples and one synchronization bit. It transmits 8000 frames per second. When a T1 service is made available in single 64 Kbps

increments, it is known as *fractional T1*.

In Europe, the comparable circuit is known as E-1, and it has a speed of 2.054 Mbps. T1 has been superseded by the CCITT *DS*-1 designation.

See also **T-carrier**.

T1 multiplexer A *statistical multiplexer* that divides the 1.544 megabits per second *T1* bandwidth into twenty-four separate 64 kilobit per second channels of digitized data or voice.

T1 small aperture terminal Abbreviated TSAT. A small satellite terminal used for digital communications that can handle *T1* data rates of up to 1.544 megabits per second.

T2 A long-distance, point-to-point, communications service, providing up to four T1 channels. T2 offers ninety-six channels of 64 kilobits per second, for a total bandwidth of 6.3 megabits per second. T2 is not available commercially, although it is used within telephone company networks.

See also **T-carrier**.

T3   A long-distance, point-to-point communications service, providing up to twenty-eight *T1* channels.

T3 can carry 672 channels of 64 kilobits per second, for a total bandwidth of 44.736 megabits per second, and is usually available over *fiber-optic cable*. T3 is used almost exclusively by AT&T and the regional telephone operating companies, although certain large private corporations are using T3 with digital microwave or fiber-optic networks.

In Europe, T3 has been superseded by the CCITT *DS*-3 designation.

See also **T-carrier.**

T4   A long-distance, point-to-point communications service, providing up to 168 *T1* channels, T4 can carry 4032 channels of 64 kilobits per second, for a total bandwidth of 274.176 megabits per second. T4 can be used for both digitized voice and data transmission.

See also **T-carrier.**

table   In a *relational database* system, a table is comparable to a database file, but more highly structured. The organization of a table is logical, not physical. Each row (or *record*) in a table

contains a unique key, or primary key, so that any item of data in the table can be retrieved by referring only to that key. Through the process known as normalization, all data items in a row are made to depend only on this primary key. View and data dictionaries in a relational database take the form of two-dimensional tables.

tap   A connector that attaches to a cable without blocking the passage of information along that cable; a connection onto the main transmission medium of the network.

tape cartridge   A self-contained tape storage module, containing tape much like that in a video cassette. Tape cartridges are primarily used to back up hard-disk systems.

See also **DC-2000, quarter-inch cartridge.**

tape drive   A computer peripheral device that reads from and writes to magnetic tape. The drive may use tape on an open reel or from an enclosed tape cartridge. Because tape-management software must search from the beginning of the tape every time it wants to find a file (a process

t

called *sequential access*), tape is too slow to use as a primary storage system; however, tapes are frequently used to back up hard disks.

See also **streaming tape.**

TAPI Abbreviation for Telephony *API.* A standard telephone interface for Microsoft Windows, developed by Intel and Microsoft, designed to allow applications to set up and control calls.

TAPI does not define the method of data transmission used once a call is in progress. It is completely independent of the telephone network itself.

See also **TSAPI.**

task Any independent running program and the set of system resources that it uses. A task may be an operating system process or part of an application.

See also **context switching, multitasking, task switching.**

task switching To switch from one running program to another quickly, either at the direction of the operating system or at the request of the user.

TB See **terabyte.**

T-carrier A digital communications service from a common carrier for voice or data transmission. The four-level, *time-division multiplexing* specification for the United States telephone system allows the bit stream of the smaller carriers to be multiplexed into the larger ones; see the illustration on the following page.

The following are the four service levels:

• **T1:** Provides twenty-four channels of 64 kilobits per second (Kbps), giving a total bandwidth of 1.544 megabits per second (Mbps). When a T1 service is made available in single 64 Kbps increments, it is known as *fractional T1.*

• **T2:** The equivalent of four T1 services, T2 offers ninety-six channels of 64 Kbps, for a total bandwidth of 6.3 Mbps.

• **T3:** The equivalent of 28 T1 circuits, T3 offers 672 channels of 64 Kbps, for a total bandwidth of 44.736 Mbps. T3 is available commercially, but is not often used for local-area networks.

• **T4:** The equivalent of 168 T1 circuits, T4 provides 4,032 channels of 64 Kbps, for a total bandwidth of 274.176 Mbps.

See also **T1, T2, T3, T4.**

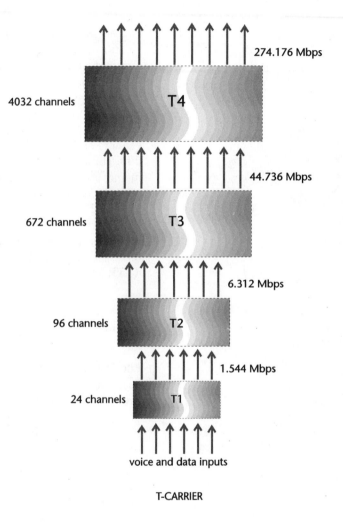

4032 channels

274.176 Mbps

T4

672 channels

44.736 Mbps

T3

96 channels

6.312 Mbps

T2

1.544 Mbps

24 channels

T1

voice and data inputs

T-CARRIER

t

T-connector   A T-shaped connector, used with coaxial cable, that connects two *thin Ethernet* cables and also provides a third connector for the network interface card; see the accompanying illustration.

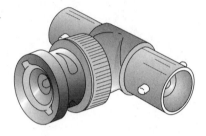

T-CONNECTOR

TCP   Abbreviation for Transmission Control Protocol. The connection-oriented, *transport-level* protocol used in the *TCP/IP* suite of protocols.
     See also **UDP**.

TCPCON   A Novell NetWare 3.1*x* and 4.*x* utility used to monitor activity on a *TCP/IP* network segment.

TCP/IP   Abbreviation for Transmission Control Protocol/Internet Protocol. A set of communications protocols first developed by the Defense Advanced Research Projects Agency (DARPA) in the late 1970s. The set of TCP/IP protocols encompasses media access, packet transport, session communications, file transfer, e-mail, and terminal emulation. Its structure is shown in the illustration on the opposite page.
     TCP/IP is supported by a large number of hardware and software vendors and is available on many different computers, from PCs to mainframes. Many corporations, universities, and government agencies use TCP/IP, and it is also the basis of the *Internet*.
     See also **Address Resolution Protocol, FTP, IP, SMTP, SNMP, TCP, TFTP, TELNET, tn3270, UDP**.

TDM   See **time-division multiplexing**.

telecommunications   A general term for the electronic transmission of all forms of information, including digital data, voice, fax, sound, and video, from one location to another over some form of communications link.

telecommuting   Working at home on a computer connected to the office by modems and telephone lines instead of commuting to the office.

Remote File Service	Server Message Block	Network File System
SMTP	FTP	TELNET	SNMP
Transmission Control Protocol		User Datagram Protocol	
Internet Control Message Protocol	Internet Protocol	Address Resolution Protocol
media access		
transmission media		

TCP/IP

Telecommuting saves time, cuts down on automobile use and pollution, and decreases stress. Some local and state governments actively encourage telecommuting to keep the number of commuters as low as possible.

A recent survey showed that more than thirty-three million people in the United States do some form of telecommuting, compared with ten million in 1985. Most studies indicate that home workers are happier and more productive. However, some jobs do not lend themselves to telecommuting; welding and brain surgery would be difficult to do via modem.

See also **SOHO**.

teleconferencing   The use of audio, video, or computer systems, linked by a communications channel, to allow widely separated individuals to take part in a discussion or meeting.

Desktop video and chalkboard programs are becoming more and more common, and *groupware* applications such as *Lotus Notes* are helping people work together.

Telephony API   See **TAPI**.

TELNET   A *terminal emulation* protocol, part of the *TCP/IP* suite of protocols, that provides remote terminal-connection services.

The most common terminal emulations are for Digital Equipment Corporation (DEC) VT-52, VT-100, and VT-220 terminals, although many companies offer additional add-in emulations.

See also **tn3270**.

temporary swap file   A *swap file* that is created every time it is needed. A temporary swap file can consist of several discontinuous pieces of hard-disk space. A temporary swap file does not occupy hard-disk space if the application that created it is not running.

See also **swap file, permanent swap file, virtual memory.**

ter   A term describing a tertiary *CCITT* recommendation, an alternative or extension to the primary or secondary recommendation.

See also **bis.**

tera-   Abbreviated T. A prefix meaning 10^{12} in the metric system, 1,000,000,000,000; commonly referred to as one trillion in the American numbering system, and one million million in the British numbering system.

terabyte   Abbreviated TB. In computing, usually 2^{40}, or 1,099,511,-627,776 bytes. Terabytes are used to represent extremely large hard-disk capacities.

terminal emulation   A method of operation or software that makes a PC or a workstation act like a terminal attached to a mainframe, usually for the purpose of *telecommunications*. Communications programs often include popular emulations, such as ANSI, VT-52, VT-100, VT-200, and TTY.

terminate-and-stay-resident program   Abbreviated TSR. A DOS program that stays loaded in memory, even when it is not actually running. A TSR can be invoked quickly to perform a specific task.

Popular TSR programs include calendars, appointment schedulers, and calculators, invoked from a word processor, spreadsheet, or other application. TSRs occupy *conventional memory* space, making that amount of memory unavailable to applications. However, with DOS 5 or 6 and an *80386* (or later) processor, TSRs can load into *upper memory blocks*, and therefore recover that conventional memory for other uses.

See also **memory management**.

terminator　A device attached to the last peripheral device in a series, or the last node on a network. For example, the last device on a *SCSI* bus must terminate the bus; otherwise, the bus will not perform properly. A 50-ohm resistor is placed at both ends of an *Ethernet* cable to prevent signals reflecting and interfering with the transmission.

text file　See **ASCII file**.

text mode　See **character mode**.

TFTP　Abbreviation for Trivial File Transfer Protocol. A simplified version of the *TCP/IP* file transfer protocol that does not include password protection or user-directory capability.

thick Ethernet　Connecting *coaxial* cable used on an *Ethernet* network. The cable is 1 centimeter (0.4 inch) thick, almost as thick as your thumb, and can be used

to connect network nodes up to a distance of approximately 1006 meters (3300 feet). Thick Ethernet is primarily used for facility-wide installations.

See also **10Base5, thin Ethernet**.

thicknet　See **thick Ethernet**.

thin Ethernet　Connecting *coaxial* cable used on an *Ethernet* network. The cable is 5 millimeters (0.2 inch) thick, about as thick as your little finger, and can be used to connect network nodes up to a distance of approximately 165 meters (500 feet). Thin Ethernet is primarily used for office installations.

See also **10Base2, thick Ethernet**.

thinnet　See **thin Ethernet**.

thrashing　An excessive amount of disk activity that causes a *virtual memory* system to spend all its time swapping pages in and out of memory, and no time executing the application.

Thrashing can be caused when poor system configuration creates a *swap file* that is too small or when insufficient memory is installed in the computer. Increasing

339

the size of the swap file or adding memory are often the best ways to reduce thrashing.

thread   A *concurrent process* that is part of a larger process or program. In a *multitasking* operating system, a single program may contain several threads, all running at the same time. For example, one part of a program can be making a calculation while another part is drawing a graph or chart.

See also **session.**

throughput   A measure of the *data-transfer rate* through a complex communications or networking scheme.

tie line   A private circuit, leased from a communications carrier, connecting two or more points in a single organization.

TIME   A Novell NetWare server utility that displays the server's time and date, as well as the daylight saving time status and other information about the time synchronization parameters used on the server.

See also **SERVMAN, SET, SET TIME.**

time-division multiplexing   Abbreviated TDM. A method of sharing a transmission channel by dividing the available time equally between competing stations. At the receiving end, the different signals are merged back into their individual streams.

See also **frequency-division multiplexing, statistical multiplexing, T1 multiplexer.**

time-domain reflectometer   Abbreviated TDR. A diagnostic tool used to detect cabling faults. A TDR calculates the length of a cable by measuring the time it takes for a reflected pulse to return to the TDR, and then multiplying that by the *nominal velocity of propagation.*

timeout   Many procedures require a device to respond or reply to an inquiry within a certain period of time; if the device does not respond, a timeout condition occurs, thus preventing the procedure from hanging up the computer. Timeouts are also used in communications to detect transmission failures. Some timeouts are fixed, such as the amount of time during which an operating system will attempt to access a modem or printer; others can be specified by the user.

time-slice multitasking A form of multitasking in which the operating system assigns the same small time period to each *process* in turn.

See also **cooperative multitasking, preemptive multitasking.**

time stamp An identification code that includes the time that an event took place. Most operating systems add a time stamp to indicate a file's create time. Automatic error logging or security auditing processes often add a time stamp to critical events such as changes to passwords or accounts.

TIMESYNC A Novell NetWare 4.*x* server utility that controls time synchronization on all servers across the network.

See also **SERVMAN.**

time synchronization In Novell NetWare 4.*x*, a method of synchronizing time across all servers on the network so that all servers in the NDS tree report the same time. By default, time is synchronized every 10 minutes by NetWare 4.*x*, but the interval can be changed if necessary.

TLI A Novell NetWare server module that provides the *transport layer* for network communications.

See also **CLIB, IPXS, SPXS, STREAMS.**

TLIST A Novell NetWare 3.*x* workstation utility that displays *trustee* rights information for files and directories. In NetWare 4.*x*, this function is provided by *RIGHTS.*

tn3270 A special version of the TELNET program specifically designed for use with large IBM computers using 3270 and 327*x* series terminals. Most of the computers on the *Internet* use *Unix*, but if you ever encounter an IBM mainframe, you will definitely need tn3270.

So how do you know when to use tn3270 rather than TELNET? It's time to load up tn3270 if you try to connect to an Internet host with TELNET and one of the following happens:

• The on-screen messages are all in uppercase letters rather than the usual Unix mix of uppercase and lowercase letters.

• You see "VM" or "MVS" anywhere in the login message.

t

These are both names of IBM operating systems.

- Your session is aborted before it really gets started.

token passing   A network access method that uses a circulating electronic token to prevent multiple nodes from transmitting on the network simultaneously. Before a node can transmit, it must be in possession of the token. *Fiber Distributed Data Interface* (FDDI), *Token Ring*, and Token Bus networks all use token passing to avoid packet collisions.

See also **CSMA/CD, token-ring network.**

Token Ring network   IBM's implementation of the *token-ring network* architecture. It uses a *token-passing* protocol transmitting at 4 or 16 megabits per second. Using standard telephone wiring, a Token Ring network can connect up to 72 devices; with *shielded twisted-pair* (STP) wiring, each ring can support up to 256 nodes. Although it is based on a closed-loop ring structure, a Token Ring network uses a star-shaped cluster of up to eight nodes, all attached to the same wiring concentrator or *Multistation Access Unit* (MAU). The MAUs are then connected to the main ring circuit; see the illustration on the next page.

A Token Ring network can include personal computers, mini-computers, and mainframes. The IEEE *802.5* standard defines token-ring networks.

token-ring network   A *local-area network* (LAN) with a ring structure that uses *token passing* to regulate traffic on the network and avoid *collisions*.

On a token-ring network, the controlling NIC generates a token that controls the right to transmit. This token is continuously passed from one node to the next around the network. When a node has information to transmit, it captures the token, sets its status to busy, and adds the message and the destination address. All other nodes continuously read the token to determine if they are the recipient of a message. If they are, they collect the token, extract the message, and return the token to the sender. The sender then removes the message and sets the token status to free, indicating that it can be used by the next node in sequence.

See also **CSMA/CD, 802.5, Token Ring network.**

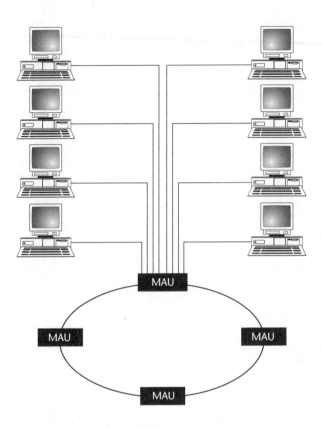

TOKEN RING NETWORK

TOP Abbreviation for Technical and Office Protocol. An *Ethernet* implementation for use in an engineering environment, developed by Boeing Corporation.

See also **MAP.**

topology The map of a network. Physical topology describes where the cables are run and where the workstations, nodes, routers, and gateways are located. Networks are usually configured in *bus*, *ring*, *star*, or *mesh* topologies. Logical topology refers to the paths that messages take to get from one user on the network to another.

343

TOPS   A local-area network
(LAN) from TOPS Corporation
that uses the *LocalTalk* protocol
to connect Apple computers, PCs,
and Sun workstations.

TP   See **twisted-pair cable.**

TPING   A Novell NetWare 4.*x*
utility similar to *PING* that transmits an *ICMP* echo request
packet to tell you if an IP node on
your network is reachable.

trackball   A device used for pointing, designed as a space-saving
alternative to the *mouse.* A
trackball contains a movable ball
that you rotate with your fingers
to move the cursor on the screen.
Because it does not need the area
of flat space that a mouse needs,
trackballs are popular with users
of *portable computers*; the Apple
PowerBook includes a trackball
as part of the keyboard case, Microsoft has released a small trackball that clips onto the side of a
laptop computer, and IBM has
developed a dual-button, touch-
sensitive pointing stick called the
TrackPoint.

TRACK OFF   A Novell Net-
Ware server utility that turns off
the router tracking display started
by *TRACK ON.*

TRACK ON   A Novell NetWare
server utility that turns on the
router tracking display. This display shows network data received
by the server, as well as data being sent from the server to workstations on the network.
See also **TRACK OFF.**

traffic   The flow of messages and
data carried by a communications
channel or link. Traffic on a data
network is normally measured in
bits transferred in a given time
period.
See also **kilobits per second,
megabits per second.**

transmission mode   The manner in which communications can
take place between a sender and a
receiver.
Several modes are defined, as
follows:
• **Simplex:** Communications
can only go in one direction, so
the sender can use the whole of
the available bandwidth.
• **Half-duplex:** Communications can go in two directions, but
only in one direction at a time.

- **Full-duplex**: Communications can go in two directions simultaneously.
- **Echo-plex**: A rare mode in which characters are retransmitted to the sender for error-checking purposes.

Transaction Tracking System

Abbreviated TTS. A *fault-tolerant* feature of Novell NetWare that maintains the integrity of databases by *backing out* or *rolling back* incomplete transactions that result from a failure in a network component.

See also **DISABLE TTS, EN-ABLE TTS, SET, SETTTS.**

transceiver   A contraction of TRANSmitter/reCEIVER. A device capable of both transmitting and receiving data. The data may be located on the network interface card that connects a workstation to a network, or it may be on a separate device. A transceiver can convert between an *AUI* (Attachment Unit Interface) *Ethernet* connection and another type of cabling, such as *fiber-optic, coaxial,* or *unshielded twisted pair* (UTP).

transfer rate   See **data-transfer rate.**

transient   See **surge.**

Transmission Control Protocol
See **TCP.**

Transmission Control Protocol/Internet Protocol
See **TCP/IP.**

transmission medium   The physical cabling used to carry network information, such as *fiber-optic, coaxial, shielded twisted-pair* (STP), or *unshielded twisted-pair* (UTP) cabling.

Transmit Data   See **TXD.**

transport layer   The fourth of seven layers of the *ISO/OSI* model for computer-to-computer communications. The transport layer defines protocols for message structure and supervises the validity of the transmission by performing some error checking.

trellis-coded modulation   Abbreviated TCM. A form of *quadrature amplitude modulation* used in modems that operate at 9600 bits per second or higher. TCM encodes data as a set of bits associated with both phase and amplitude changes.

t

345

Trivial File Transfer Protocol
See TFTP.

trustee   A user or group who has been granted rights to work in a network directory or file.

trustee rights   The means by which you control what a user can do to a particular directory or file. For example, trustee rights regulate whether a user can read a file, change it, change its name, delete it, or control other users' trustee rights to it. Trustee rights are assigned to individual users, and one user's rights can be different from another user's rights to the same directory. Also known as trustee assignments.

TSAPI   Abbreviation for Telephony Services API. A standard telephone interface developed by AT&T and Novell, designed to allow applications to set up and control calls. TSAPI is available as a *NetWare Loadable Module* for NetWare 4.01 and above.

TSAPI requires that the *PBX* is linked to a server, and so has greater control over the call than does *TAPI*.

TSAT   See **T1 small aperture terminal.**

TSR   See **terminate-and-stay-resident program.**

TTS   See **Transaction Tracking System.**

tunneling   The *encapsulation* of one *protocol* within another, often used to transport a local-area network (LAN) protocol across a *backbone* that does not support that particular protocol.

twinaxial cable   A cable with two coaxial cables inside a single insulating shield; see the accompanying illustration. Twinaxial cable is used with IBM *AS/400* minicomputers.

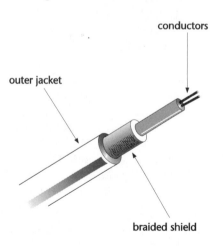

TWINAXIAL CABLE

twisted-pair cable   Abbreviated TP. Cable that comprises two or more pairs of insulated wires twisted together, at six twists per inch. In twisted-pair cable, one wire carries the signal and the other is grounded. The cable may be shielded or unshielded. Telephone wire installed in modern buildings is often twisted-pair wiring.

TXD   Abbreviation for Transmit Data. A hardware signal defined by the *RS-232-C* standard that carries information from one device to another.
See also **RXD**.

Type 1–9 cable   IBM Cabling System specifications, as follows:

- **Type 1 cable:** Shielded, twisted, dual-pair cable with 22-gauge solid conductors and a braided shield. Used with *Token Ring networks*.
- **Type 2 cable:** Two-pair, shielded cable with solid conductors and a braided shield. Type 2 also includes four pairs of unshielded voice-grade lines, giving a total of six pairs in the same sheath.
- **Type 3 cable:** Four unshielded, solid, twisted pairs, used for voice or data. IBM's variant of twisted-pair telephone wire.
- **Type 4 cable:** No published specification.
- **Type 5 cable:** Dual 100/140 micron *fiber-optic cable*; IBM now recommends 125-micron fiber-optic cable, which is the current industry standard for fiber-optic cable.
- **Type 6 cable:** Shielded, two-pair, braided cable used for patch cables. Type 6 is more flexible than Type 1 cable.
- **Type 7 cable:** No published specification.
- **Type 8 cable:** Shielded, dual-pair cable with no twists, housed in a flat jacket; commonly used under carpets.
- **Type 9 cable:** Shielded, dual-pair, *plenum cable* with solid or braided conductors and a fire-resistant outer coating, for use between floors in a building.

See also **AWG, cabling standards, riser cable.**

type-ahead buffer   See **keyboard buffer.**

U

UART Acronym for universal asynchronous receiver/transmitter, pronounced "you-art." An electronic module that combines the transmitting and receiving circuitry needed for asynchronous communications over a serial line. See also **asynchronous transmission**.

UDP Abbreviation for User Datagram Protocol. The connectionless, *transport-level* protocol used in the *TCP/IP* suite of protocols, usually bundled with IP-layer software. Because UDP does not add overhead, as does connection-oriented *TCP*, UDP is often used with *SNMP* (Simple Network Management Protocol) applications.

UIMPORT A Novell NetWare 4.*x* workstation utility that allows users to create, delete, or update user objects and their properties. UIMPORT can also import data from an existing database into the *NetWare Directory Services* (NDS) database.

UMB See **upper memory block**.

unauthorized access To gain entry to a computer system using a stolen or guessed *password*. See also **hacker, intruder**.

UNBIND A Novell NetWare server command used to unbind a network protocol from a network interface card so that the card or the protocol can be changed. See also **BIND**.

unbundled software

1. Software sold with a computer system that is priced separately, rather than included as part of a package.

2. A feature in an application repackaged and sold by itself at a lower price. See also **bundled software**.

undelete To recover an accidentally deleted file. Many operating systems include commands you can use to recover a deleted file; forever, once the file has been overwritten on your hard disk by a new file, the original is lost, and

the only way to get it back is to reload it from a recent backup.

See also **file recovery**.

Unicode A 16-bit character code,
defined by the Unicode Consor-
tium and by ISO 10646, that supports up to 65,536 unique
characters rather than the 256 characters available in the current *AS-
CII character set*.

Unicode allows for the representation of multiple language
characters using a single code; for
example, the Chinese language defines almost 10,000 basic ideo-
graphs. When universally
adopted, Unicode will make
multilingual software much
easier to write and maintain.

The Directory database in
Novell Directory Services uses
Unicode to store information
about objects and their properties
or attributes.

See also **ASCII, EBCDIC**.

Uniform Resource Locator
See **URL**.

uninterruptible power supply
See **UPS**.

**universal asynchronous
receiver/transmitter** See **UART**.

**universal synchronous
receiver/transmitter** See **USRT**.

Unix Pronounced "you-nix." A
32-bit, *multiuser, multitasking*,
portable operating system, originally developed by AT&T. Since
the purchase of UNIX System
Laboratories, Inc., Unix is owned
by Novell.

Unix was developed by Dennis
Ritchie and Ken Thompson at
Bell Laboratories in the early
1970s. It has been enhanced over
the years, particularly by computer scientists at the University
of California, Berkeley. Networking, in the form of the *TCP/IP* set
of protocols, has been available in
Unix from its early stages. During
the 1980s, AT&T began the work
of consolidating the many versions of Unix. In January 1989,
the UNIX Software Operation
was formed as a separate AT&T
division. In November 1989, that
division introduced a significant
new release, Unix System V 4.0.
In June 1990, the UNIX Software
Operation became known as
UNIX System Laboratories, Inc.,
which was bought by Novell in
1993.

Unix is available on a huge
range of computational hardware,
ranging from a PC to a Cray super-
computer, and is also available in

other related forms. For example, *AIX* runs on IBM workstations, A/UX is a graphical version that runs on powerful Macintosh computers, and *Solaris* from SunSoft runs on Intel processors.

See also **BSD Unix, UnixWare.**

Unix client   Any computer running *Unix* that connects to the network.

UnixWare   A version of the Unix operating system, based on Unix System V release 4.2, available from Novell. UnixWare is available in two versions:

• **Personal Edition:** A two-user system that supports up to two processors.

• **Application Server:** A multi-user, server system that can scale up to twelve processors.

UnixWare also supports multiple *threads,* and uses *preemptive multitasking.*

In 1993, Novell acquired UNIX System Laboratories, Inc. from AT&T, and as part of the deal, secured all rights to the System V Release 4.2 source code.

See also **SuperNOS, System V Interface Definition, Unix.**

UNLOAD   A Novell NetWare 4.*x* server utility used to unload

NetWare Loadable Modules (NLMs) from a server and return the memory space to the operating system.

See also **LOAD, MODULES.**

unshielded cable   Any cable not protected from electromagnetic interference or *radio-frequency interference* (RFI) by an outer foil shield.

unshielded twisted-pair cable   Abbreviated UTP. Cable that contains two or more pairs of twisted copper wires; see the accompanying illustration. The greater the number of twists, the lower the *crosstalk*. UTP is offered in both voice grade and data grade. The advantages of UTP include ease of installation and low cost of materials. Its drawbacks are limited

outer jacket

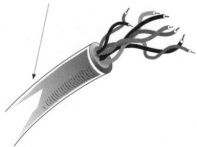

UNSHIELDED TWISTED-PAIR CABLE

351

signaling speeds and shorter maximum cable-segment lengths.

See also **shielded twisted-pair cable.**

upgradable computer   A computer system specifically designed to be upgraded as technology advances. The amount of circuitry that must be changed when you make the upgrade and the method of upgrading differ from one upgradable computer to another.. At a minimum, you must replace the processor; at most, you need to change nearly all the circuitry installed in the computer. In some systems, the use of a ZIF socket to hold the main processor makes an upgrade easy; in other systems, replacing the main processor can be extremely difficult.

upgrade

1.   The process of installing a newer and more powerful version of a software or hardware product. For example, you may upgrade to a newer and more capable version of a software package, such as Microsoft Word version 6, or OS/2 Warp, or to a larger hard disk. In the case of hardware, an upgrade is often called an upgrade kit.

2.   A new and more powerful version of software (a noun referring to the improved software itself).

uplink   The transmission of information from an earth station to a communications satellite.

See also **downlink.**

upload   In communications, sending a file or files from one computer to another over a network or via a modem. For example, you might upload a file to a network server or a bulletin board system.

See also **download.**

upper memory   See **reserved memory.**

upper memory block   Abbreviated UMB. The memory between 640 kilobytes and 1 megabyte in an IBM-compatible computer running DOS. This area was originally reserved for system and video use; however, not all the space is used. The unused portions are the UMBs.

With an *80386* (or later) processor, up to 120 kilobytes of additional memory can be gained by accessing UMBs. This space can be used to load *device drivers* and *terminate-and-stay-resident programs*.

See also **memory management**.

UPS

1. Abbreviation for uninterruptible power supply, pronounced "you-pea-ess." An alternative power source, usually consisting of a set of batteries, used to power a computer system if the normal power service is interrupted or falls below acceptable levels. An online UPS continuously monitors and modifies the power flowing through the unit. If an outage occurs, the UPS continues to provide regulated power.

An offline UPS monitors the AC level, but only switches in when the power drops below a preset level, so there is the possibility of a slight time lag. Because a UPS system is expensive, it is usually applied only to the most critical devices on the network, such as servers, routers, gateways, and independent hard disks.

2. A Novell NetWare 4.*x* server utility that links a UPS system to a server.

See also **power conditioning, UPS monitoring, UPS STATUS, UPS TIME.**

UPS monitoring The process that a server uses to make sure that an attached *UPS* (uninterruptible power supply) system is functioning properly.

See also **power conditioning**.

UPS STATUS A Novell NetWare server utility that displays information about the linked *UPS* (uninterruptible power supply) system.

UPS TIME A Novell NetWare server utility that lets a network administrator change the recharge, discharge, and wait settings for a linked *UPS* (uninterruptible power supply) system.

uptime The length or percentage of time during which a computer system is functioning and available for use.

See also **downtime, POH**.

upward compatibility The design of software that incorporates the capability to function with other, more powerful, products likely to become available in the near future. Adherence to design standards makes upward compatibility possible.

u

URL Abbreviation for Uniform Resource Locator, pronounced "earl" or "you-are-ell." A method of accessing *Internet* resources.

URLs contain information about both the access method to use and also about the resource itself, and are used by *Web browsers* to connect you directly to a specific document or *home page* on the *World Wide Web,* without you having to know where that resource is located physically. A sample URL might look like this:

```
http://www.ibm.com/search
```

The first part of the URL, before the colon, specifies the access method. On the Web, this is usually *HTTP* (for hypertext transmission protocol), but you might also see file, *FTP,* or *Gopher* instead. The second part of the URL, after the colon, specifies the resource. The text after the two slashes usually indicates a *server* name, and the text after the single slash defines the directory or individual file you will connect to. If you are linking to a document, it will usually have the file-name extension .html, the abbreviation for hypertext markup language.

URLs are always case-sensitive, so pay particular attention to uppercase and lowercase letters, and to symbols as well.

USENET Contraction of USEr NETwork. An international, noncommercial network, linking many thousands of Unix sites. Although there is a very close relationship between the *Internet* and USENET, they are not the same thing by any means. USENET predates the Internet; in the early days, information was distributed by dial-up connections and *UUCP* software. Not every Internet computer is part of USENET, and not every USENET system can be reached from the Internet.

Like the Internet, USENET has no central governing body; USENET is run by the people who use it. With well over ten thousand newsgroups, USENET is accessed by millions of people every day, in more than one hundred countries.

USENET newsgroups The individual discussion groups within *USENET.* USENET newsgroups contain *articles posted* by other

Internet and USENET subscribers; very few of them contain actual hard news. Most newsgroups are concerned with a single subject; the range of subjects available through USENET is phenomenal—there are over ten thousand newsgroups from which to choose. If people are interested in a subject, you are sure to find a newsgroup for it somewhere.

Newsgroups are like the online forums found on CompuServe or America Online; you can post your own articles and browse through similar items posted by others. When you reply to a post, you can reply to the newsgroup so that other subscribers can read your reply, or you can respond directly to the originator in a private e-mail message.

If you see the word "binary" in a newsgroup name, that newsgroup specializes in pictures. The picture files are first converted to text with the *Unix uuencode* utility; you will need a copy of the Unix utility *uudecode* to turn this text back into a graphical image you can view.

user   Any person allowed to access a computer system or network.

user account   A security mechanism used to control access to a network or to a multiuser computer system, established and maintained by the network administrator. Elements of a user account include password information, rights, and information about the groups to which the user belongs.

USERDEF   A Novell NetWare 3.*x* workstation utility that employs a template consisting of a default set of rights and properties to assist the network administrator in creating new network users. In NetWare 4.*x*, this function is provided by *UIMPORT*.

user group   A group of users of a specific computer or software package who meet to share tips and listen to industry experts. Some PC user groups hold large, well-attended monthly meetings, run their own bulletin board systems, and publish newsletters of exceptional quality.

See also **special interest group**.

USERLIST   A Novell NetWare 3.*x* workstation utility that displays information about users logged in to the server, including each user's network address, node

u

355

address, connection number, and login time. In NetWare 4.*x*, this function is provided by *NLIST*.

USRT   Abbreviation for universal synchronous receiver/transmitter. An electronic module that combines the transmitting and receiving circuitry needed for synchronous communications over a serial line.

See also **synchronous transmission**.

UTP   See **unshielded twisted-pair cable**.

UUCP   A standard Unix utility that manages the transmission of information between Unix systems, using serial connections and regular telephone lines. The name is derived from "Unix-to-Unix copy."

uudecode   Pronounced "you-you-de-code."

1. To convert a *text file* created by the *Unix uuencode* utility back into its original *binary* form.

Graphical images and other binary files are often sent to *USENET newsgroups* in this form, because the newsgroups can only handle text and don't know how to manage binary files.

2. The name of the utility program that performs a text-to-binary file conversion. Originally a Unix utility, uudecode is now available for most operating systems.

uuencode   Pronounced "you-you-en-code."

1. To convert a *binary file* such as a graphical image into a *text file* so the file can be sent over the *Internet* or to a *USENET newsgroup* as a part of an *e-mail* message. When you receive a uuencoded text file, you must process it through the *Unix uudecode* utility to turn it back into a graphical image that you can view.

2. The name of the utility that performs a binary-to-text file conversion. Originally a Unix utility, uuencode is now available for most operating systems.

V.17   A *CCITT Group 3* fax modulation standard for transmitting fax data at up to 14,400 bits per second (bps), with a fallback to 12,000 bps as line conditions deteriorate.

V.21   A *CCITT* standard for 300-bit-per-second modems using *full-duplex* transmission over dial-up lines. This standard is not compatible with the Bell 103 standard widely used in the United States.

V.22   A *CCITT* standard for 600-bit-per-second (bps) and 1200-bps *full-duplex* modems over two-wire, dial-up, or leased lines.

V.22 bis   A *CCITT* standard for 2400-bit-per-second (bps) *full-duplex* modems over dial-up and two-wire leased lines, with fallback to 1200- and then 600-bps operation.

V.23   A *CCITT* standard for 600- or 1200-bit-per-second synchronous or asynchronous *half-duplex* modems used on dial-up lines.

V.24   A *CCITT* definition of the interface between a modem and a computer system. V.24 is functionally equivalent to the *RS-232-C* standard, but does not specify connectors or pin assignments; those are defined in ISO 2110.

V.25   A *CCITT* standard for automatic calling and answering circuits over dial-up lines using a parallel interface. V.25 includes the disabling of echo suppression on manually dialed calls.

V.25 bis   A *CCITT* standard for automatic calling and answering circuits over dial-up lines with three modes: asynchronous, character-oriented synchronous, and bit-oriented synchronous (HDLC/SDLC). V.25 bis does not include modem configuration commands.

V.26   A *CCITT* standard for 1200-bit-per-second, *full-duplex* modems used over four-wire leased lines.

V.26 bis   A *CCITT* standard for 1200-bit per second (bps) and 2400-bps *full-duplex* modems used on dial-up lines.

V.27   A *CCITT* standard for 4800-bit-per-second, *full-duplex* modems used with four-wire leased lines, with a manual equalizer.

V.27 bis   A *CCITT* standard for 2400- or 4800-bit-per-second, *full-duplex* modems used with four-wire leased lines. The main advance over *V.27* is the addition of an automatic adaptive equalizer for use on leased circuits.

V.27 ter   A *CCITT* standard for 2400- or 4800-bit-per-second, *full-duplex* modems used with dial-up lines. Used in some *CCITT Group 3* fax transmissions.

V.29   A *CCITT* standard for 9600-bit-per-second (bps) modems used with *point-to-point*, four-wire leased lines. This standard has been adopted for *CCITT Group 3* fax transmissions over dial-up lines at 9600 and 7200 bps.

V.32   A *CCITT* standard for 9600-bit-per-second (bps) modems, with fallback to 4800 bps, used over two-wire, dial-up lines or two-wire or four-wire leased lines, with echo canceling to remove any telephone-line echo. V.32 encodes four data bits for each baud to give an effective throughput of 9600 bps and includes *trellis-coded modulation* error correcting techniques. V.32 is the first standard for 9600-bps modems using standard lines anywhere in the world.

V.32 bis   A *CCITT* standard extending *V.32* to 7200, 12,000, and 14,400 bits per second.

V.32 terbo   A pseudo-standard proposed by AT&T and others that supports transmission at up to 19,200 bits per second. The name is a pun; the next revision of the *V.32* standard after V.32 *bis* will be V.32 *ter*.

See also **V.fast.**

V.33   A *CCITT* standard for 12,000-bit-per-second (bps) and 14,400-bps modems used over four-wire, leased circuits, with *time-division multiplexing* available for line sharing.

V.34   A *CCITT* standard for 28,800-bit-per-second (bps) modems using *trellis-encoding* techniques and advanced data compression to speed effective data-transfer rates to 100,000 bps.

V.42 A *CCITT* standard for error correction rather than for a modem. V.42 uses LAP-M (Link Access Procedure-Modem) as the primary error-correcting protocol, with *MNP* (Microcom Networking Protocol) classes 2 through 4 as an alternative.

V.42 bis A *CCITT* standard that adds a British Telecom Lempel-Ziv *data-compression* technique to *V.42* error correction, usually capable of achieving a compression ratio of 3.5 to 1.

V.54 A *CCITT* standard that specifies the *loopback* tests incorporated into modems for testing the telephone circuit and isolating any transmission problems.

V.110 A *CCITT* standard that specifies how *DTE* (data terminal equipment) using synchronous or asynchronous serial interfaces is supported on an *ISDN* (Integrated Services Digital Network).

V.120 A *CCITT* standard that specifies how *DTE* (data terminal equipment) using synchronous or asynchronous serial interfaces is supported on an *ISDN* (Integrated Services Digital Network) using a protocol to *encapsulate* the transmitted data.

value-added process Abbreviated VAP. In Novell NetWare 2.*x*, an application that adds functions to the network operating system, such as print server or communications server software.

NetWare Loadable Modules (NLMs) provide a similar function in later versions of NetWare. See also **Virtual Loadable Module**.

value-added reseller See **VAR**.

VAP See **value-added process**.

vaporware A slang term for a product that has been announced but has missed its release date, often by a large margin, and so is not actually available.

VAR Acronym for value-added reseller. A company that adds value to a system, repackages it, and then resells it to the public. This added value can take the form of better documentation, user support, service support, system integration, or sometimes just a new nameplate on the box. For example, Canon makes the print engine used in many laser printers, including those from Hewlett-Packard (HP); in this case, Canon is an *OEM* (original equipment manufacturer) and HP is the VAR.

VAX   Digital Equipment Corporation's (DEC's) popular line of minicomputers and workstations.
See also **VMS**.

vector graphics   See **object-oriented graphics**.

vendor   The person or company that manufactures, supplies, or sells computer hardware, software, or related services.

Veronica   A search service built into the *Gopher Internet* application. When you use Veronica to search a series of Gopher menus (files, directories, and other items), the results of the search are presented as another Gopher menu, which you can use to access the resources your search has located. Veronica allegedly stands for Very Easy Rodent-oriented Net-wide Index to Computer Archives.
See also **Archie, Gopherspace**.

VERSION   A Novell NetWare server utility that displays the current version number of the network operating system.

version number   A method of identifying a particular software or hardware release, assigned by the developer, that often includes numbers before and after a decimal point; the higher the number, the more recent the release.

The number before the decimal point indicates the major revision levels (as in DOS 5 and DOS 6), and the part after the decimal indicates a minor revision level (as in DOS 6.1 and DOS 6.2). In some cases, a minor revision can produce a significant difference in performance.

Many people steer clear of any release labeled 1.0, because this number implies the first release of a product that may not have had extensive real-world use. Microsoft avoided this issue with the first release of Windows NT by taking the unusual step of calling it version 3.1 (instead of 1.0) to associate it in the minds of buyers with the successful Windows 3.1. And the upgrade to Windows 3.1, rather than being Windows 4.0, is known as Windows 95, after the release year.

vertical application An application specifically created for a narrow and specialized market or profession. Software designed for veterinary hospital management is an example of a vertical application.

very low-frequency emission Abbreviated VLF. Radiation emitted by a computer monitor and other common household electrical appliances, such as televisions, hair dryers, electric blankets, and food processors. VLF emissions range from 2 to 400 kHz and decline with the square of the distance from the source. Emissions are not constant around a computer monitor; they are higher from the sides and rear, and weakest from the front of the screen.

Sweden is the only country to have defined a set of standards for monitor emissions. In 1990, Mat Oct Provadet (MPR), the Swedish National Board for Meterology and Testing, revised its guidelines for acceptable VLF emissions as less than or equal to 25 nanoTesla (nT). A nanoTesla is a unit of measurement for small magnetic fields.

See also **extremely low-frequency emission, radio-frequency interference.**

very small aperture terminal Abbreviated VSAT. A small satellite terminal used for digital communications, from 1 to 3 meters (3.3 to 10 feet) in diameter, capable of managing digital transmissions of up to 56 kilobits per second. Satellites that can handle T1 data rates of up to 1.544 megabits per second are known as TSATs.

VESA Abbreviation for Video Electronics Standards Association. An association of video graphics adapter and monitor manufacturers that sets standards for PC video. VESA is most notable for its role in standardizing Super VGA (SVGA) hardware.

VESA local bus See **VL bus.**

V.fast A pseudo standard from Hayes and Rockwell for modems transmitting at data rates of up to 28,800 bits per second, developed in anticipation of the long-awaited V.34 standard. Some V.fast modems can be upgraded or converted to the V.34 standard. Also known as V.FC, an abbreviation of V.Fast Class.

See also **V.32 terbo.**

video adapter   An *expansion board* that plugs into the *expansion bus* in a DOS computer and provides the text and graphics output to the monitor. Some later video adapters, such as the SVGA, are included in the circuitry on the motherboard rather than as separate plug-in boards.

video conferencing   A method used to allow people at remote locations to join in a conference and share information. In a networked environment, video conferencing has gone way beyond looking at a picture of a person; users can look at and update charts, make drawings or sketches on a chalkboard, update spreadsheets, and so on, all online.

A video camera and a speakerphone are linked to a PC at each site, and the PC in turn is linked to the network.

See also **desktop video**.

Video Electronics Standards Association   See **VESA**.

video RAM   Abbreviated VRAM, pronounced "vee-ram." Special-purpose *RAM* random-access memory) with two data paths for access (conventional RAM has just one). These two paths let a VRAM board manage two functions at once: refreshing the display and communicating with the processor. VRAM does not require the system to complete one function before starting the other, so it allows faster operation for the whole video system.

VINES   See **Banyan VINES**.

virtual 8086 mode   A mode found in the *80386* and later processors that lets the processor emulate several separate PC environments simultaneously. The operating system controls the external elements, such as *interrupts* and input/output.

Applications running in this mode are protected from the applications running in all the other virtual 8086 environments, and they behave as though they have control of the whole 8086 environment. To the user, it appears that several 8086 systems are running side by side, but under the control of the operating system. Both *OS/2* and *Windows NT* use this feature of the processor to multitask multiple DOS sessions.

virtual circuit   A temporary shared communications path that appears to the user as a dedicated connection. A virtual circuit is maintained only for as long as the customer requires a connection; the next time a call is placed, a different virtual circuit may be used.

virtual data network
A method used to provide full interconnection of all LAN segments without using dedicated circuits, so that customers only pay for the services they use. Also known as a virtual LAN.

See also **bandwidth on demand, virtual circuit.**

virtual drive
See **RAM disk.**

virtual LAN
See **virtual data network.**

Virtual Loadable Module
Abbreviated VLM. A Novell NetWare modular program that runs on each *DOS client* and allows that workstation to communicate with the server. The *NetWare DOS Requester* consists of several VLMs that replace and provide backward compatibility with the *NetWare shells* used in earlier versions of NetWare.

See also **NetWare Loadable Module.**

virtual machine
An environment created by the operating system that gives each executing application the illusion that it has complete control of an independent computer and can access all the system resources that it needs. For example, the Intel *80386* (and higher) processor can run multiple DOS applications in completely separate and protected address spaces using *virtual 8086 mode.*

virtual memory
A memory-management technique that allows information in physical memory to be swapped out to a hard disk if necessary. This technique provides applications with more memory space than is actually available in the computer. True virtual-memory management requires specialized hardware in the processor for the operating system to use; it is not just a matter of writing information out to a *swap file* on the hard disk at the application level.

In a virtual memory system, programs and their data are divided into smaller pieces called pages. When more memory is needed, the operating system decides which pages are least likely to be needed soon (using an algorithm based on frequency of use,

V

most recent use, and program priority), and it writes these pages out to disk. The memory space that they used is now available to the rest of the system for other applications. When these pages are needed again, they are loaded back into real memory, displacing other pages.

virus   A program intended to damage a computer system without the user's knowledge or permission. A virus may attach itself to another program or to the partition table or boot track on a hard disk. When a certain event occurs, a date passes, or a specific program executes, the virus is triggered into action.

Not all viruses are harmful; some are just annoying. The most famous virus is probably the Israeli or Jerusalem virus, also known as Friday the 13th, first seen on a computer at the University of Jerusalem in July 1987. This virus slows down the system and draws black boxes on the lower-left portion of the screen. If the virus is in memory on any Friday 13th, every program executed is erased from the hard disk.

See also **anti-virus program.**

VL bus   Also known as VL local bus. Abbreviation for VESA local bus.

A local bus architecture introduced by *VESA* (Video Electronics Standards Association), in which up to three VL bus adapter slots are built into the motherboard. The VL bus allows for *bus mastering.* The most common VL bus adapters are video adapters, hard-disk controllers, and network interface cards.

See also **PCI local bus, PCMCIA.**

VLF   See **very low-frequency emission.**

VL local bus   See **VL bus.**

VLM   See **Virtual Loadable Module.**

VM   An IBM operating system, usually run on smaller mainframe computers.

VMS   A *multiuser, multitasking, virtual memory* operating system from Digital Equipment Corporation (DEC) for the VAX line of computers.

voice mail   A computerized *store-and-forward* system for voice messages. A voice-mail system uses prerecorded messages to route the caller to the correct person, department, or *mailbox,* and then digitizes the incoming messages and stores them on disk for review by the recipient. Users can often forward voice-mail messages to another department or person after attaching their own comments.

See also **e-mail.**

VOLINFO   A Novell NetWare 3.*x* workstation utility that displays information about the volumes on a server, including volume names, storage capacity, and the maximum number of directory entries allowed for each volume. In NetWare 4.*x*, this function is provided by *FILER*.

volume   In networking, a volume is the highest level of the file server directory and file structure. Large hard disks can be divided into several different volumes when the network operating system is first installed.

See also **MAP, MOUNT, VOLINFO.**

volume label   In many operating systems, the name assigned to a disk by the user, displayed on the first line of a directory listing. The Macintosh, where disks are often referred to by name, uses the term volume name instead.

VOLUMES   A Novell NetWare server utility that displays a list of all the *volumes* currently mounted on the server.

volume serial number   In several operating systems, a unique number assigned to a disk during the formatting process. This number is displayed at the beginning of a directory listing. In the Macintosh, System 7 assigns a similar number, known as a volume reference number, that programs can use when referring to disks.

VRAM   See **video RAM.**

VREPAIR   A Novell NetWare server utility that finds and corrects volume problems.

See also **DISMOUNT, MOUNT.**

VSAT   See **very small aperture terminal.**

VT-52, VT-100, VT-200   A series of asynchronous terminals manufactured by Digital Equipment Corporation (DEC) that uses a specific set of control codes for display management. Many communications and *terminal-emulation*

V

packages include emulations of these terminals.

VTAM   Abbreviation for Virtual Telecommunications Access Method. IBM software that runs on a mainframe computer running the MVS or *VM* operating system.

VTAM controls communications in an *SNA* (Systems Network Architecture) environment. VTAM supports a range of network protocols, including *SDLC* (Synchronous Data Link Control) and *Token Ring*.

W

W3 See World Wide Web.

WAIS Abbreviation for Wide Area Information Service, pronounced "ways." A service used to access text databases or libraries on the *Internet*. WAIS uses simple natural-language queries, and takes advantage of index searches for fast retrieval. Unlike *Gopher*, which only searches through the names of Gopher resources, WAIS can search the content of all documents retrievable from WAIS databases. WAIS is particularly adept at searching through collections of *USENET newsgroups*, electronic texts, and newspaper archives.

wait state A clock cycle during which no instructions are executed, because the processor is waiting for data from memory.

Static RAM chips and *paged-mode RAM* chips are becoming popular because they can store information without being constantly refreshed by the processor, thus eliminating the wait state. A computer that can process information without wait states is known as a *zero-wait-state computer*.

WAN See wide-area network.

warm boot A *reboot* performed after the operating system has been running for some period of time, by pressing *Ctrl-Alt-Delete* rather than cycling the computer.

Warp See OS/2.

Warp Connect See OS/2.

WATS Abbreviation for Wide Area Telephone Service. Unlimited use of a telephone circuit for specified periods for a fixed charge.

Web browser A *World Wide Web* client application that lets you look at *hypertext* documents and follow links to other *HTML* documents on the Web.

When you find something that interests you as you browse through a hypertext document, you can click your mouse on that object, and the system automatically takes care of accessing the

Internet host that holds the document you requested; you don't need to know the IP address, the name of the host system, or any other details.

The NCSA *Mosaic* program, created by the National Center for Supercomputing Applications, is an example of a popular Web browser.

See also URL.

WHOAMI A Novell NetWare workstation utility that displays connection information, including effective rights, security information, and the groups to which a user belongs.

wide-area network Abbreviated WAN. A network that connects users across large distances, often crossing the geographical boundaries of cities or states.

See also **local-area network, metropolitan-area network.**

wideband In communications, a channel capable of handling more frequencies than a standard 3-kHz voice channel.

wideband transmission See **broadband network.**

wildcard character A character that represents one or more unknown characters. In many operating systems, a *question mark* (?) represents a single unknown character in a file name or file-name extension, and an *asterisk* (*) represents any number of unknown characters.

See also **star-dot-star.**

window In a *graphical user interface*, a rectangular portion of the screen that acts as a viewing area for applications. Windows can be tiled, so they are displayed side by side, or cascaded, so their individual title bars are always visible. They then can be individually moved and sized on the screen. Some programs can open multiple document windows inside their application window to display several word-processing or spreadsheet data files at the same time.

See also **social interface, X Window.**

Windows See **Microsoft Windows.**

Windows 95 The long-awaited replacement for the DOS and Windows 3.1 operating systems, from Microsoft Corporation. Windows 95 is a *32-bit, multitasking,* multithreaded operating system capable of running DOS, Windows 3.1, and Windows 95 applications. It supports *Plug-and-Play* (on the appropriate hardware), and adds an enhanced FAT file system in the Virtual FAT, which allows file names of up to 255 characters while also supporting the DOS 8.3 file-naming conventions.

Applets include WordPad (a word processor), Paint, and WinPad (a personal information manager), as well as system tools such as Backup, ScanDisk, Disk Defragmenter, and DriveSpace. Access to *Microsoft Network* is available directly from the Windows 95 desktop. A new Start button and desktop TaskBar make application management easy and straightforward.

Rather than follow a normal software version numbering scheme, Microsoft decided to associate the first release of this operating system (which would normally be version number 1.0) with the year 1995 by naming the operating system Windows 95.

Windows accelerator   An expansion card or a chip containing circuitry dedicated to speeding up the performance of PC video hardware so that Microsoft Windows appears to run faster. Standard display adapters do not handle the throughput required by Windows particularly well, so they rapidly become *input/output bound*. An accelerator card specifically tuned for Windows can improve overall performance considerably.

See also **graphics accelerator board, graphics coprocessor.**

Windows client   A workstation that loads Windows and gains access to the network by using either a *NetWare shell* (for NetWare versions 2.*x* and 3.*x*) or the *NetWare DOS Requester* (for NetWare 4.*x*).

Windows for Pen Computing A software product from Microsoft, based on the Windows *graphical user interface*, installed on portable computers that work with an electronic pen or stylus that is used to write directly onto the screen.

Windows for Workgroups   A Microsoft software product based on the Windows *graphical user interface*, with added functions for *peer-to-peer* networking of computers. Users can share files, exchange e-mail, maintain a

W

collective calendar of meetings, and so on. Windows for Workgroups requires DOS (not *Windows NT*) to run.

Windows NT   A 32-bit, *multitasking*, portable operating system developed by Microsoft, first released in 1993.

Windows NT runs on Intel *80386* (or later) processors and *reduced instruction set computing* (RISC) processors, such as the *MIPS R4000* and *DEC Alpha,* the *PowerPC*, and Hewlett-Packard's PA-RISC systems.

Windows NT contains the graphical user interface from Microsoft Windows 3.1. It can run Windows 3.1 and DOS applications, as well as OS/2 16-bit, character-based applications and new 32-bit programs specifically developed for Windows NT. Multitasking under Windows NT is *preemptive*, and applications can execute multiple *threads*.

Windows NT supports several file systems, including the DOS *file allocation table* (FAT) system, installable systems such as CD-ROMs, and its own native *NTFS*. Windows NT also supports *multiprocessing*, *Object Linking and Embedding* (OLE), and *peer-to-peer* networking.

Instead of giving the first version of Windows NT the version number 1.0, Microsoft called it version 3.1, to associate it in the minds of buyers with the successful Windows 3.1. Also known as Windows NT Workstation.

See also **Windows NT Server.**

Windows NT Server   A version of Windows NT that provides centralized network management and *security* functions. It has *fault-tolerant* features, such as *disk mirroring, disk duplexing, RAID* level 5 (redundant array of inexpensive disks), and *UPS* (uninterruptible power supply) monitoring. Previously known as Windows NT Advanced Server. The illustration on the opposite page shows the Windows NT Server architecture.

Windows NT Server supports connections to *LAN Manager, LAN Server*, Unix, Macintosh, and NetWare, along with *TCP/IP, IPX/SPX, PPP*, and *SLIP.*

See also **Microsoft BackOffice, Solaris, Unix, Windows NT.**

Windows Sockets API   An *Application Program Interface* for writers of TCP/IP-related software. Also known as Winsock or the Windows Network Transit Protocol. The Windows Sockets API allows Windows programmers to

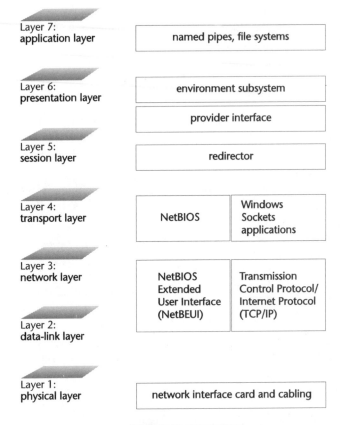

Layer 7: application layer	named pipes, file systems	
Layer 6: presentation layer	environment subsystem	
	provider interface	
Layer 5: session layer	redirector	
Layer 4: transport layer	NetBIOS	Windows Sockets applications
Layer 3: network layer	NetBIOS Extended User Interface (NetBEUI)	Transmission Control Protocol/ Internet Protocol (TCP/IP)
Layer 2: data-link layer		
Layer 1: physical layer	network interface card and cabling	

WINDOWS NT SERVER

W

ignore the intricacies of program-ming to dissimilar *TCP/IP* protocol stacks by providing an intermediate layer of software. Similarly, developers of TCP/IP software also program to the API rather than directly to the application.

wireless communications   A

method of connecting a node or a group of nodes into the main network using a technology other than conventional cabling.

The following methods are in use:

• **Infrared line of sight:** High-frequency light waves are used to transmit data between nodes up to 24.4 meters (80 feet) apart using an unobstructed path; infra-red beams cannot pass through masonry walls. Data rates are relatively high, in the tens of megabits per second range.

- **High-frequency radio:** High-frequency radio signals transmit data to nodes from 12.2 to 39.6 meters (40 to 130 feet) apart, depending on the nature of obstructions separating them; the signal can penetrate thin walls but not supporting masonry. Data rates are usually less than 1 megabit per second.

- **Spread-spectrum radio:** A small set of frequencies are available for wireless LANs without *FCC* approval. The 902 to 928 megahertz (Mhz) band is known as the Industrial, Scientific, Medical (ISM) band and is not regulated. The 2.4 to 2.483 gigahertz (Ghz) band is regulated and requires an FCC license for use. Spread-spectrum nodes can be up to 243.8 meters (800 feet) apart in an open environment, and these radio waves can pass through masonry walls. However, in an environment with fully enclosed offices, distances are limited to 33.5 meters (110 feet). Data rates are usually less than 1 megabit per second.

Wireless LANs are not always completely wireless. They may be used to replace the cabling on certain network segments or to connect groups of networks that use conventional cabling.

See also **mobile computing**.

word length

1. The standard data unit in a particular computer. The most common words are 8, 16, 32, or 64 bits.

2. In communications, the number of data bits in a data word.

workflow software
Software that allows users to move and manage information among themselves, combining the functions of e-mail, imaging, and document management.

A document moves through various stages of processing as it is edited, signed, or validated by the various members of the workgroup. Each stage is orchestrated and validated by workflow software.

See also **Lotus Notes**.

workgroup
A group of individuals who work together and share the same files and databases over a local-area network (LAN). Special software coordinates the workgroup and allows users to edit and exchange files and update databases as a group.

See also **workflow software**.

workstation

1. In networking, any personal computer (other than the file server) attached to the network.

2. A high-performance computer optimized for graphics applications, such as computer-aided design (CAD), computer-aided engineering (CAE), or scientific applications.

See also **diskless workstation.**

World Wide Web

Abbreviated WWW, W3, or simply the Web. A huge collection of *hypertext* pages on the *Internet*. World Wide Web concepts were developed in Switzerland by the European Laboratory for Particle Physics (known as CERN), but the Web is not just a tool for scientists; it is one of the most flexible and exciting tools in existence for surfing the Internet.

Hypertext links connect pieces of information (text, graphics, audio, or video) in separate *HTML* pages located at the same or at different Internet sites, and you explore these pages and links using a *Web browser* such as the NCSA *Mosaic* application.

You can also access a WWW resource directly if you specify the appropriate *URL* (Uniform Resource Locator). The illustration on the following page shows an HTML page of the Exploratorium *home page* displayed by an OS/2 Web browser.

World Wide Web traffic is growing faster than most other Internet services, and the reason for this becomes obvious once you try a capable Web browser; it is very easy to access World Wide Web information.

WORM

Acronym for Write Once Read Many. A high-capacity optical storage device that can only be written to once, but that can be read a number of times. WORM devices can store from 200 to 700 MB of information on a 5.25" disk, and so are well suited to archival and other non-changing storage.

write-back cache

A technique used in cache design for writing information back into main memory. In a write-back cache, the cache stores the changed block of data, but only updates main memory under certain conditions, such as when the whole block must be overwritten because a newer block must be loaded into the cache, or when the controlling algorithm determines that too much time has elapsed since the last update. This method is rather complex

W

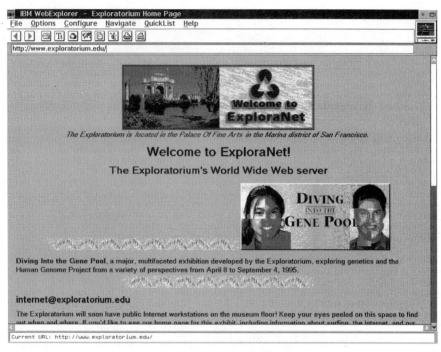

WORLD WIDE WEB

to implement, but is much faster than other designs.

See also **cache, write-through cache**.

write-through cache   A technique used in cache design for writing information back into main memory. In a write-through cache, each time the processor returns a changed bit of data to the cache, the cache updates that information in both the cache and in main memory. This method is

simple to implement, but is not as fast as other designs; delays can be introduced when the processor must wait to complete write operations to slower main memory.

See also **cache, write-back cache**.

WSUPDATE   A Novell NetWare workstation utility used to search for and replace workstation files. WSUPDATE can update files in multiple directories on many workstations, as well as those that have the read-only flag set,

374

and it can search mapped as well as local drives.

WSUPGRD A Novell NetWare workstation utility used to upgrade workstations from *IPX* device drivers to *ODI* drivers. WSUPGRD can also modify a workstation's *AUTOEXEC.BAT*

file so that the ODI driver is loaded automatically in place of the IPX driver.

In NetWare 4.x, WSUPGRD also lets you update workstation files by comparing the data and time of files on the server.

WWW See **World Wide Web.**

W

X

X.21   A *CCITT* standard that defines a *protocol* used in a *circuit-switching* network.

X.25   A *CCITT* standard, developed in 1976, that defines the connection between a terminal and a public *packet-switched network*. X.25 describes the electrical connections, the transmission protocol, error detection and correction, and other aspects of the link. X.25 standards parallel the lowest three levels of the *ISO/OSI model* for computer-to-computer communications: the *physical layer*, *data-link layer*, and *network layer*.

X.25 gateway   See X.75.

X.28   A *CCITT* standard, developed in 1977, that defines a *DTE/DCE* (data terminal equipment/data communications equipment) interface for accessing a *PAD* (packet assembler/disassembler) in a public data network that does not cross an international boundary but is confined within one country.

X.29   A *CCITT* standard, developed in 1977, for user data and the exchange of control information between a *PAD* (packet assembler/disassembler) and packet-mode *DTE* (data terminal equipment) or another PAD.

X.75   A *CCITT* standard that defines the procedures used to connect two separate *packet-switched networks*, such as those located in separate countries; often referred to as an X.25 gateway.

X.200   A *CCITT* standard that documents the seven-layer *ISO/OSI model* for computer-to-computer communications.

X.400   A *CCITT* and OSI (*Open Systems Interconnection*) recommended standard, released in 1984 and revised in 1988, for public or private international *e-mail* distribution systems, defining how messages will be transferred across the network or between two or more connected heterogeneous networks. X.400 defines the components of an electronic address as well as the

details of the envelope surrounding the message and the rules to follow when converting between message types, such as text or fax.
See also **X.500**.

X.500 A *CCITT* and OSI (*Open Systems Interconnection*) recommended standard, first released in 1988 and revised in 1992, for a global directory system for locating e-mail users, to be used with the *X.400* e-mail services. X.500 is similar to a worldwide telephone book.

Xerox Network Services

Abbreviated XNS. A multilayer communications *protocol*, first developed by Xerox, and later used by Novell and other network software suppliers. XNS also supports a distributed file system that lets users access other computers' files and printers as if they were local.

Xmodem A popular *file transfer protocol* available in many off-the-shelf and shareware communications packages, as well as on many bulletin board systems. Xmodem was originally developed by Ward Christiansen for early PCs using the CP/M operating system. Xmodem divides the data for a transmission into blocks. Each block consists of the start-of-header character, a block number, 128 bytes of data, and a *checksum*. An acknowledgment byte is returned to the sender if the checksum calculation is identical to the sender's checksum; however, this requirement to acknowledge every transmitted block can lead to poor performance.

An extension to Xmodem, called Xmodem-CRC, adds a more stringent error-checking method by using a *cyclical redundancy check* (CRC) to detect transmission errors rather then Xmodem's simple additive checksum.

Another variation is Xmodem-1K, which transfers data in 1,024-byte blocks.

See also **Kermit, Ymodem, Zmodem**.

XMS See **Extended Memory Specification**.

XNS See **Xerox Network Services**.

XON/XOFF In *asynchronous transmissions* between two PCs, a simple method of *flow control*. The receiving PC sends an XOFF control character (ASCII 19, Ctrl-S) to pause the transmission of data when the receive buffer is full, and then sends an XON character (ASCII 17, Ctrl-Q) when it is ready to continue the transmission.

See also **flow control, handshaking.**

X/Open An independent international organization with more than forty member companies, established in Europe in 1984 to develop an open, multivendor Common Applications Environment (CAE), based on industry and de facto standards. The X/Open CAE is based on the interfaces defined in IEEE 1003.1, the 1988 *POSIX* standard, extended to cover additional open systems requirements. Novell transferred its ownership of the Unix trademarks to X/Open in 1993.

XT See **crosstalk.**

X Window A windowing environment developed at MIT for Unix workstations. Often referred to simply as "X." X Window is an open and nonproprietary bit-mapped graphics system, designed to be independent of both the display hardware and the underlying operating system. It is supported by all the major workstation vendors. The Open Software Foundation (OSF) implementation is known as Motif; Sun and Hewlett-Packard use a version called OpenLook.

X

Yellow Pages A name for the security and file-access databases on Unix systems. These databases are now known as *Network Information Services* (NIS).

Ymodem A popular *file transfer protocol* available in many off-the-shelf and shareware communications packages, as well as on many bulletin board systems. Ymodem, a variation of the *Xmodem* protocol, divides the data to be transmitted into blocks; each block consists of the start-of-header character, a block number, 1 kilobyte of data, and a *checksum*. Ymodem's larger data block means less overhead for error control when compared with Xmodem, but if the block has to be retransmitted because the protocol detects an error, there is more data to resend. Ymodem also incorporates the capabilities to send multiple files in the same session and to abort file transfer during the transmission.

See also **Kermit, Zmodem.**

Zero Insertion Force socket
See ZIF socket.

zero-slot LAN   A *local-area network* (LAN) that uses one of the existing serial or parallel ports on the computer rather than a special network interface card plugged in to the computer's expansion bus. Because zero-slot LANs can only transmit as fast as the computer's output port, they are considerably slower than networks that use network-specific hardware and software. The maximum length of each cable segment is also severely limited, so zero-slot LANs can network only two or three computers. The advantage of a zero-slot LAN is its low cost compared with dedicated network systems; however, the prices of newer *peer-to-peer networks* are beginning to negate this advantage.

zero-wait-state computer   A computer that can process information without processor *wait*

states, which are clock cycles during which no instructions are executed because the processor is waiting for data from a device or from memory. *Static RAM* chips and *paged-mode RAM* chips are becoming popular because they can store information without being constantly refreshed by the processor, thus eliminating the wait state.

ZIF socket   Abbreviation for Zero Insertion Force socket. A specially designed chip socket that makes replacing a chip easier and safer. To change a chip in a ZIF socket, you raise a lever beside the socket to free the original chip's pins from the socket. Then slide the old chip out and slide in the replacement chip, taking care to align the pins and holes. Finally, lower the lever again. A ZIF socket minimizes damage to the delicate pins that connect the chip to the rest of the system.

Zmodem   A popular *file transfer protocol* available in many off-the-shelf and shareware communications packages, as well as on many bulletin board systems. Zmodem is similar to *Xmodem* and *Ymodem* but is designed to handle larger data transfers with fewer errors. Zmodem also includes a feature called checkpoint restart, which allows an interrupted transmission to resume at the point of interruption, rather than starting again at the beginning of the transmission.

See also **Kermit, Xmodem, Ymodem.**

zone   On a local-area network (LAN) such as AppleTalk, a logical subgroup of users within a larger group of interconnected networks.

ASCII and EBCDIC Character Sets

ASCII and EBCDIC Character Sets   Table A.1 shows the first 32 ASCII characters (0–31), also known as the control characters.

Table A.2 shows the 7-bit standard ASCII character set (comprising characters 0–127), which is implemented on all computers that use ASCII.

Table A.3 shows characters 128–255 of the 8-bit IBM extended ASCII character set.

Table A.4 shows all 256 characters that make up the EBCDIC character set.

TABLE A.1: *ASCII Control Characters*

DECIMAL	CHARACTER	CONTROL COMBINATION
0	NUL (Null)	Ctrl+@
1	SOH (Start of heading)	Ctrl+A
2	STX (Start of text)	Ctrl+B
3	ETX (End of text)	Ctrl+C
4	EOT (End of transmission)	Ctrl+D
5	ENQ (Enquire)	Ctrl+E
6	ACK (Acknowledge)	Ctrl+F
7	BEL (Bell)	Ctrl+G
8	BS (Backspace)	Ctrl+H
9	HT (Horizontal tab)	Ctrl+I
10	LF (Line feed)	Ctrl+J

TABLE A.1: *ASCII Control Characters*

DECIMAL	CHARACTER	CONTROL COMBINATION
11	VT (Vertical tab)	Ctrl+K
12	FF (Form feed)	Ctrl+L
13	CR (Carriage return)	Ctrl+M
14	SO (Shift out)	Ctrl+N
15	SI (Shift in)	Ctrl+O
16	DLE (Data link escape)	Ctrl+P
17	DC1 (Device control 1)	Ctrl+Q
18	DC2 (Device control 2)	Ctrl+R
19	DC3 (Device control 3)	Ctrl+S
20	DC4 (Device control 4)	Ctrl+T
21	NAK (Negative acknowledgement)	Ctrl+U
22	SYN (Synchronous idle)	Ctrl+V
23	ETB (End transmission block)	Ctrl+W
24	CAN (Cancel)	Ctrl+X
25	EM (End of medium)	Ctrl+Y
26	SUB (Substitute)	Ctrl+Z

TABLE A.1: *ASCII Control Characters*

DECIMAL	CHARACTER	CONTROL COMBINATION
27	ESC (Escape)	Ctrl+[
28	FS (File separator)	Ctrl+/
29	GS (Group separator)	Ctrl+]
30	RS (Record separator)	Ctrl+^
31	US (Unit separator)	Ctrl+_

TABLE A.2: *Standard 7-Bit ASCII Character Set*

DECIMAL	CHARACTER	DECIMAL	CHARACTER
01	☺	05	♣
02	☻	06	♠
03	♥	07	•
04	♦	08	◘

TABLE A.2: *Standard 7-Bit ASCII Character Set*

DECIMAL	CHARACTER	DECIMAL	CHARACTER
09	●	20	¶
10	◘	21	§
11	♂	22	▬
12	♀	23	↕
13	♪	24	↑
14	♫	25	↓
15	☼	26	→
16	►	27	←
17	◄	28	∟
18	↕	29	↔
19	‼	30	▲

TABLE A.2: *Standard 7-Bit ASCII Character Set*

DECIMAL	CHARACTER	DECIMAL	CHARACTER
31	▼	42	*
32	space	43	+
33	!	44	,
34	"	45	–
35	#	46	.
36	$	47	/
37	%	48	0
38	&	49	1
39	'	50	2
40	(	51	3
41	)	52	4

TABLE A.2: *Standard 7-Bit ASCII Character Set*

DECIMAL	CHARACTER	DECIMAL	CHARACTER
53	5	65	A
54	6	66	B
55	7	67	C
56	8	68	D
57	9	69	E
58	:	70	F
59	;	71	G
60	<	72	H
61	=	73	I
62	>	74	J
63	?	75	K
64	@	76	L

TABLE A.2: *Standard 7-Bit ASCII Character Set*

DECIMAL	CHARACTER	DECIMAL	CHARACTER
77	M	89	Y
78	N	90	Z
79	O	91	[
80	P	92	\
81	Q	93	]
82	R	94	^
83	S	95	_
84	T	96	`
85	U	97	a
86	V	98	b
87	W	99	c
88	X	100	d

TABLE A.2: *Standard 7-Bit ASCII Character Set*

DECIMAL	CHARACTER	DECIMAL	CHARACTER
101	e	113	q
102	f	114	r
103	g	115	s
104	h	116	t
105	i	117	u
106	j	118	v
107	k	119	w
108	l	120	x
109	m	121	y
110	n	122	z
111	o	123	{
112	p	124	¦

TABLE A.2: *Standard 7-Bit ASCII Character Set*

DECIMAL	CHARACTER	DECIMAL	CHARACTER
125	}	127	DEL
126	~		

TABLE A.3: *IBM Extended ASCII Character Set*

DECIMAL	CHARACTER	DECIMAL	CHARACTER
128	Ç	135	ç
129	ü	136	ê
130	´	137	ë
131	â	138	è
132	ä	139	ï
133	à	140	î
134	å	141	ì

TABLE A.3: *IBM Extended ASCII Character Set*

DECIMAL	CHARACTER	DECIMAL	CHARACTER
142	Ä	153	Ö
143	Å	154	Ü
144	É	155	¢
145	æ	156	£
146	Æ	157	¥
		158	₧
147	ô	159	ƒ
148	ö	160	á
149	ò	161	í
150	û	162	ó
151	ù	163	ú
152	ÿ	164	ñ

TABLE A.3: *IBM Extended ASCII Character Set*

DECIMAL	CHARACTER	DECIMAL	CHARACTER
165	Ñ	177	▒
166	ª	178	▓
167	º	179	│
168	¿	180	┤
169	┌	181	╡
170	┐	182	╢
171	½	183	╖
172	¼	184	╕
173	¡	185	╣
174	«	186	║
175	»	187	╗
176	░	188	╝

TABLE A.3: *IBM Extended ASCII Character Set*

DECIMAL	CHARACTER	DECIMAL	CHARACTER
189	⅃	200	╚
190	⅃	201	╔
191	┐	202	╩
192	└	203	╦
193	┴	204	╠
194	┬	205	═
195	├	206	╬
196	─	207	╧
197	┼	208	╨
198	╞	209	╤
199	╟	210	╥

TABLE A.3: *IBM Extended ASCII Character Set*

DECIMAL	CHARACTER	DECIMAL	CHARACTER
211	╚	223	▀
212	╘	224	∝
213	╒	225	β
214	╓	226	Γ
215	╫	227	π
216	╪	228	Σ
217	┘	229	σ
218	┌	230	μ
219	█	231	τ
220	▄	232	Φ
221	▌	233	Θ
222	▐		

TABLE A.3: *IBM Extended ASCII Character Set*

DECIMAL	CHARACTER	DECIMAL	CHARACTER
234	Ω	245	\
235	δ	246	÷
236	∞	247	≈
237	φ	248	°
238	ε	249	°
239	∩	250	·
240	≡	251	√
241	±	252	η
242	≥	253	^{2}
243	≤	254	■
244	⌠	255	

TABLE A.4: *EBCDIC Character Set*

DECIMAL	CHARACTER	DECIMAL	CHARACTER
0	NUL (null)	16	DLE (data length escape)
1	SOH (start of heading)	17	DC1 (device control 1)
2	STX (start of text)	18	DC2 (device control 2)
3	ETX (end of text)	19	DC3 (device control 3)
4	SEL (select)	20	RES/ENP (restore/enable presentation)
5	HT (horizontal tab)	21	NL (new line)
6	RNL (required new line)	22	BS (backspace)
7	DEL (delete)	23	POC (program-operator communication)
8	GE (graphic escape)	24	CAN (cancel)
9	SPS (superscript)	25	EM (end of medium)
10	RPT (repeat)	26	UBS (unit backspace)
11	VT (vertical tab)	27	CU1 (customer use 1)
12	FF (form feed)		
13	CR (carriage return)		
14	SO (shift out)		
15	SI (shift in)		

TABLE A.4: *EBCDIC Character Set*

DECIMAL	CHARACTER	DECIMAL	CHARACTER
28	IFS (interchange file separator)	38	ETB (end of transmission block)
29	IGS (interchange group separator)	39	ESC (escape)
30	IRS (interchange record separator)	40	SA (set attribute)
31	IUS/ITB (interchange unit separator/ intermediate transmission block)	41	SFE (start field extended)
		42	SM/SW (set mode/switch)
		43	CSP (control sequence prefix)
32	DS (digit select)	44	MFA (modify field attribute)
33	SOS (start of significance)	45	ENQ (enquiry)
34	FS (field separator)	46	ACK (acknowledge)
35	WUS (word underscore)	47	BEL (bell)
		48–49	not assigned
36	BYP/INP (bypass/inhibit presentation)	50	SYN (synchronous idle)
37	LF (line feed)	51	IR (index return)

TABLE A.4: *EBCDIC Character Set*

DECIMAL	CHARACTER	DECIMAL	CHARACTER
52	PP (presentation position)	66–73	not assigned
		74	¢
53	TRN (transport)	75	.
54	NBS (numeric backspace)	76	<
55	EOT (end of transmission)	77	(
		78	+
56	SBS (subscript)	79	| (Logical OR)
57	IT (indent tab)	80–89	not assigned
58	RFF (required form feed)	90	!
		91	$
59	CU3 (customer use 3)	92	*
60	DC4 (device control 4)	93	)
		94	;
61	NAK (negative acknowledge)	95	¬ (Logical NOT)
62	not assigned	96	–
63	SUB (substitute)	97	/
64	SP (space)	98–105	not assigned
65	RSP (required space)	106	¦ (broken pipe)
		107	,

TABLE A.4: *EBCDIC Character Set*

DECIMAL	CHARACTER	DECIMAL	CHARACTER
108	%	135	g
109	_	136	h
110	>	137	i
111	?	138–144	not assigned
112–120	not assigned	145	j
121	`	146	k
122	:	147	l
123	#	148	m
124	@	149	n
125	'	150	o
126	=	151	p
127	"	152	q
128	not assigned	153	r
129	a	154–160	not assigned
130	b	161	~
131	c	162	s
132	d	163	t
133	e	164	u
134	f	165	v

TABLE A.4: *EBCDIC Character Set*

DECIMAL	CHARACTER	DECIMAL	CHARACTER
166	w	209	J
167	x	210	K
168	y	211	L
169	z	212	M
170–191	not assigned	213	N
192	{	214	O
193	A	215	P
194	B	216	Q
195	C	217	R
196	D	218–223	not assigned
197	E	224	\
198	F	225	NSP (numeric space)
199	G		
200	H	226	S
201	I	227	T
202	SHY (syllable hyphen)	228	U
		229	V
203–207	not assigned	230	W
208	}	231	X

TABLE A.4: *EBCDIC Character Set*

DECIMAL	CHARACTER	DECIMAL	CHARACTER
232	Y	245	5
233	Z	246	6
234–239	not assigned	247	7
240	0	248	8
241	1	249	9
242	2	250–254	not assigned
243	3	255	EO (eight ones)
244	4		